1001 EASY
INEXPENSIVE
GRILLING
RECIPES

**Easy and Inexpensive Recipes for
Grilling Almost Everything**

Cookbook Resources, LLC
Highland Village, Texas

1001 Easy Inexpensive Grilling Recipes

Easy and Inexpensive Recipes for Grilling Almost Everything

10 9 8 7 6 5 4 3 2 1

ISBN: 978-1-4351-5221-2

This 2014 edition printed for Barnes & Noble, Inc.

Printed in the United States of America

Cover by Rasor Design

Edited, Designed, Published and Manufactured in the United States of America
Cookbook Resources, LLC
541 Doubletree Drive
Highland Village, Texas 75077
Toll Free 866-229-2665

www.cookbookresources.com

Bringing Family and Friends to the Table

1001 Easy Inexpensive Grilling Recipes

Grilling and smoking foods is one of the most rewarding and relaxing backyard pastimes we have. We all have childhood memories of July 4th backyard barbecues with hot dogs and hamburgers and fireworks.

This cookbook gives you some basic and fun recipes to get you back in the yard with your grilling tools and your imagination. A good barbecue sauce or a juicy, slightly charred but medium rare steak are sources of great pride for any backyard chef.

Mastery of backyard barbecues just takes time and a little patience. Grilling is hot and fast. Smoking is low and slow. Choose your specialty and delight others with fabulous food right off the grill.

Table of Contents

    Appetizing pre-dinner nibbles and hearty
    between-meal snacks are terrific.

    Easy, tasty beverages are always a welcome
    sight at a fun, casual, backyard barbecue.

    Yes, even breads are great on the grill. Check
    out the variety.

    You can easily grill your whole meal with
    these easy, delicious side dishes.

    Pizzas, sandwiches, brats and burgers give
    lots of ideas for inexpensive meals and snacks.

Table of Contents

Cooking Times

How Hot Is the Fire?

How Hot?	Hand over fire	Temperature	Description
High	2 seconds	400° - 450°	Red hot coals
Medium	3 seconds	350° - 375°	Some gray ash
Low	4 - 5 seconds	300° - 350°	Covered in ash

Note: Many of the newer gas grills have a temperature sensor, but the "hand over fire" method works for all grills.

How Long Do You Grill It?

Meat	Internal Temperature	Desired Doneness	Direct Medium Heat	Indirect Medium Heat
Beef				
Sirloin- 1 inch thick	145°	Medium rare	14 - 18 minutes	22 - 26 minutes
Flank - ¾ inch thick	145°	Medium rare	12 - 14 minutes	18 - 22 minutes
Ground meat	160°	No pink	14 - 18 minutes	20 - 24 minutes
Chicken				
Breast Half	165°	No pink	15 - 18 minutes	20 - 30 minutes
Half Chicken	165°	No pink	40 - 50 minutes	1 - 1¼ hours
Quarter	165°	No pink	30 - 40 minutes	50 - 60 minutes
Pork				
Pork chops- ¾ inch	145°	Medium	8 - 11 minutes	18 - 20 minutes
Pork tenderloin- 1 pound	145°	Medium	25 - 45 minutes	
Pork loin - 3 pounds	145°	Medium	1 hour 30 minutes	

Meat	Internal Temperature	Desired Doneness	Direct Medium Heat	Indirect Medium Heat
Baby Back ribs	145°	Medium	1 - 2 hours	
Ham slice	145°	Medium	20 - 24 minutes	
Seafood				
Whole, dressed		Flakes	20 - 25 minutes	
Salmon Steaks		Flakes	5 - 8 minutes	15 - 25 minutes
Halibut Steaks		Flakes	6 - 10 minutes	20 - 30 minutes
Shrimp		Turns pink	5 - 8 minutes	10 - 12 minutes

How Long Do You Smoke It?

Meat	Size	Doneness	Temperature of Grill	Time
Brisket	3 - 4 lbs	Tender	225° - 250°	4 - 5 hours
Rib Roast	4 - 5 lbs	140° - 160°	225° - 250°	3 - 4 hours
Pork Shoulder	4 - 5 lbs	Tender	250° - 300°	4 - 5 hours
Pork Ribs	2 racks	Tender	250° - 300°	2 - 4 hours
Whole Chicken	2½ - 3 lbs	No pink	300° - 375°	1 - 2 hours
Whole Turkey	10 - 12 lbs	No pink	250° - 300°	4 - 5 hours

Note: It's a good idea to use an oven thermometer to check your grill temperature.

For more information, e-mail: mphotline.fsis@usda.gov

Best Meats for Grilling

Beef

Steaks . . . . New York Strip, rib-eye, T-bone, porterhouse, sirloin, flatiron, filet, club, sirloin tip, rump, skirt, flank

Ground . . . . Round, sirloin

Pork

Hams . . . . Picnic, shoulder, butt, shank

Chops . . . . Loin, center-cut, blade, shoulder steaks

Ribs . . . . Spareribs, country-style ribs, baby back

Ground . . . . Picnic, shoulder

Chicken

Whole, quarters, breasts, legs, thighs

Fish

Flounder . . . . Whole dressed, pan-dressed (without head), fillets

Halibut . . . . Steaks, scallops

Red Snapper . . . (Also black sea bass, grouper) Fillets, brochettes

Rockfish . . . . (Also cod, haddock, ocean perch) Fillets, brochettes

Salmon . . . . Steaks, fillets, brochettes

Sea Bass . . . . (Also striped bass, redfish, speckled trout) Fillets, brochettes

Sole . . . . Whole dressed, pan-dressed (without head), fillets

Swordfish . . . . . . Steaks, brochettes

Trout . . . . Whole, dressed (with or without head)

Tuna . . . . (Also yellowtail, bluefish, mahi-mahi, bonito) Steaks, whole dressed (small without head), fillets, brochettes

Appetizers and Snacks

Appetizing pre-dinner nibbles and
hearty between-meal snacks are terrific.

Baked Brie with Maple Glaze

3 tablespoons real maple syrup
3 tablespoons butter, melted
⅓ cup sliced almonds
1 (4 inch) round brie

- In small saucepan over low-medium heat, combine maple syrup, butter and almonds. Stir constantly and heat just until it mixes well. Place brie on sprayed heavy-duty foil to make pouch.

- Spoon syrup-butter mixture over brie. Fold foil so it doesn't touch top of brie and no juices leak out. Cook away from direct medium fire, close lid, until warm throughout, about 15 minutes. Serves 4 to 6.

Grilled Feta

This is great served with pita chips or crusty breads.

1 (6 ounce) package feta cheese
3 sprigs fresh thyme
1 tablespoon olive oil

- Bring feta to room temperature. Preheat grill to low-medium heat. Place feta in center of sprayed heavy-duty foil. Top with thyme, oil and ½ teaspoon pepper.

- Fold loosely for air to circulate. Grill about 15 minutes until cheese is soft. Serves 4.

Jalapeno Grillers

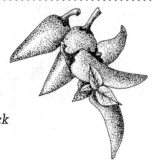

Prepare day before grilling.

Small onion, chopped
¼ pound ground beef
1 (8 ounce) package shredded Monterey Jack
10 - 12 large jalapenos
½ - 1 pound bacon

- Cook onion several minutes in sprayed skillet. Add ground meat, brown until there's no pink and drain thoroughly. Let meat cool a little and combine with cheese.

- Cut top off jalapenos and cut down 1 side almost to bottom. Spread sides and remove seeds and veins. Stuff each jalapeno with hamburger-cheese mixture. Wrap ½ to 1 slice bacon around jalapeno and secure with toothpick. Refrigerate overnight in covered container.

- Bring to room temperature. Cook on oiled grill or sprayed foil over medium fire for about 5 to 10 minutes per side until bacon is crispy. Serves 4 to 6.

Pimento-Stuffed Jalapenos

1 (5 ounce) container pimento cheese
10 large fresh jalapenos
5 slices bacon, halved

- Wear rubber gloves to remove jalapeno stems, slice down one side of jalapenos (but don't go through both sides) and remove seeds and veins. Stuff jalapenos with pimento cheese so jalapenos still close.

- Wrap with half slice of bacon and secure with toothpick. Cook on oiled grill or sprayed foil over medium heat. Turn frequently and cook until bacon is done, about 10 minutes per side. Remove from grill, cool and serve. Makes 10.

$ave Money! *Scan your fridge and pantry before going to the store.*

Veggie-Stuffed Jalapenos

2 - 3 sweet potatoes, peeled, cooked
10 - 16 large fresh jalapenos
5 - 8 slices bacon, halved

- Cook sweet potatoes and set aside to cool. Wear rubber gloves to remove jalapeno stems, slice down one side of jalapenos (but don't go through both sides) and remove seeds and veins. Mash sweet potatoes, stuff jalapenos with sweet potatoes, but jalapenos should still close.

- Wrap with half slice of bacon and secure with toothpick. Cook on oiled grill or sprayed foil over medium heat. Turn frequently and cook until bacon is done. Remove from grill, cool and serve. Makes 10 to 16.

Grilled Cheesy Chicken Jalapenos

10 - 16 large fresh jalapenos
1 (8 ounce) package cream cheese, softened
1 cup shredded Monterey Jack cheese
1 cup cooked chicken, chopped
1 bunch fresh cilantro
5 - 8 slices bacon, halved

- Wear rubber gloves to remove stems, slice down one side of jalapenos (but don't go through both sides) and remove seeds and veins. Combine cream cheese, Monterey Jack cheese, chicken and about ¼ cup chopped cilantro in blender and process just enough to mix well.

- Stuff jalapenos with cheese mixture, wrap with half slice of bacon and secure with toothpick. Cook on oiled grill or sprayed foil over medium heat. Turn frequently and cook until bacon is done, about 10 minutes per side. Remove from grill, cool and serve. Makes 10 to 16.

> *$ave Money!* Plan at least a week's worth of meals at a time. This will cut down on the number of trips to the store and avoid impulse buys.

Jalapenos and Onions

2 large sweet onions
10 mild fresh jalapenos
Olive oil

- Peel and quarter onions. Wear rubber gloves to remove jalapeno stems, slice jalapenos down center and remove seeds and ribs. Thread onion and jalapenos alternately on skewers. Brush with olive oil and sprinkle with salt and pepper.

- Cook over oiled grill or sprayed foil over medium fire until grill marks appear and onions and jalapenos are tender, about 10 to 20 minutes. Serves about 4 to 6.

Grilled Nachos

5 cups tortilla chips
1 (15 ounce) can refried beans
2 teaspoons taco seasoning mix
½ cup salsa
2 cups shredded Mexican blend cheese
2 tablespoons chopped green onions

- Place tortilla chips in sprayed 12 x 18-inch foil pan. Combine beans and taco seasoning and mix well. Spoon beans, salsa, cheese and onions over chips. Cover with foil. Cook on preheated grill about 10 minutes until cheese melts; rotate once. Serves 4.

TIP: When removing foil pan from grill, slide onto baking sheet for more stability.

Green Chile Nachos

- Use recipe for *Grilled Nachos (page 12)* and add 1 (4.5 ounce) can diced green chilies before grilling. Serves 4.

$ave Money! *The more you see, touch, feel, smell or taste an item, the more likely you are to buy it. Stick to your grocery list and don't be persuaded by special displays or samples.*

Fire-Roasted Nachos

36 corn tortilla chips
5 pickled jalapeno peppers, sliced
1 cup diced tomatoes, drained
2 (8 ounce) packages shredded Monterey Jack cheese
4 green onions with tops, chopped

- Arrange chips on sprayed, disposable baking pan. Sprinkle with jalapenos, tomatoes and cheese. Cover pan with foil.

- Place baking pan on grill away from direct medium-high heat, close lid and cook until cheese melts, about 10 minutes. Sprinkle with green onions. Serves 4 to 6.

Portobello Quesadillas

4 portobello mushrooms
2 tablespoons olive oil, divided
8 flour tortillas
2 cups shredded Monterey Jack cheese

- Coat mushrooms with 1 tablespoon oil and ½ teaspoon each salt and pepper. Cook on oiled grill or sprayed foil about 6 minutes per side until tender. Slice into thin strips.

- Brush tortillas with remaining oil. Evenly distribute mushrooms and cheese on 4 tortillas; top with remaining tortillas. Carefully place on grill. Cook each side about 3 minutes until cheese melts. Serves 4.

Green Chile Portobello Quesadillas

- Use recipe for *Portobello Quesadillas (page 13)* and add 1 (4 ounce) can diced green chilies to mushroom-cheese mixture before grilling. Serves 4.

Peppery Portobello Quesadillas

- Use recipe for *Portobello Quesadillas (page 13)* and substitute Pepper jack cheese for Monterey Jack cheese. Serves 4.

Chicken Quesadillas

These are great served with guacamole, sour cream and salsa.

8 large flour tortillas
1 tablespoon olive oil
1 - 2 cups cooked, shredded chicken
2 cups shredded Monterey Jack cheese

- Brush tortillas with oil. Combine chicken and cheese. Distribute evenly on 4 tortillas and top with remaining tortillas.

- Carefully place on preheated, oiled grill or sprayed foil. Cook over medium heat for about 3 minutes on each side until cheese melts. Serves 3 to 4.

Chicken-Spinach Quesadillas

- Use recipe for *Chicken Quesadillas (page 14)* and add 3 cups baby spinach to chicken and cheese mixture. Serves 3 to 4.

Green Chile Chicken Quesadillas

- Use recipe for *Chicken Quesadillas (page 14)* and add 1 (4 ounce) can diced green chilies to chicken and cheese mixture. Serves 3 to 4.

Curried Sport Wings

2 pounds chicken wings
¼ cup (½ stick) butter, melted
¼ cup honey
¼ cup mustard
1¼ teaspoons curry powder

- Cut off wing tips and discard. Cut wings in half at joint. Combine remaining ingredients in large sealable bag. Add chicken, seal and refrigerate for at least 2 hours; turn chicken occasionally.

- Remove chicken from marinade and discard marinade. Cook on oiled, preheated grill (or on foil-lined grill) over indirect medium fire for about 30 minutes to 1 hour until juices are clear and internal temperature is 165°. Turn occasionally. Serves 6 for appetizers; 3 for main dish.

Raspberry-Glazed Wings

3 pounds chicken wings
1½ cups seedless raspberry jam
½ cup cider vinegar
½ cup soy sauce
2 teaspoons garlic powder

- Cut chicken wings into 3 sections and discard wing tips. Sprinkle wings with a little salt and pepper. Cook on oiled, preheated grill over medium-hot fire for about 20 to 30 minutes until juices are clear and internal temperature is 165°; turn several times.

- Combine remaining ingredients in large saucepan and heat, but do not boil. Place wings in saucepan and toss to coat.

- Place back on foil-lined grill over indirect heat and cook for about 20 minutes at low temperature. Turn several times. Don't let sauce burn. Use slotted spoon to serve wings. Serves 10 for appetizers; 4 for main dish.

How Many Wings Should I Prepare?

Figure about 5 wings or 10 pieces per pound. If you discard the wing tip and cut the wing at the joint leaving 2 pieces, you can figure 10 pieces per pound. As an appetizer, people will eat about 2 to 3 pieces. As a main dish, people will eat about 6 to 10 pieces.

No. of People	Appetizer Pieces (3 per person)	Main Dish Pieces (8 per person)
2	6	16
4	12	32
8	24	64

No. of People (Appetizers)	No. of People (Main Dish)	Approximate Pounds Wings
6	3	2
10	4	3
12	6	4
14	7	5

Call-the-Fire-Department Hot Wings

2 pounds chicken wings
½ cup (1 stick) butter, melted
½ cup red wine vinegar
¼ cup ketchup
1 (2 ounce) bottle hot pepper sauce
1 tablespoon lemon juice
1 tablespoon honey
1 clove garlic, pressed

- Trim off tips of wings and cut in half at joint. Season with salt and pepper. Cook on oiled grill away from medium heat for about 30 to 40 minutes until juices are clear and internal temperature in thickest part is 165°. Cook until outside of wings is crispy.

- Mix remaining ingredients in small bowl. Remove wings from grill and place in large bowl. Pour sauce over wings and stir to coat well. Serves 6 for appetizers; 3 for main dish.

Desert Buffalo Wings

Not too hot, but still gets your attention. Very flavorful.

3 pounds chicken wings
¾ cup Frank's® RedHot Thick™ Cayenne Pepper Sauce
½ cup (1 stick) butter, melted
3 - 4 cloves garlic, pressed
1 large onion, minced

- Trim off tips of wings and cut in half at joint. Season with salt and pepper. Cook on oiled grill away from medium heat for about 20 to 35 minutes per side and turn frequently. Cook until juices are clear and internal temperature in thickest part is 165°. Cook until outside of wings is crispy.

- Mix Frank's, butter, garlic and onion in small bowl. Remove wings from grill and place in large bowl. Pour sauce over wings and stir to coat well. Serves 10 for appetizers; 4 for main dish.

Easy Grilled Chicken Wings

3 pounds chicken wings, tips removed
1 (12 ounce) bottle Italian dressing
3 - 4 lemons
½ cup (1 stick) butter, melted
1 teaspoon hot sauce

- Trim off tips of wings and cut in half at joint. Place wings in sealable plastic bag. Mix dressing, juice of 3 lemons, butter and hot sauce in bowl. Taste, add more lemon juice and hot sauce, if needed. Pour over wings and marinate in refrigerator for about 1 hour.

- Cook on oiled grill over medium-hot fire for about 10 to 20 minutes per side until juices are clear and internal temperature in thickest part is 165°. Serves 10 for appetizers; 4 for main dish.

Easy Hot-Hot Wings

3 pounds chicken wings
Oil
Garlic powder
Pinch brown sugar

- Rub chicken wings with oil and sprinkle with seasonings and a little salt. Refrigerate for 15 to 20 minutes. Cook on oiled grill over medium-hot fire for about 10 to 20 minutes per side until juices are clear and internal temperature is 165°.

Sauce:

½ cup (1 stick) butter, melted
¼ cup olive oil
¼ cup hot sauce
2 tablespoons red wine vinegar

- Mix all sauce ingredients, pour over wings and stir well. Serve wings with celery, carrot sticks and ranch dressing. Serves 10 for appetizers; 4 for main dish.

Frank's Terrific Top-of-the-Line Hot Wings

3 pounds chicken wings
½ cup Frank's® RedHot Thick™ Cayenne Pepper Sauce
½ cup (1 stick) butter, melted
2 tablespoons apple vinegar

- Trim off tips of wings and cut in half at joint. Season with salt and pepper. Cook on oiled grill away from medium heat for about 1 hour until juices are clear and internal temperature in thickest part is 165°. Cook until outside of wings is crispy.

- Mix Frank's, butter and vinegar in small bowl. Remove wings from grill and place in large bowl. Pour sauce over wings and stir to coat well. Serves 10 for appetizers; 4 for main dish.

Honey Hot Wings

2 pounds chicken wings
¾ cup hot pepper sauce
¼ cup butter, melted
1 teaspoon fresh lemon juice
1 - 2 teaspoons honey

- Trim off tips of wings and cut in half at joint. Season with salt and pepper. Cook on oiled grill away from medium heat for about 1 hour until juices are clear and internal temperature in thickest part is 165°. Cook until outside of wings is crispy.

- Mix hot pepper sauce, butter, lemon juice and honey in small bowl. Remove wings from grill and place in large bowl. Pour sauce over wings and stir to coat well. Serves 6 for appetizers; 3 for main dish.

Smoking refers to cooking meats with indirect heat and smoke at lower temperatures for longer periods of time. It is sometimes difficult to keep the heat source consistent, but well worth the effort.

Lemon-Garlic Wings

Not hot, but very tasty and great wings.

3 pounds chicken wings
½ cup (1 stick) butter, melted
½ cup shredded parmesan cheese
¼ cup lemon juice
3 - 4 cloves garlic, pressed

- Trim off tips of wings and cut in half at joint. Season with salt and pepper. Cook on oiled grill away from medium heat for about 1 hour at 250° until juices are clear and internal temperature in thickest part is 165°. Cook until outside of wings is crispy.

- Mix butter, parmesan, lemon juice and garlic in small bowl. Remove wings from grill and place in large bowl. Pour sauce over wings and stir to coat well. Serves 10 for appetizers; 4 for main dish.

TIP: This is really good when you sprinkle grated parmesan on wings before serving.

Louisiana Hot Wings

2 pounds chicken wings
1 cup (2 sticks) butter, melted
1 (2 ounce) bottle Louisiana Hot Sauce
2 cloves garlic, pressed
1 teaspoon lemon juice

- Trim tips of wings and cut in half at joint. Season with salt and pepper. Cook on oiled grill away from medium heat for about 1 hour with lid closed until juices are clear and internal temperature in thickest part is 165°. Cook until outside of wings is crispy.

- Mix butter, Louisiana Hot Sauce, garlic and lemon juice in small bowl. Remove wings from grill and place in large bowl. Pour sauce over wings and stir to coat well. Serves 6 for appetizers; 3 for main dish.

Pete's Best Hot Wings

3 pounds chicken wings
1 cup Texas Pete® Buffalo Wing Sauce
1 cup (2 sticks) butter, melted
1 cup lemon juice

- Trim off tips of wings and cut in half at joint. Season with salt and pepper. Cook on oiled grill away from medium heat for about 1 hour with lid closed until juices are clear and internal temperature in thickest part is 165°. Cook until outside of wings is crispy.

- Mix Texas Pete® Buffalo Wing Sauce, butter and lemon juice in small bowl. Remove wings from grill and place in large bowl. Pour sauce over wings and stir to coat well. Serves 10 for appetizers; 4 for main dish.

Spicy Brown Ale Wings

4 pounds chicken wings
½ cup packed brown sugar
1 tablespoon kosher salt
2 (12 ounce) bottles brown ale
1 cup (2 sticks) butter
2 - 3 cloves garlic, minced
½ - 1 cup Frank's® RedHot Buffalo Wings Sauce
1 teaspoon finely ground black pepper

- Trim small tips off wings and discard. Separate remaining 2 parts of wings. Mix brown sugar, salt and ale in large bowl and whisk until sugar and salt dissolve. Place wings in bowl and stir to coat. Cover and refrigerate for 4 to 8 hours.

- Melt butter in large skillet and saute garlic until translucent. Add Frank's wings sauce and ground black pepper. Mix well and simmer for 3 minutes. Remove wings from marinade, drain on paper towels and discard marinade.

- Cook on oiled grill over medium fire for about 5 minutes per side. Turn and brush liberally cooked side with butter-garlic sauce.

- Continue to turn, cook and brush on garlic-butter mixture until wing juices are clear and internal temperature in thickest part is 165°. Serves about 12 for appetizers; 5 for main dish.

Touchdown Wings

3 pounds chicken wings
1 cup soy sauce
¼ cup ketchup
¼ cup rice wine vinegar
¼ cup packed brown sugar
4 cloves garlic, pressed
1 tablespoon ground ginger

- Trim tips off chicken wings and split sections. Place in large bowl or sealable plastic bag. In separate bowl, mix all remaining ingredients and pour over wings.

- Seal and move wings around in bag to distribute marinade. Leave in refrigerator for about 24 hours before grilling.

- Cook on oiled grill over medium-hot fire for about 5 to 10 minutes per side until juices are clear and internal temperature is 165°. If wings start to burn or flame up, move to outside of fire. Serves 10 for appetizers; 4 for main dish.

Chicken Lickers

2 white onions, sliced
10 - 12 chicken livers
4 strips bacon
⅓ cup sherry

- Place onion slices in shallow pan. Top each onion slice with chicken liver and one-third strip bacon; secure with toothpick. Pour sherry over all.

- Cook on oiled, preheated medium grill (or on foil-lined grill) over indirect fire for about 45 minutes until juices are clear and internal temperature is 165°. Turn occasionally. Serves 5 to 6.

It is healthier to grill chicken or turkey without the skin. If you prefer to cook with the skin, grill with skin side up so that natural juices soak through the meat while it cooks.

Party Bourbon Bites

½ cup (1 stick) butter, melted
¼ cup dijon-style mustard
¼ cup packed dark brown sugar
3 tablespoons bourbon whiskey
4 boneless, skinless chicken breasts cut into 1½-inch, square pieces

- In medium bowl, blend butter, mustard, sugar and whiskey. Reserve half of marinade in separate bowl. Add chicken pieces to remaining half and toss to coat.

- Grill chicken on oiled foil over medium heat for about 7 to 10 minutes per side until juices are clear and internal temperature is 165°.

- While grilling chicken, pour reserved marinade into small saucepan and bring to a boil. Reduce heat to medium-low and stir often. Cook about 10 minutes.

- Pour heated marinade into small decorative dip bowl. Place chicken on platter with party picks and bowl of dipping sauce. Dip each bite before eating. Serves 6 to 8.

Brat-Pineapple Bites

1 (14 ounce) package chicken brats
2 (15 ounce) cans pineapple chunks, drained

- Slice brats in 1-inch pieces and place on skewers. Cook on oiled grill over medium heat for about 10 minutes per side until crispy on outside.

- Run 2 skewers through each pineapple chunk to keep them from spinning. Cook on sprayed foil on grill away from direct heat for about 5 minutes per side until hot.

- Place both on serving platter with toothpicks through 1 brat slice and 1 pineapple chunk. Serves 8 to 10.

Brat Bites

1 (14 ounce) package brats
1 (8 ounce) rectangular block cheddar cheese
Ritz® crackers
Deli-style ground mustard

- Cut brats in ½-inch pieces. Cut cheese into about ½-inch cubes to fit on brat slices. Cook brats on oiled foil over medium-high heat for about 10 minutes until sides start to curl up.

- Arrange cheese pieces on top of each brat slice, move away from direct heat and close lid. Cook just long enough for cheese to melt. Spread mustard on crackers and place 1 brat slice with cheese on top of each. Serves about 10 to 12.

Brat Skewers

1 (14 ounce) package brats
1 (16 ounce) package thin bacon slices
12 - 18 jalapenos

- Cut brats into small pieces to stuff into jalapenos. Cut bacon slices in half to wrap around jalapenos. Cut stem end off jalapeno and scrape out seeds and veins without breaking open the jalapeno.

- Stuff jalapenos with brats and wrap in bacon. Slide on skewers with room in between each and cook on oiled grill over medium direct heat for about 5 minutes per side until bacon is crispy.

- (If you don't want to use skewers, spray foil and cook jalapenos on foil.) Turn several times. Serves 6 to 10.

According to the National Pork Producers Council, a pork packer, named Uncle Sam Wilson, shipped a boatload of pork to U.S. troops in the War of 1812. The pork was packed in barrels and marked U.S. on each one. Talk around the docks was that U.S. stood for Uncle Sam and it has eventually grown to mean the U.S. government.

Turkey Brat Kebabs

1 (14 ounce) package turkey brats
1 red and 1 yellow bell pepper, cored, quartered
1 large yellow onion, quartered
Honey mustard

- Cut brats into 1-inch pieces and place on skewers with space in between each. Cook on oiled grill over medium heat until outsides begin to blister and bubble, about 10 minutes per side.

- Place peppers and onion on 2 skewers to keep them from spinning. Cook on oiled grill over medium heat until vegetables are tender about 5 minutes per side. Place all on serving dish with toothpicks. Serves 8 to 10 as appetizers.

Brat Toast Bites

1 (14 ounce) package brats
1 (1 pound) loaf French bread
½ cup extra virgin olive oil
4 - 5 cloves garlic, pressed

- Cook brats on oiled grill over medium heat for about 10 minutes per side until brats cook through. Slice bread ¼ to ½ inch thick. Place bread on sprayed foil on grill away from direct heat and toast both sides, about 5 to 8 minutes per side.

- Heat oil in skillet and sauté garlic until translucent. Brush garlic oil on bread and top with slice of brat. Serves 8 to 10.

Franks in Chili Sauce

1 (10 count) package wieners
½ cup chili sauce
½ cup packed brown sugar
½ cup bourbon

- Cook wieners on oiled, preheated grill over medium-hot fire for about 15 minutes until slightly charred on outside. Remove wieners, cut in bite-size pieces

- Combine chili sauce, sugar and bourbon in saucepan. Add wieners to sauce and simmer for 30 minutes. Serve in chafing dish. Serves 8 to 10.

Sausage Rounds

1 (8 ounce) package crescent dinner rolls
1 pound sausage

- Open package of rolls, smooth out dough with rolling pin and seal seams. Break up sausage with hands and spread thin layer of sausage over rolls. Roll into log. Wrap in wax paper and freeze for several hours.

- When ready to cook, preheat grill to about 350°. Slice into ¼-inch rounds. Place on oiled, foil-lined grate over indirect heat, close lid and grill for 20 minutes until light brown. Serves 8.

Bacon Candy

People enjoy a familiar taste with a little surprise.

½ pound bacon slices
Brown sugar
Hot pepper flakes

- Prepare bacon by rubbing each slice with brown sugar and red pepper flakes. Cook on sprayed foil over medium-hot fire about 10 minutes, turn and continue to cook until crispy. Drain and pat dry. Break into bite-size pieces. Serves 4 to 6.

Maple-Sugar Bacon

½ pound bacon slices
Maple syrup
Brown sugar

- Prepare bacon by rubbing each slice with maple syrup and brown sugar. Cook on sprayed foil over medium-hot fire for about 10 minutes, turn and continue to cook until crispy. Drain and pat dry. Break into bite-size pieces. Serves 4 to 6.

Oyster Bites

1 (5 ounce) can smoked oysters, drained, chopped
⅔ cup herb-seasoned stuffing mix, crushed
8 slices bacon, halved, partially cooked

- Combine oysters, stuffing mix and ¼ cup water in bowl. Add another teaspoon of water if mixture seems too dry. Form into balls with about 1 tablespoon mixture for each.

- Wrap half slice bacon around each ball and secure with toothpick. Cook on oiled, preheated grill over medium fire until grill marks show, about 5 to 8 minutes. Turn and repeat. Cook until bacon is crisp. Serves 6 to 8.

Grilled Fruit Appetizers

Grilled fruit is a great appetizer. Grilling brings out the flavors and people really enjoy a flavorful, healthy treat. You'll find grilled fruit recipes on pages 335-343.

Beverages

Easy, tasty beverages are always a welcome
sight at a fun, casual, backyard barbecue.

Lemonade Tea

2 family-size tea bags
½ cup sugar
1 (12 ounce) can frozen lemonade concentrate
1 quart ginger ale, chilled

- Steep tea in 3 quarts water and mix with sugar and lemonade. Add ginger ale just before serving. Serves 6 to 8.

Refrigerator Fresh Brewed Tea

Tea bags
Lemon
Sugar

- Fill pitcher with cold water and add number of tea bags from directions on box. Refrigerate overnight and serve with lemon slices and sugar or sugar substitute.

Raspberry Iced Tea

4 individual tea bags
1 (11 ounce) can frozen cranberry-raspberry juice concentrate,
  thawed

- Place tea bags in teapot and add 4 cups boiling water. Cover and steep for 5 minutes. Remove and discard tea bags. Refrigerate tea.

- Just before serving, combine cranberry-raspberry concentrate and 4 cups cold water in 2½-quart pitcher. Stir in tea and serve with ice cubes. Serves 6 to 8.

Pineapple-Citrus Punch

1 (46 ounce) can pineapple juice, chilled
1 quart apple juice, chilled
1 (2 liter) bottle lemon-lime soda, chilled
1 (6 ounce) can frozen lemonade concentrate, thawed
1 orange, sliced

- Combine pineapple juice, apple juice, lemon-lime soda and lemonade in punch bowl. Add orange slices for decoration. Serves 24.

Use leftover red wine to marinate beef. If you don't have enough wine to cover, place meat in sealable plastic bag, add wine and about half as much oil and marinate for about 1 hour. Turn bag several times. If you marinate in refrigerator, leave meat at room temperature for about 30 minutes before cooking.

Strawberry Punch

2 *(10 ounce) boxes frozen strawberries, thawed*
2 *(6 ounce) cans frozen pink lemonade concentrate*
2 *(2 liter) bottles ginger ale, chilled*

- Process strawberries through blender. Pour lemonade into punch bowl and stir in strawberries. Add chilled ginger ale and stir well. (It would be nice to make an ice ring out of another bottle of ginger ale.) Serves 30.

Easiest Grape Punch

2 *liters ginger ale*
Red seedless grapes
3 *(25 ounce) bottles sparkling white grape juice, chilled*

- To make ice ring, fill circular gelatin mold with hole in center with ginger ale and seedless grapes and freeze. (Use any shape for ice mold.) When ready to serve, pour sparkling white grape juice in punch bowl with ice ring. Serves 20.

Ginger Ale Nectar Punch

1 *(12 ounce) can apricot nectar*
1 *(6 ounce) can frozen orange juice concentrate, thawed, undiluted*
2 *tablespoons lemon juice*
1 *(2 liter) bottle ginger ale, chilled*

- Combine apricot nectar, orange juice concentrate, 1 cup water and lemon juice in pitcher and refrigerate. When ready to serve, stir in ginger ale and pour into punch bowl. Serves 24.

Kid's Cherry Sparkler

2 *(6 ounce) jars red maraschino cherries, drained*
2 *(6 ounce) jars green maraschino cherries, drained*
1 *(2 liter) bottle cherry 7UP®, chilled*

- Place 1 red or green cherry in each compartment of 4 ice cube trays. Fill trays with water and freeze for 8 hours. Serve soft drink over ice cubes. Serves 6 to 8.

Amaretto

3 cups sugar
1 pint vodka
3 tablespoons almond extract
1 tablespoon real vanilla

- Combine sugar and 2¼ cups water in large pan. Bring mixture to a boil and reduce heat. Simmer for 5 minutes, stirring occasionally. Remove from stove.

- Add vodka, almond extract and vanilla and stir to mix. Cool and store in airtight jar. Makes 1½ quarts.

Sangria Tropics

1 (2 liter) bottle white wine
6 cups fresh fruit (mango, papaya, pineapple, watermelon,
*   honeydew melon, oranges)*

- Prepare fruit and slice enough fruit for 6 cups. Pour white wine into pitcher, add fruit and refrigerate overnight. Serves about 10.

Kahlua

1 cup instant coffee granules
4 cups sugar
1 quart vodka
1 vanilla bean, split

- Combine 3 cups hot water, coffee and sugar in large saucepan and mix well. Boil for 2 minutes and cool. Add vodka and vanilla bean. Pour into bottle or jar and let rest for 30 days before serving. Shake occasionally. Makes 2 quarts.

TIP: If you have some Mexican vanilla, make "instant" Kahlua®
by using 3 tablespoons Mexican vanilla instead of 1 vanilla
bean. You don't have to wait 30 days.

If you drink a diet soda and eat a candy bar, will they cancel out each other?

Kahlua Frosty

1 cup Kahlua® liqueur
1 pint vanilla ice cream
1 cup half-and-half cream
⅛ teaspoon almond extract
1⅔ cups crushed ice

- Combine all ingredients in blender and process until smooth. Serve immediately. Serves 4 to 6.

Breads

Yes, even breads are great on
the grill. Check out the variety.

Thyme Breadsticks

1 package refrigerated pizza dough
4 tablespoons olive oil, divided
3 tablespoons fresh thyme leaves

- Spread pizza dough out and sprinkle olive oil on both sides. Grill both sides over medium heat until it cooks through and chars a little, about 8 minutes per side.

- Combine remaining olive oil, thyme and ¼ teaspoon each of salt and pepper. Spread generously on bread. Cut into breadsticks and serve immediately. Serves 4.

*Use three times more fresh herbs than dried herbs.
(3 tablespoons minced fresh herbs = 1 tablespoon
dried herbs)*

Stuffed French Bread

1 loaf French bread
½ cup basil pesto
1 cup mozzarella cheese, shredded

- Cut loaf into 12 slices but don't cut all the way through (only cut about two-thirds the way through so slices stay connected to loaf). Spread pesto on each slice and evenly distribute cheese in between each slice.

- Place loaf in large piece of oiled foil and seal. Grill over medium heat about 10 minutes away from direct heat with lid closed until cheese thoroughly melts; rotate halfway through. Serves 4 to 6.

Sun-Dried Tomato Stuffed Bread

- Follow instructions for *Stuffed French Bread (page 31)* and substitute basil pesto with sun-dried tomato pesto. Serves 4 to 6.

Parmesan Bread

1 (16 ounce) loaf French bread
Butter
Garlic powder
Shredded parmesan

- Slice bread, but don't cut all the way through. Spread butter liberally on both sides of each slice and sprinkle with garlic powder and parmesan. Wrap bread in foil and place at back of medium-hot grill while cooking other food. Rotate several times and serve when cheese melts. Serves 6 to 8.

Bastes are brushed on meats, breads and vegetables while they cook and flavor the outside of the food. Warm basting sauces go on more smoothly than cold ones.

Toasted Garlic Bread

1 (1 pound) loaf French bread
½ cup extra virgin olive oil
4 - 5 cloves garlic, pressed

- Slice bread about ¼ to ½ inch thick. Cook bread on oiled foil over medium heat and toast both sides, about 5 to 8 minutes per side.

- Heat oil in skillet and sauté garlic until translucent. Brush garlic oil on both sides of bread. Serves 8 to 10.

Crusty Garlic Bread

1 long loaf French bread
½ cup - 1 cup (1 - 2 sticks) butter, softened
3 cloves garlic, pressed
¼ cup chopped fresh parsley
1 teaspoon paprika
¼ cup shredded parmesan cheese

- Slice bread down center to make 2 halves. Combine butter, garlic and parsley and spread over bread. Sprinkle paprika and parmesan over buttered side.

- Place bread buttered side up on oiled grill. Cook over low-medium heat with lid closed for about 5 to 10 minutes until bread gets crusty. Serves 6.

Smoky Gouda Bread

1 (1 pound) loaf French bread
2 (6 ounce) rounds smoky gouda cheese, sliced

- Slice bread about ¼ to ½ inch thick. Place bread on oiled foil over medium heat and toast on 1 side, about 3 to 5 minutes. Turn and add slice of gouda on top and cook until cheese melts. Serves 8 to 10.

Always place food on a clean plate after grilling.
Never use the same plate that held raw foods.

Garlic-Herb Grilled Bread

½ cup (1 stick) butter, melted
4 cloves garlic, minced
2 teaspoons paprika
1 teaspoon oregano
½ teaspoon cayenne
1 loaf sourdough bread, sliced

- Spray and preheat grill to medium-high heat. Combine butter, garlic and spices and mix well. Spread bread with butter mixture on both sides and place directly on oiled grill over medium heat. Toast bread 2 to 3 minutes per side until golden brown. Serves 6 to 8.

Herb Butter French Bread

Men go for French bread wrapped in foil and heated on a grill over coals.

½ cup (1 stick) butter, softened
¼ teaspoon paprika
¼ teaspoon dried savory or 2 teaspoons chopped parsley
½ teaspoon dried thyme
Few grains red pepper
1 (13 - 16 ounce) loaf French or Vienna bread

- Cream butter with ½ teaspoon salt, paprika, savory or parsley, thyme and red pepper. Cut bread diagonally, almost through to bottom crust in 12 equal slices. Spread herb butter between slices. Wrap loaf snugly in foil.

- Cook on grill over medium fire and turn frequently; heat about 20 to 25 minutes. Serves 6.

Onion Butter French Bread

- Use recipe for *Herb Butter French Bread (page 33)*, but omit paprika, herbs and red pepper and add 3 tablespoons minced onion. Serves 6.

Always preheat a gas grill for about 5 to 10 minutes.

Cheesy Grilled Bread

1 cup shredded cheddar cheese
½ cup (1 stick) butter, melted
1½ teaspoons paprika
1 teaspoon garlic powder
1 loaf French bread

- Heat half of grill to medium heat. Combine all ingredients except bread. Slice bread into 2 halves lengthwise. Spread cheese mixture evenly on both halves.

- Wrap loaf in large piece of foil, fold and seal. Cook about 15 to 20 minutes with indirect heat while grilling other foods. Turn to heat evenly. Serves 6 to 8.

Cream Cheesy Grilled Bread

- Use recipe for *Cheesy Grilled Bread (page 34)* and substitute cream cheese for cheddar cheese. Also substitute Italian seasoning for paprika. Serves 6 to 8.

Crusty Bread

1 loaf crusty bread (sourdough, French baguette, ciabatta, etc.)
Butter or olive oil

- Slice bread into thick slices. Oil or butter both sides of slices. Toast on preheated, oiled grill over medium heat for about 3 minutes per side until bread turns light brown. Serves 6 to 8.

Garlic Bread

- Follow instructions for *Crusty Bread (page 34)*. Rub each side of bread slices with garlic cloves or sprinkle lightly with minced garlic. Serves 6 to 8.

Tomato Bread

- Follow instructions for *Crusty Bread (page 34)*. Immediately top grilled bread with sliced tomato and salt and pepper. Serves 6 to 8.

Balsamic-Tomato Bread

- Follow instructions for *Crusty Bread (page 34)*. Immediately top grilled bread with sliced tomato and a little balsamic vinegar. Serves 6 to 8.

Roasted Red Pepper Bread

- Follow instructions for *Crusty Bread (page 34)*. Immediately top grilled bread with sliced roasted red peppers. Serves 6 to 8.

Basil Bread

- Follow instructions for *Crusty Bread (page 34)*. Immediately top grilled bread with fresh basil, mozzarella and chopped onion. Serves 6 to 8.

Grilled Bruschetta

- Follow instructions for *Crusty Bread (page 34)*. Before grilling add 2 teaspoons dried basil and 2 cloves minced garlic to a little oil and spread on bread. After grilling, top with thin tomato slices. Serves 6 to 8.

Grilled Tomato-Basil Flatbread

Extra-virgin olive oil
1 (11 ounce) package flatbread
1 large tomato, seeded, diced, drained
2 green onions with tops, chopped
¼ cup basil leaves
1 cup shredded mozzarella cheese

- Spread light coating of olive oil on both sides of flatbread. Place on oiled grill over medium-low heat and toast one side until slightly brown, about 5 minute. Remove from grill.

- Spread tomatoes, onions and basil on top of toasted side of bread. Cover with cheese and grill with lid closed until cheese melts. Break into smaller pieces or serve whole. Serves 4 to 6.

Zucchini-Ricotta Grilled Bread

4 tablespoons olive oil or butter, divided
1 cup fresh basil
3 zucchini, thinly sliced lengthwise
1 (1 pound) loaf French bread, sliced
2 cups ricotta

- In large bowl combine 2 tablespoons oil or butter with basil and 1 teaspoon salt and set aside.

- Cook zucchini on oiled grill over medium heat for about 4 minutes per side until grill marks show and zucchini is tender. Place zucchini in basil-oil mixture and coat both sides.

- Spread bread slices with remaining oil (or butter) and grill about 2 minutes per side until golden brown. Top grilled bread with dollop of ricotta and zucchini slice. Serves 6 to 8.

Zucchini-Ricotta Grilled Bread with a Kick

- Use recipe for *Zucchini-Ricotta Grilled Bread (page 36)*, but replace basil with crushed red pepper, drained sliced green chilies or sliced canned jalapenos. Serves 6 to 8.

Cheesy-Onion Focaccia

3 tablespoons butter
1 large onion, chopped
6 slices provolone cheese (or Swiss, Colby-Jack, shredded parmesan)
1 loaf focaccia bread

- Heat grill to medium-high heat. Melt butter in skillet and add onion. Cook until onion pieces turn a little brown, about 10 minutes. Cut bread in half horizontally. Place cheese and onions on bottom half and top with other half. Place in foil and wrap tightly.

- Turn one side of grill off, place bread away from heat and close lid. Grill for 15 to 20 minutes until cheese melts; rotate often. Cut into wedges and serve immediately. Serves 4 to 6.

Barbecue Focaccia Bread

1 loaf focaccia
1 tablespoon olive oil
4 ounces barbecue sauce
8 ounces cream cheese, softened

- Slice focaccia ¼-inch thick and lightly brush with olive oil.
  Cook on oiled grill over medium heat until toasted, about
  5 minutes per side. Combine barbecue sauce and cream
  cheese, mix well and serve as dip. Serve at room temperature.
  Serves 8 to 10.

Homemade Pizza Dough

2 teaspoons active dry yeast
2¾ cups bread flour, divided
1 tablespoon plus 2 teaspoons olive oil, divided
1 tablespoon sugar

- Dissolve yeast in 1 cup warm water (110° to 115°). Add 1 cup
  flour, 1 tablespoon oil and 1 teaspoon salt mix well. Add
  remaining flour and mix well. Turn on to floured counter top
  and knead about 6 to 8 minutes until smooth.

- Transfer dough to sprayed bowl, cover and place in warm area
  for about 1 hour to double in size. Punch down and roll out into
  15-inch circle. Oil both sides of dough.

- Place dough on oiled grill away from direct medium heat
  and cook until grill marks appear and bread is crusty, about
  15 minutes.

- Remove from heat, add toppings to cooked side and return
  to grill. Cook until cheeses melt and pizza is hot throughout.
  Serves 8.

Vegetables

You can easily grill your whole meal
with these easy, delicious side dishes.

Buttered-Almond Asparagus

1 - 1½ pounds fresh asparagus
⅓ cup butter
⅔ cup slivered almonds
1 tablespoon lemon juice

- Place asparagus in 2 heavy-duty, sprayed foil packets. Divide butter and almonds equally between packets. Wrap tightly to hold juices. Place on preheated grill over medium-hot fire for about 3 to 5 minutes.

- Shake packets to distribute butter. When packets sizzle, move to indirect heat and cook until tender-crisp, about 10 minutes. Sprinkle lemon juice and a little salt and pepper over asparagus. Serve hot. Serves 4 to 6.

TIP: If you want grill marks on asparagus, rub with olive oil and cook directly on grill for about 10 minutes.

Grilled Sweet Asparagus

1¼ pounds asparagus, trimmed
2 - 3 tablespoons virgin olive oil
1 lemon, sliced

- Rub asparagus with olive oil. Cook on oiled, preheated grill over medium-hot fire until grill marks show about 5 minutes. Turn and grill on other side. When asparagus is tender, remove from grill. Serve with lemon slices. Serves 4.

Black Bean and Rice Stuffed Peppers

1 (15 ounce) can black beans, drained
1 cup cooked rice
1 cup shredded Monterey jack cheese
½ cup salsa
1 tablespoon oil
1 clove garlic, minced
3 large bell peppers, halved lengthwise, seeds removed

- Combine black beans, rice, cheese, salsa, oil, garlic and ½ teaspoon salt in bowl. Place bell pepper halves on large, sprayed heavy-duty sheet of foil.

- Fill all bell peppers with bean-rice mixture. Fold loosely in foil and seal tightly. Cover and grill over medium fire for about 20 minutes until peppers are tender. Serves 6.

Salsa Verde Stuffed Peppers

- Use recipe for *Black Bean and Rice Stuffed Peppers (page 39)* and substitute salsa verde for regular salsa. Serves 6.

Roasted Bell Pepper Medley

3 - 4 green, red and yellow bell peppers, cored, halved

- Cook on oiled, preheated grill or on sprayed foil over direct medium heat. Cook until outside of pepper chars. Rotate until all sides are slightly charred. Place peppers in plastic bag and seal for about 10 minutes to steam. Remove peppers and slice. Serves 4.

Many vegetables are excellent cut in large, bite-size pieces and placed on a skewer. It may be easier to cook all the larger, firmer vegetables on the same skewer because they need to cook longer than softer, smaller vegetables like zucchini and mushrooms.

Bok Choy Howdy

If you haven't tried this Chinese cabbage before, try it on the grill. This is a very simple way to expand your horizons.

2 - 4 large stems bok choy, trimmed
Sesame oil or canola oil
Soy sauce

- Rub bok choy with oil. Cook on oiled, preheated grill over medium heat until tender, about 5 to 10 minutes per side. Turn once after grill marks appear. Trim to smaller bite-sized pieces and drizzle soy sauce over top before serving. Serves 4.

Lemon-Peppered Broccoli

2 large stalks broccoli
½ cup (1 stick) butter, melted
Lemon-pepper seasoning

- Remove broccoli leaves, cut into bite-sized pieces and place in center of sprayed, heavy-duty foil. Pour half of melted butter over broccoli and sprinkle generously with lemon-pepper.

- Fold foil loosely for air to circulate and seal tightly. Cook on preheated grill over medium fire, about 10 to 15 minutes until tender. Shake packet several times to redistribute broccoli. Place broccoli in bowl and pour remaining butter over top. Serves 4.

Cauliflower and Carrot Packs

1 small head cauliflower, cut into small florets
1 cup baby carrots, halved lengthwise
1 small onion, sliced
2 tablespoons olive oil
1 teaspoon garlic powder

- Combine all ingredients and ½ teaspoon each salt and pepper; stir to coat well. Place cauliflower mixture on sprayed heavy-duty foil. Fold foil loosely so air can circulate and seal tightly.

- Cook on grill over medium heat for about 15 minutes until vegetables are tender; rotate once. Serves 4.

Olive-Cauliflower Packs

- Use recipe for *Cauliflower and Carrot Packs (page 40)*. Top grilled mixture with ¼ cup sliced olives and fresh basil leaves. Serves 4.

Crunchy Grilled Baby Carrots

1 (1 pound) package baby carrots
3 tablespoons olive oil

- Rub carrots with oil and place in basket, wok or heavy-duty foil on preheated grill over medium-hot fire. Cook carrots until tender, about 20 minutes; turn several times.

- The sugars in carrots will caramelize and make sugar crust on outside. Sprinkle with a little salt and serve immediately. Serves 4 to 6.

Crunchy Cauliflower

1 head cauliflower
¼ cup prepared Italian vinaigrette salad dressing
3 tablespoons olive oil

- Trim stems of cauliflower and slice into bite-sized pieces. Pour salad dressing over cauliflower and marinate for about 30 minutes. Sprinkle with oil and place in basket, wok or sprayed heavy-duty foil on preheated grill over medium-hot fire.

- Cook cauliflower until tender, about 20 minutes, and turn several times. Serve immediately. Serves 4 to 6.

If you use bamboo skewers for grilling, be sure to soak them in water for at least 30 minutes before putting them over heat source.

Grilled Anaheim Chili Peppers

4 - 6 large green Anaheim chili peppers
2 - 3 tablespoons vegetable oil

- Rub chili peppers with oil. Place on oiled, preheated grill over hot coals until grill marks show. Turn and grill on other side. When skin blisters all over, remove from grill. Place in bowl and seal with plastic wrap. Peppers steam and skin is easy to remove. Serves 4.

TIP: Anaheim chili peppers are large and look like they might do some damage to taste buds, but they are very mild.

Grilled Whole Anaheim Chilies

Serve these delicious chilies whole or sliced in strips called rajas. Anaheims are very mild, but remove seeds for milder flavor.

8 - 10 fresh, whole Anaheim green chilies
Shredded parmesan cheese

- Place chilies on lightly oiled grill over low heat. Turn frequently because chilies blister and char on outside. Grill for about 2 to 3 minutes per side.

- Remove from grill and slide peel away from chilies. Serve whole or cut into narrow strips with a sprinkle of parmesan on top. Serves 6 to 8.

> *Before 1911, salt clumped in damp weather and dispensing was difficult. In 1911 the Morton Salt Company added magnesium carbonate to its salt so that it would flow freely. The girl with umbrella, illustrating that the salt flows even in the rain, was introduced in 1914.*
>
> *The company has updated the girl's appearance to be in keeping with times about every ten years or so. The girl with the umbrella, holding free-flowing salt, and walking in the rain is one of the most recognized icons in the world. The old saying, "It never rains, but it pours," was the inspiration for the company slogan, "When it rains, it pours."*

Roasted Corn-on-the-Cob

The arrival of corn-on-the-cob lets us know that summer is definitely here. Here are the simplest ways to grill or roast corn-on-the-cob.

Tips for Grilling or Roasting Corn:

- Always soak corn with husks in water for 30 minutes to 1 hour. Shake off excess water before cooking. The remaining water will steam corn while it cooks.

- Use tongs to turn and to remove corn from grill.

- Direct or indirect heat works well for corn. You can place corn away from direct heat or on upper rack while other foods cook.

- It usually takes between 12 to 30 minutes for corn to be tender. If you overcook corn, it will be mushy.

- Some silks will burn off while grilling.

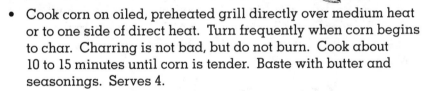

Basic Grilled Corn

4 ears corn-on-the-cob
Butter

- Cook corn on oiled, preheated grill directly over medium heat or to one side of direct heat. Turn frequently when corn begins to char. Charring is not bad, but do not burn. Cook about 10 to 15 minutes until corn is tender. Baste with butter and seasonings. Serves 4.

TIP: You can also spread butter on corn, sprinkle it with salt and pepper and wrap it in foil to grill. It will take a little longer to cook.

Always clean grill very well before cooking fruits and vegetables or they may taste like hamburger. You can also use foil over the grate to avoid extra cleaning.

Basic Grilled Corn in Husks

4 ears corn-on-the-cob

- Remove several of the thick, outer leaves. Pull back other leaves, but do not remove. Pull off silks and fold leaves back over corn. Separate narrow strips from outer leaves and tie leaves on. Soak corn in water for about 1 hour. Shake off excess water. Water inside husks will steam corn.

- Cook corn on oiled, preheated grill directly over medium heat or to one side of heat. Turn frequently when corn begins to char.

- Cook about 15 to 30 minutes until corn is tender and steams. Serve with butter and seasonings. Serves 4.

Compound Butters for Roasted Corn-on-the-Cob

These are simple recipes for flavored butters. It's a great way to add exciting bursts of unexpected flavors for vegetables, steaks, chicken and seafood.

- Choose any of the flavored butters for grilled corn-on-the-cob. Stir together all ingredients. Place mixture on parchment or waxed paper and roll into log shape. Twist ends together to seal. Refrigerate for 1 month or freeze for 3 months. Makes 1 cup.

Cilantro-Lime Butter

1 cup (2 sticks) unsalted butter, softened
¼ cup minced fresh cilantro
Zest of 1 lime
1 teaspoon kosher salt
½ teaspoon cayenne pepper

To spread out the work on cooking day, make sauces ahead of time. Store in refrigerator for up to one week.

Gorgonzola-Flavored Butter

1 cup (2 sticks) unsalted butter, softened
¼ cup gorgonzola, softened
½ - 1 teaspoon Kosher salt

Parslied Green Onion Butter

1 cup (2 sticks) unsalted butter, softened
¼ - ⅓ cup minced green onion with tops
1 - 2 tablespoons minced parsley
½ teaspoon kosher salt

Sun-Dried Tomato Butter with Basil

1 cup (2 sticks) unsalted butter, softened
2 - 3 tablespoons diced sun-dried tomatoes
1 tablespoon minced fresh basil leaves
½ teaspoon kosher salt, optional

Seasoned Butters for Grilled Corn

Seasoned butters make grilled corn taste like gourmet fare and it's so easy.

- For ½ cup (1 stick) butter, softened, mix with one or more of the following seasonings, enough for about 6 ears of grilled corn.

1 teaspoon chili powder
1 teaspoon curry powder
1 teaspoon chopped chives or chopped green onions.
1 teaspoon chopped parsley
1 teaspoon lemon pepper
1 teaspoon seasoned salt
½ teaspoon onion salt
½ teaspoon garlic salt

Smokin' Corn-on-the-Cob

12 ears fresh corn-on-the-cob with husks
2 quarts light beer
1 (10 pound) bag ice

- Peel husks back three-fourths down cob, but do not remove.
  Pull off as many silks as possible and wrap husks around corn.
  Place in cooler and pour beer over corn. Pour ice into cooler,
  close cooler and marinate corn for 5 or 6 hours.

- Drain corn and place on rack in oiled grill, cook over medium
  heat and close lid. Cook about 15 to 20 minutes per side
  until corn is tender. Peel back husks and use as handles.
  Serves 8 to 10.

Grilled Corn Coblets

4 ears fresh corn-on-the-cob
Olive oil

- Slice or break corn in 2 to 3-inch pieces. Rub with olive oil and
  sprinkle salt and pepper on liberally. Cook on sprayed foil on
  grill over medium fire for about 5 to 10 minutes per side until
  tender. Serves 6 to 8.

The best charcoal briquettes are plain, natural and compressed charcoal without any starter additions. Pile coals in charcoal chimney or pyramid fashion with paper for starter. Petroleum-based starter or lighter fluids leave a residual smell and taste.

Mexican Street-Corner Corn

This recipe is for a very popular grilled food sold by street vendors in Mexico City.

8 ears corn
1 cup mayonnaise
2 cups queso cotija
2 limes, halved
1 - 2 tablespoons chili powder

- Cook corn on oiled, preheated grill over medium fire for about 10 to 20 minutes until tender; turn frequently. Corn will have some charring.

- Spread mayonnaise on corn and roll in queso cotija* to cover. Sprinkle lime juice and chili powder over corn before serving. Serves 8.

TIP: You may substitute shredded parmesan for queso cotija (a traditional cheese from Mexico that is often used in ways similar to parmesan).

Eggplant Vinaigrette

1 medium eggplant
½ cup balsamic vinaigrette

- Peel and slice eggplant into ¼ to ½-inch slices. Pour balsamic vinaigrette over slices and marinate for about 30 minutes. Drain and pat dry. Grill eggplant on sprayed foil or across oiled grate over medium fire for about 5 to 8 minutes per side. Remove when tender. Serves 4.

Start gas grills with the lid open. Heat long enough to bring grate and unit to optimum cooking temperature. If you want a smoky flavor, soak wood chips for about 1 hour and place in aluminum pan next to gas burners. Grate should be about 4 to 5 inches from heat source. Adjust flame height according to what you are cooking.

Grilled Purple Eggplant Slices

1 large purple eggplant
2 - 3 tablespoons virgin olive oil
Garlic powder

- Slice eggplant into ½-inch thick slices lengthwise. Rub with olive oil and sprinkle with a little garlic powder.

- Cook on oiled, preheated grill over medium heat until grill marks show, about 5 minutes per side. Turn and grill on other side until it browns slightly, about 5 minutes. Serves 4.

Sliced Eggplant with Red Sauce

2 eggplants

- Slice eggplants lengthwise, sprinkle with salt and set aside for about 20 to 30 minutes. Wipe dry and cook on oiled grill over medium fire for about 5 minutes per side until grill marks appear.

Red Sauce:

¼ cup (½ stick) butter
3 cloves garlic, pressed
½ cup chopped celery
½ cup chopped green onions with tops
¼ cup chopped bell pepper
1 tablespoon chili powder
1 - 2 tablespoons Louisiana hot sauce
1 (28 ounce) can crushed Italian tomatoes

- In large saucepan, melt butter and sauté garlic, celery, onions and bell pepper until garlic and onions are translucent. Add chili powder, hot sauce and crushed tomatoes and bring to a boil.

- Cook for several minutes and reduce heat to low. Cook 30 to 45 minutes until sauce thickens. Pour over eggplant slices before serving. Serves about 4.

Parmesan Garlic Bake

4 baking potatoes with peel
⅓ cup Italian-style breadcrumbs
¼ cup shredded parmesan
3 tablespoons butter, melted
2 cloves garlic, pressed

- Cut potatoes in ¼-inch horizontal slices. Place equally on 2 sheets of sprayed heavy-duty foil. Combine breadcrumbs, parmesan, butter and garlic and pour over potatoes. Wrap potatoes loosely, but seal foil package tightly to hold juices.

- Cook on preheated grill over medium-hot fire for about 10 minutes with lid closed. Reposition packets and cook another 8 to 12 minutes until potatoes are tender. Serves 4 to 6.

Grilled Elephant Garlic

3 - 6 elephant garlic bulbs
2 - 3 tablespoons canola oil
2 - 3 tablespoons butter, melted

- Preheat grill for indirect medium-hot heat. Remove skin from outside of bulbs and trim ends. Coat garlic with oil. Place bulbs on sprayed heavy-duty foil. Fold and seal foil allowing for air expansion.

- Grill away from direct heat until cloves are tender, about 20 to 30 minutes; rotate often. Separate cloves in garlic bulbs, slice in half lengthwise and drizzle with melted butter. Serve immediately. Serves 4.

If something goes wrong, you can usually fix it by adding butter, bacon or a little salt. Try it before you surrender to defeat.

Lemon Green Beans

1½ - 2 pounds fresh green beans, cleaned
Oil
4 tablespoons (½ stick) butter
1 lemon, sliced

- Place green beans in bowl, pour a little oil over top and stir well to coat beans. Place in 4 individual packages of heavy-duty, sprayed foil. Season with salt and pepper.

- Add 1 tablespoon butter on top and 1 slice of lemon. Fold foil loosely, but seal tightly. Cook on grill, away from direct medium heat, for about 10 to 15 minutes until tender-crisp. Turn bundles once or twice. Serves 4.

Smoked Jalapenos

10 - 12 medium fresh jalapenos
½ cup (1 stick) butter, softened
3 - 4 cloves garlic, minced
2 tablespoons liquid smoke

- Slice jalapenos in half and remove seeds. Spread butter on each half and sprinkle minced garlic over each. Place jalapenos on sprayed heavy-duty foil. Sprinkle liquid smoke over jalapenos. Fold loosely and seal tightly.

- Cook jalapeno packages on preheated grill to one side of medium-hot fire for about 30 minutes until tender. Serves 8 to 10.

TIP: Wear rubber gloves when removing seeds from jalapenos.

It is best to scrape the grate of your grill or smoker before and after you cook. After you start the fire, some of the residue from the last grilling burns off. When you oil or spray the grill before you use it and clean it afterwards, it always makes cleanup easier.

Grilled Jalapeno Wraps

6 - 8 fresh jalapenos, seeded, halved lengthwise
1 (8 ounce) carton cream cheese
6 - 8 thin slices bacon

- Fill each jalapeno half with cream cheese. Wrap bacon around each and secure with toothpick. (If your bacon is thick, you may use ½ slice for each jalapeno half.)

- Refrigerate until ready to grill. Grill over medium heat until bacon is crispy. Makes about 6 to 8 wraps.

TIP: Refrigerate cheese before grilling so cream cheese is very firm and won't melt too quickly.

Garden-Stuffed Mushrooms

1 (12 ounce) carton button mushrooms
½ cup seasoned stuffing mix
¼ cup (½ stick) butter, softened
¼ cup diced celery
2 tablespoons diced green onions with tops

- Remove stems from mushrooms. Mix stuffing, butter, celery, green onions and dash of salt and pepper. Stuff mixture into mushroom cavities.

- Cook on oiled grill away from direct medium heat with lid closed for about 12 to 15 minutes until mushrooms are tender. Serves about 4 to 6.

Grilled Portobello Mushrooms

4 large portobello mushrooms, stemmed
2 - 3 tablespoons virgin olive oil

- Rub mushrooms with olive oil. Cook on oiled preheated grill over or to one side of medium fire until grill marks show, about 5 minutes. Turn and grill on other side until tender, about 3 to 5 minutes. Serves 4.

Grilled Button Mushrooms

1 (12 ounce) package button mushrooms, stemmed
2 - 3 tablespoons canola oil
¼ cup melted butter

- Rub mushrooms with oil. Place on wok or sprayed, heavy-duty foil on preheated grill over medium fire. Cook until grill marks show, turn and grill on other side until tender, about 3 to 5 minutes. Drizzle melted butter over mushrooms and serve. Serves 4.

Easy Onions

6 medium white onions, peeled
6 beef bouillon cubes
Worcestershire sauce
¼ cup (½ stick) butter, melted

- Cut out center of onion, but do not go through bottom. Place 1 bouillon cube in each onion cavity and several drops of Worcestershire. Fill cavity with butter. Fold foil loosely around onions and seal each tightly.

- Cook on grill over medium-high heat and cook, with lid closed, for about 30 to 45 minutes until onions are tender. Serves 6.

Caramelized Onions

This is very good served with grilled meats.

4 - 5 sweet onions, thinly sliced
2 tablespoons butter, chopped
¼ teaspoon garlic powder

- Place onion slices, butter, garlic powder and a little salt and pepper in sprayed foil pan. Place on grill away from direct medium heat and cook for 30 to 45 minutes until onions are soft, dark golden brown and liquid is syrupy. Stir occasionally. Serves 6.

Cheesy Roasted Sweet Onions

4 medium *Texas SuperSweet or Vidalia® sweet onions*
½ cup (1 stick) butter
¼ cup shredded sharp cheddar cheese

- Remove outer skin of onions. Remove very thin slice from bottom of onion so onions sit flat. Make 2 vertical crisscross slices from top almost cutting down to core but not all the way.

- Insert butter into center slit of each onion. Add ½ teaspoon salt and ¼ teaspoon pepper and sprinkle heaping tablespoon cheese in each slit. Wrap onions loosely in sprayed, heavy-duty foil to avoid touching cheese.

- Place on preheated grill over medium fire or off to one side of medium-hot fire until onions are tender, about 30 minutes. Serves 4.

Grilled Sweet Vidalia Onions

4 medium *Vidalia® onions, peeled*
2 - 3 tablespoons virgin olive oil
Worcestershire sauce

- Cut onions in ¾-inch slices horizontally. Rub slices with olive oil. Place in basket or on sprayed, heavy-duty foil and cook on preheated grill over medium heat until grill marks show, about 5 minutes.

- Turn each slice with spatula, drizzle Worcestershire sauce over top and grill until tender, about 3 to 5 minutes. Serve warm. Serves 4.

Grilled Fresh Green Onions

2 bunches green onions with tops, trimmed
2 tablespoons canola oil

- Rub onions and green stems with oil. Place on oiled, preheated grill or on sprayed heavy-duty foil over grill and cook over medium heat until grill marks show. Turn and grill on other side until tender, about 5 to 10 minutes total. Serves 4 to 6.

Grilled Shallots

Similar to onions, shallots are a little milder than onions and easy to grill.

6 - 8 shallots, peeled
2 tablespoons virgin olive oil

- Rub shallots with olive oil and place on oiled grill. Cook away from direct medium-high heat for about 10 to 15 minutes. Turn and continue to cook until outside is slightly charred and inside is tender-crisp, about 10 to 15 minutes. Serves 4.

Baked Potatoes over an Open Fire

Baked potatoes are a great favorite because there are so many ways of achieving a good baked potato!

Campfire Baked Potatoes

- For an outdoor outing, pierce clean potatoes with a fork and wrap in several layers of heavy-duty foil; bake on bonfire coals. Turn several times, for about 40 to 50 minutes until potatoes are tender. Serve with butter, sour cream, grated cheese, chives, freshly ground pepper and salt.

Backyard Grill Baked Potatoes

- For a backyard barbecue, pierce clean whole potatoes and wrap in heavy-duty foil. Cook on preheated grill, over direct or indirect medium heat, until potatoes are tender, about 50 minutes.

Cook fresh pork slowly, 20 to 25 minutes per inch of thickness, over medium-low heat.

Baked Potato Slices

Potatoes, sliced
Butter, divided
Vegetables (onion, celery, mushrooms, bell peppers)

- Grill sliced potatoes, with or without peel, in sprayed foil packet with butter. Cook over medium-hot fire for about 20 minutes and shake packet.

- Continue to cook until potatoes are tender, about 10 to 20 minutes. Add sliced or chopped vegetables, butter, and salt and pepper to packet during last 20 minutes of cooking.

Twice Grilled Potatoes

2 baking potatoes, baked
¼ cup (½ stick) butter
2 cloves garlic, pressed
1 cup shredded cheddar cheese

- Halve potatoes, scoop out flesh to within ¼ inch of skin and mash flesh with butter, garlic and a little salt and pepper. Place skins, cut side down, on oiled grill over medium-hot fire for about 5 to 10 minutes per side until crispy.

- Pour mashed potatoes back into shells. Top with cheddar cheese, place back on grill and cook until cheese melts, about 5 to 7 minutes. Serves 4.

Roasted Surprise Potatoes

8 - 10 new (red) potatoes, sliced
½ cup (1 stick) butter
1 bunch fresh green onions with tops, chopped
2 - 3 ribs celery, chopped
1 - 2 red bell peppers, cored, seeded, chopped

- Place potatoes equally in 4 large pieces of heavy-duty foil. Add butter to packets and seal so liquid will not leak. Cook on preheated grill over medium-hot fire for about 10 to 15 minutes. (Move away from direct heat if packet begins to burn.)

- Carefully open packet, stir and add vegetables. Sprinkle with a little salt and pepper, reseal packets and continue to cook until potatoes and vegetables are tender, about 10 minutes. Serve in packets or empty contents onto individual plates. Serves 4.

Pouch Potatoes

1 cup (2 sticks) butter, melted
2 (4 ounce) cans diced green chilies
¼ cup fresh snipped parsley
1 teaspoon garlic powder
½ teaspoon paprika
12 - 14 small, red potatoes with peels

- In saucepan, combine butter, green chilies, parsley, garlic powder, paprika, 1 teaspoon salt and ½ teaspoon black pepper, heat and stir well. Place potatoes in 4 sprayed, heavy-duty foil packages, pour butter sauce over potatoes and seal so liquid does not leak.

- Cook on preheated grill over low direct heat or away from heat until potatoes are tender, about 20 to 30 minutes. Turn pouches and shake a little to stir butter sauce. Serves 4 to 6.

Grilled New Potatoes

1 pound new (red) potatoes
3 tablespoons orange marmalade
1 teaspoon brown sugar
2 tablespoons butter, melted

- Cook new potatoes in medium saucepan covered in boiling water until tender-crisp. Drain and cut in half. Thread on skewers. Combine marmalade, brown sugar and butter and brush mixture over potatoes.

- Cook on oiled grill over medium hot coals until potatoes are brown, about 5 minutes on each side. Add a little salt and pepper. Baste frequently. Serves 4 to 6.

Cook smoked pork slowly, 15 to 20 minutes per inch of thickness, over medium-low heat.

Cheddar Potato Packs

4 potatoes
3 tablespoons butter, melted
1 cup shredded cheddar cheese
2 tablespoons bacon bits

- Cut potatoes into 1-inch cubes and place on sprayed heavy-duty foil. Pour butter over potatoes. Sprinkle with cheese, bacon and ½ teaspoon each salt and pepper.

- Fold and seal foil allowing for expansion. Punch a few holes in top of foil packet. Cover and grill over direct or indirect heat for about 50 minutes until potatoes are tender; rotate at least once. Serves 4.

Onion-Cheddar Potato Packs

- Use recipe for *Cheddar Potato Packs (page 57)* and add 2 tablespoons chopped green onions to foil packs before grilling. Serves 4.

Swiss Potato Packs

- Use recipe for *Cheddar Potato Packs (page 57)* and substitute Swiss cheese for cheddar cheese. Serves 4.

Colorful Potato Packs

- Use recipe for *Cheddar Potato Packs (page 57)* and add ½ cup chopped red bell pepper. Serves 4.

Potatoes, onions, zucchini and bell peppers are perfect to grow in the garden and to grill. Cube potatoes, chop onions, mince a little garlic or sprinkle on garlic salt, salt and pepper and several pats of butter. Wrap in a pouch of foil, poke several holes on top and place on grill. Remove when potatoes are soft. For peppers, add a little oil to outside and cook on grill until slightly charred. Place in plastic bag for about 10 minutes, peel and serve.

Grilled New Potatoes and Onions

2 tablespoons olive oil
6 - 10 red potatoes with peel, quartered
2 sweet onions, quartered
½ teaspoon lemon pepper

- Rub oil over potatoes and onions. Sprinkle with lemon pepper and ½ teaspoon salt. Place in vegetable basket or on sprayed foil on grill. Grill about 30 minutes over medium heat, turning frequently, until tender. Serves 4.

Grilled Potato Skin Bites

4 baking potatoes, baked
½ cup (1 stick) butter, melted
3 cloves garlic, pressed
¼ - ½ cup Real Bacon Pieces
1 cup shredded cheddar cheese
Sour cream

- Halve potatoes, scoop out flesh to within ¼ to ½ inch of skin. (Save flesh for Twice Grilled Potatoes or mashed potatoes.) Place skins, upside down, on oiled grill over medium-hot fire for about 5 to 10 minutes to brown.

- Fill skins with butter, garlic, bacon, a little salt and pepper and cheddar cheese. Place back on grill and cook until cheese melts. Cut in half and top with sour cream. Serves 4 to 6.

Special grill racks or toppers are available to cook vegetables, shrimp or any small pieces that might fall through the grill grate, but foil works just as well.

Mediterranean Potato Salad

2 pounds new (red) potatoes, quartered
Olive oil
1 cup chopped roasted red peppers
¾ - 1 cup Caesar dressing
½ cup grated parmesan cheese
¼ cup chopped fresh parsley

- Place potatoes equally into 2 sprayed, heavy-duty foil packets. Pour several drops of olive oil in each packet and wrap tightly to hold juices.

- Place on preheated grill over medium-hot fire for about 10 minutes. Shake packet to redistribute, add red peppers and continue cooking until potatoes are tender, about 10 to 15 minutes.

- Remove from fire and pour potatoes in large bowl. Toss lightly with remaining ingredients and serve warm or refrigerate potatoes before mixing. Serves 6 to 8.

Grilled Sweet Potato Chips

2 - 3 sweet potatoes
Olive oil
Sweet Hungarian paprika
Sea salt

- Cut sweet potatoes into ¼-inch slices to make chip-size pieces. Rub with a little oil and place on sprayed heavy-duty foil on grill.

- Sprinkle sweet paprika over chips and cook over medium-hot fire for about 7 minutes per side. Turn, sprinkle a little sea salt on top of each chip and cook until crispy. Serve immediately. Serves 6 to 8.

Always brush grill with oil or use non-stick spray
before the grill heats up to avoid foods sticking to it.

Sweet Potato Packs

2 tablespoons butter, melted
2 tablespoons honey
2 sweet potatoes, peeled

- In large bowl combine butter, honey and 1 teaspoon salt. Cut sweet potatoes into 1-inch cubes and add to butter honey mixture; stir to coat well.

- Pour potato mixture on large heavy-duty, sprayed foil. Fold foil loosely so air can circulate and seal edges. Grill over medium heat until tender, about 20 minutes. Serves 4.

TIP: You can also grill this in a disposable foil pan and cover with foil.

Sweet Potato and Bell Pepper Packs

- Use recipe for *Sweet Potato Packs (page 60)* and add 1 cubed bell pepper for a colorful flavor-burst. Serves 4.

Apricot-Glazed Sweet Potatoes

1½ cups apricot preserves
2 teaspoons lemon juice
½ teaspoon cinnamon
3-4 sweet potatoes, peeled, halved lengthwise
1 tablespoon olive oil

- In saucepan combine preserves and ½ cup water over medium heat until mixture begins to boil. Reduce heat and simmer 5 minutes, stirring constantly. Remove from heat and stir in lemon juice and cinnamon.

- Coat sweet potatoes with oil. Place on oiled grill over medium heat for about 15 minutes per side until tender; turn once. Cut into bite-size pieces and toss with apricot glaze. Serves 6 to 8.

Nutty Apricot Sweet Potatoes

- Use recipe for *Apricot-Glazed Sweet Potatoes (page 60)* and top with toasted almond slices or pecans. Serves 6 to 8.

Stuffed Yellow Squash

5 large crookneck yellow squash
1 (16 ounce) package frozen chopped spinach, thawed
1 (8 ounce) package cream cheese, cubed
1 (1 ounce) packet onion soup mix
Shredded cheddar cheese

- Cut squash lengthwise and remove seeds with spoon. Cook on oiled, preheated grill over medium-low fire until grill marks show and squash is tender, about 10 minutes per side. Set aside shells.

- Cook spinach according to package directions and press between paper towels to drain thoroughly. Add cream cheese to spinach and stir until it melts. Do not boil. Add soup mix and mix well.

- Fill squash shells with spinach mixture and top with few sprinkles cheddar cheese. Place squash back on grill, close lid and cook until cheese melts, about 5 minutes. Serves 4 to 6.

Grilled Yellow Squash

3 large yellow squash with peel
2 tablespoons virgin olive oil

- Slice in half lengthwise. Rub with olive oil. Cook on oiled, preheated grill away from medium-hot fire until grill marks show, about 5 to 10 minutes per side. Turn and grill on other side until tender-crisp. Serves 4.

I started with nothing and still have most of it.

Maple-Pecan Butternut Squash

2 small butternut squash, halved lengthwise, seeds removed
3 tablespoons butter, melted
5 tablespoons maple syrup, divided
⅓ cup chopped pecans

- Place each squash half, cut side up, on large, sprayed heavy-duty foil. Sprinkle with salt. Combine butter and 3 tablespoons syrup; pour over squash. Fold foil loosely and seal tightly.

- Grill over medium heat for about 1 hour until squash is tender; rotate once. Remove squash from foil and sprinkle with pecans and remaining syrup to serve. Serves 4.

Grilled Roma Tomatoes

4 - 6 Roma tomatoes
2 - 3 tablespoons virgin olive oil

- Rub tomatoes with olive oil. Cook on oiled, preheated grill over medium heat until grill marks show, about 3 to 5 minutes per side. When tomatoes are soft and slightly charred, remove from grill. Sprinkle with salt and pepper and serve hot. Serves 4.

Grilled Grape Tomatoes

1 (8 ounce) package grape tomatoes

- Place tomatoes in grill basket, on sprayed foil or oiled grill and cook over medium heat until grill marks show. Turn and grill on other side about 3 minutes until tomatoes are tender. Sprinkle with salt and pepper and serve warm. Serves 4.

Don't worry about the world coming to an end. It's already tomorrow in Australia.

–Charles Schulz

Grilled Homegrown Jumbo Tomatoes

4 fresh large homegrown or hot house tomatoes
2 tablespoons virgin olive oil
Shredded parmesan cheese

- Slice tomatoes in half horizontally and rub with olive oil. Cook on oiled, preheated grill away from direct high heat until grill marks show, about 5 minutes per side. (This works best if lid is closed.)

- Turn tomatoes so flat, cut side is up. Sprinkle shredded cheese on top of each half and cook until cheese melts a little. Serves 4.

Broccoli-Stuffed Tomatoes

4 medium tomatoes
1 (10 ounce) package frozen chopped broccoli
1 (6 ounce) roll garlic cheese, softened
½ teaspoon garlic salt

- Cut tops off tomatoes and scoop out flesh, but do not pierce bottom. Cook broccoli in saucepan according to package directions and drain thoroughly.

- Combine broccoli, cheese and garlic salt in saucepan and heat just until cheese melts. Stuff broccoli mixture into tomatoes and cook on oiled, preheated grill over indirect medium heat for about 10 minutes until tomatoes are tender. Serves 4.

Tomato Bread Salad

1 loaf crusty bread, sliced
1 (14.5 ounce) can diced Italian tomatoes, drained well
¼ cup olive oil
2 tablespoons lemon juice

- Cook bread on oiled grill over medium heat for about 3 minutes per side until golden brown.

- In large bowl combine tomatoes, olive oil, lemon juice and salt and pepper to taste. Cut bread into 1-inch cubes and add to tomato mixture. Mix well and set aside for 15 to 20 minutes. Serves 4 to 6.

Grilled Zucchini

2 large zucchini with peel
2 tablespoons virgin olive oil

- Slice zucchini lengthways about 1 inch thick. Rub with olive oil and place on oiled grill. Cook to one side of hot coals until grill marks show, about 5 to 7 minutes. Turn and grill on other side until tender-crisp, about 5 to 7 minutes. Serves 4.

Peppered Bacon-Zucchini Rolls

2 zucchini
12 slices peppered bacon
2 ounces goat cheese or ¼ cup cream cheese, softened
1 teaspoon lemon juice
1 teaspoon dried parsley

- Slice zucchini lengthwise about ¼ inch thick. Cook bacon, but not crisp and still soft; drain well. Mix cheese, lemon juice and parsley. Arrange bacon on each zucchini slice. Spread cheese mixture down middle of bacon and roll up. Secure with toothpick if needed.

- Cook on oiled grill over medium-hot fire for about 5 minutes until grill marks show and zucchini is tender. Remove from grill before cheese melts. Makes about 12 rolls.

Zucchini Patties

1½ cups grated zucchini
1 egg, beaten
2 tablespoons flour
⅓ cup finely minced onion
½ teaspoon seasoned salt

- Mix all ingredients in bowl. Form mixture into small patties. Place on sprayed, heavy-duty foil on grill. Cook over medium-hot fire for about 5 minutes until crispy on bottom. Turn, continue to cook until crispy, about 5 to 10 minutes. Serves 4.

Zucchini Dijon

3 zucchini
2 tablespoons dijon-style mustard
2 tablespoons white wine vinegar
2 teaspoons extra virgin olive oil

- Slice zucchini lengthwise about ¼ inch to ½ inch thick. Cook on oiled grill or on sprayed, heavy-duty foil over medium heat for about 5 to 7 minutes per side until grill marks show and zucchini is tender. Mix remaining ingredients and pour over zucchini before serving. Serves 4 to 6.

Omit and substitute. That's how recipes should be written. Please don't ever get so hung up on published recipes that you forget that you can omit and substitute.

–Jeff Smith, The Frugal Gourmet

Baja Grilled Vegetables

Vegetables are great when you cook them on the grill. Everyone is surprised by the flavors an open fire brings out.

Grape tomatoes
Roma tomatoes
Button mushrooms, stemmed
Bell pepper, green, yellow and red, seeded, quartered
Zucchini, sliced lengthwise
Yellow squash, sliced lengthwise
Sweet onions, peeled, quartered
Jalapenos, seeded, veined
Portobello mushrooms, stemmed
Asparagus
Eggplant, sliced lengthwise
Poblano peppers
Olive oil

- Lightly coat your choice of vegetables with oil and a little salt and pepper. Skewer and alternate small vegetables like tomatoes and button mushrooms and place larger, denser vegetables directly on grill.

- Cook on oiled, preheated grill over medium-hot fire until grill marks appear and vegetables are tender, but crisp, about 5 minutes for soft vegetables and about 10 minutes for harder vegetables.

TIP: *Skewers with onion slice, green bell pepper, grape tomato, button mushroom, yellow bell pepper, another onion slice, etc. make a beautiful vegetable medley. Keep vegetables with same density on skewers.*

Use canola oil if it is in a marinade. Use olive oil only when it goes on grill directly. Olive oil will congeal if refrigerated.

Grilled Mixed Vegetables

1 yellow squash, cubed
1 green bell pepper, seeded, quartered
1 small onion, quartered
1 (8 ounce) bottle Italian dressing

• Mix vegetables and spread on heavy-duty foil. Sprinkle
  dressing over all. Seal foil tightly and place on grill rack.
  Grill for about 10 minutes until vegetables are tender-crisp.
  Serves 4.

TIP: You could also add sliced zucchini and mushrooms.

Herb-Seasoned Vegetables

1 (16 ounce) package frozen vegetables
½ teaspoon garlic salt
2 tablespoons butter
¼ cup grated parmesan cheese

• Place frozen vegetables on sprayed heavy-duty foil large
  enough to hold all vegetables. Sprinkle with garlic salt and
  butter and seal foil tightly to hold in juices. Cook on preheated
  grill away from direct medium-high heat for about 10 minutes.

• Shake packet to redistribute vegetables and cook additional 10
  minutes until tender-crisp. (Drain liquid if needed.) Pour into
  bowl and sprinkle cheese on top. Serves 4 to 6.

*Bacon was sold in solid slabs until 1924 when Oscar
Mayer pre-sliced bacon and packaged it for consumer
sales. In 1950 Oscar Mayer was the first company
to offer pre-sliced meat as cold cuts in vacuum-
sealed packages.*

Grilled Veggie Kebabs

Extra-virgin olive oil
8 small white onions, peeled
2 green and 2 yellow bell peppers, seeded, quartered
Button mushrooms
1 pint grape tomatoes

- Use extra-virgin olive oil to coat vegetables. Place all veggies except tomatoes on skewers or in grilling basket. Put veggies on grill over medium heat.

- When veggies begin to soften, about 10 to 15 minutes, move to cooler part of grill and place tomatoes (in grilling basket) over medium heat for about 5 minutes per side. Do not overcook. Serves 4 to 6.

Grilled Veggies

Use any combination of vegetables below.

2 red peppers, quartered, seeded
2 green peppers, quartered, seeded
2 yellow peppers, quartered, seeded
2 zucchini, sliced lengthwise
2 yellow squash, sliced lengthwise
Olive oil
Garlic salt
Parsley

- Place vegetables in resealable plastic bags. Pour enough olive oil into each bag to coat vegetables. Season with garlic salt, parsley, pepper and salt. Shake bags until olive oil mixture coats vegetables.

- Lay bags flat to marinate for 1 hour on counter. Remove from bags and place on sprayed, heavy-duty foil on grill.

- Cook slowly away from medium heat until vegetables cook through and are tender-crisp. Serves about 8.

Mixed Veggie Packs

2 Yukon gold potatoes, sliced thin
1 cup baby carrots
1 cup fresh green beans
2 tablespoons butter, melted
½ teaspoon garlic powder
½ teaspoon oregano

- Combine all ingredients plus ½ teaspoon each salt and pepper.
  Pour onto large sprayed, heavy-duty foil. Fold loosely so air
  will circulate and seal foil tightly. Grill 5 inches from medium-
  hot heat for about 20 minutes until vegetables are tender, turn
  once. Serves 4.

TIP: Potatoes turn brown quickly so slice right before grilling.

Vegetable Medley

Sometimes it's better to cook vegetables alone on skewers without
meat because meat and vegetables don't cook at the same rate.

1 large Texas SuperSweet or Vidalia® onion, quartered
2 zucchini, cut in 1-inch slices
2 bell peppers, quartered, seeded
1 (12 ounce) carton button mushrooms, stemmed
1 (12 ounce) carton grape or cherry tomatoes
Olive oil

- Cover all vegetables with a little olive oil. Alternate vegetables
  on 2 parallel skewers to keep vegetables from turning.

- Cook on oiled grill over medium fire for about 7 minutes
  per side. Or, cook away from direct heat while meat cooks
  (vegetables will take a little longer to cook this way). Remove
  from grill and salt and pepper before serving. Serves 6 to 8.

$ave Money! *If you're dashing into the store for just
a few items, don't use a cart. If you're limited to what
you can carry, you're more likely to avoid impulse buys.*

Vegetable Seasoning Specialties

- Rub each vegetable with olive oil and sprinkle with seasonings listed below. Cook vegetable on oiled grill or on sprayed heavy-duty foil over medium heat for 10 minutes or away from direct heat while meat is cooking. Vegetables are ready when they are tender-crisp.

- (1 tablespoon fresh herbs equals 1 teaspoon dried herbs)

Vegetable	Seasonings
Artichoke Hearts	Season with crumbled bay leaves, savory or tarragon.
Asparagus	Season with garlic, allspice, chives, lemon balm, sage, savory, tarragon, thyme, chervil, dill and tarragon, thyme or basil.
Beans	Season with cumin, savory, garlic, mint, oregano, parsley, sage, or thyme.
Beets	Season with cloves, allspice, basil or dill.
Broccoli	Season with allspice, lemon pepper, basil, dill, garlic, marjoram, oregano, tarragon or thyme.
Brussels Sprouts	Season with dill, sage, thyme or savory.
Cabbage	Season with basil, caraway, cayenne, cloves, cumin, dill, fennel, marjoram, sage, savory, dill seed, mint, oregano or savory.
Carrots	Season with allspice, caraway, coriander, rosemary, basil, chervil, chives, cinnamon, cloves, cumin, dill, sage, ginger, marjoram, mint, parsley, savory, tarragon, thyme or chervil.
Cauliflower	Season with ginger, basil, caraway, chives, chili powder, cumin, dill, garlic, marjoram, parsley, rosemary, savory, tarragon, thyme or fennel.
Corn	Season with cilantro, chili powder, chives, cumin, dill, sage or thyme.
Cucumbers	Season with mint.
Eggplant	Season with lemon pepper, basil, cinnamon, dill, garlic, marjoram, mint, oregano, parsley, sage, savory or thyme.
Green Beans	Season with tarragon, savory, basil, caraway, cloves, dill, marjoram, mint, sage, tarragon or thyme.
Mushrooms	Season with coriander, marjoram, oregano, rosemary, tarragon, thyme, basil, dill, lemon balm, parsley, rosemary or savory.

Vegetable	Seasonings
Onions	Season with basil, marjoram, oregano, sage, tarragon or thyme.
Peas	Season with allspice, caraway, chives, rosemary, savory, tarragon, thyme, basil, chervil, dill, marjoram, mint, parsley or sage.
Potatoes	Season with bay leaves, cumin, paprika, parsley, basil, caraway, chives, coriander, dill, fennel, garlic, sage, marjoram, oregano, rosemary, tarragon or thyme.
Spinach	Season with nutmeg, basil, caraway, chives, cinnamon, dill, rosemary, thyme, marjoram, mint, sage or tarragon.
Squash	Season with cloves, allspice, basil, caraway, cardamom, cinnamon, cloves, ginger, marjoram, oregano, rosemary, sage, savory or dill.
Sweet potatoes	Season with cloves, allspice, cinnamon or ginger.
Tomatoes	Season with cumin, basil, bay leaf, chives, chili powder, chervil, coriander, dill, garlic, sage, marjoram, oregano, parsley, rosemary, savory, tarragon or thyme.
Zucchini	Season with allspice, basil, dill, marjoram, rosemary or tarragon.

It is best to sear beef, chicken and vegetables on outside for several minutes to hold in juices. Don't stick foods with fork before grilling. It will just cause juices to run out while grilling.

Burgers and More

Pizzas, sandwiches, brats and burgers give
lots of ideas for inexpensive meals and snacks.

Pepperoni Pizza

1 (12 - 14 inch) pre-baked pizza crust
½ - 1 cup pizza sauce
1 (3.5 ounce) package pepperoni
1 tablespoon Italian seasoning
1½ cups shredded Italian blend cheese

- Cook one side of pizza crust on oiled grill over medium-hot
  heat until grill marks appear, about 5 to 10 minutes. Spread
  pizza sauce on grilled-side of pizza crust. Add pepperoni,
  seasoning and cheese.

- Cook pizza on grill away from direct heat with lid closed for
  5 to 10 minutes until cheese melts and pizza is hot throughout.
  Makes 1 (12 - 14 inch) pizza.

Hawaiian Pizza

- Use recipe for *Pepperoni Pizza (page 72)*. Substitute Canadian
  bacon for pepperoni and add 1 cup small pineapple chunks.
  Makes 1 (12 - 14 inch) pizza.

Italian Delight Pizza

- Use recipe for *Pepperoni Pizza (page 72)* and add cooked,
  crumbled Italian sausage, 1 cup sliced bell pepper and 1 cup
  sliced mushrooms. Makes 1 (12 - 14 inch) pizza.

Artichoke Pizza

- Use recipe for *Pepperoni Pizza (page 72)*. Substitute cooked, crumbled Italian sausage for pepperoni and add 1 cup sliced artichoke hearts. Makes 1 (12 - 14 inch) pizza.

Chicken Alfredo Pizza

1 (12 - 14 inch) pre-baked pizza crust
½ - 1 cup alfredo sauce
1-2 cups cooked, chopped chicken
1 tablespoon Italian seasoning
1½ cups shredded Italian blend cheese

- Cook one side of pizza crust on oiled grill over medium-hot heat until grill marks appear, about 5 to 10 minutes. Spread alfredo sauce on grilled-side of pizza crust. Add chicken, seasoning, ½ teaspoon salt and cheese.

- Cook pizza on grill away from direct heat with lid closed for 5 to 10 minutes until cheese melts and pizza is hot throughout. Makes 1 (12 - 14 inch) pizza.

Spinach Alfredo Pizza

- Use recipe for *Chicken Alfredo Pizza (page 73)* and add 1 cup spinach leaves before topping pizza with cheese. Makes 1 (12 - 14 inch) pizza.

Mushroom Alfredo Pizza

- Use recipe for *Chicken Alfredo Pizza (page 73)* and add 1 cup sliced mushrooms before topping pizza with cheese. Makes 1 (12 - 14 inch) pizza.

Chicken Pesto Pizza

- Use recipe for *Chicken Alfredo Pizza (page 73)*. Replace alfredo sauce with pesto and omit salt. Makes 1 (12 - 14 inch) pizza.

Grilled Chicken Pizza with Spinach and Cashews

1 (12 - 14 inch) pre-baked pizza crust
1 (6 ounce) jar prepared pesto sauce
1 - 2 cups cooked, chopped chicken
1 tablespoon Italian seasoning
1 cup spinach leaves
½ cup chopped cashews
1 roma tomato, sliced
2 cups shredded Italian blend cheese

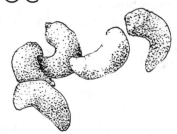

- Cook one side of pizza crust on oiled grill over medium-hot heat until grill marks appear, about 5 to 10 minutes. Spread pesto sauce on grilled-side of pizza crust. Add chicken, seasoning, spinach, cashews, tomato and cheese.

- Cook pizza on grill away from direct heat with lid closed for 5 to 10 minutes until cheese melts and pizza is hot throughout. Makes 1 (12 - 14 inch) pizza.

Margherita Pizza

1 (12 - 14 inch) pre-baked pizza crust
3 tablespoons olive oil
2 teaspoons minced garlic
1 teaspoon Italian seasoning
1 tomato, sliced
1½ cups shredded mozzarella cheese

- Cook one side of pizza crust on oiled grill over medium-hot heat until grill marks appear, about 5 to 10 minutes. Spread olive oil on grilled-side of pizza crust and add garlic, seasoning, tomato and cheese.

- Cook pizza on grill away from direct heat with lid closed for 5 to 10 minutes until cheese melts and pizza is hot throughout. Makes 1 (12 - 14 inch) pizza.

Chicken Margherita Pizza

- Use recipe for *Margherita Pizza (page 74)* and add 1 to 2 cups cooked, chopped chicken. Makes 1 (12 - 14 inch) pizza.

Garden Fresh Margherita Pizza

- Use recipe for *Margherita Pizza (page 74)* and add ¼ cup fresh basil leaves. Makes 1 (12 - 14 inch) pizza.

Olive-Margherita Pizza

- Use recipe for *Margherita Pizza (page 74)* and add ¼ cup sliced black olives and ¼ cup sliced green olives. Makes 1 (12 - 14 inch) pizza.

Sun-Dried Tomato Pizza

1 (12 - 14 inch) pre-baked pizza crust
½ - 1 cup pizza sauce
1 - 2 cups cooked, chopped chicken
1 teaspoon Italian seasoning
1 (4 ounce) jar sun-dried tomatoes, sliced
2 cups shredded Monterrey Jack cheese

- Cook one side of pizza crust on oiled grill over medium-hot heat until grill marks appear, about 5 to 10 minutes. Spread pizza sauce on grilled-side of pizza crust. Add chicken, seasoning, tomatoes and cheese on top.

- Cook pizza on grill away from direct heat with lid closed for 10 to 15 minutes until cheese melts and pizza is hot throughout. Makes 1 (12 - 14 inch) pizza.

The first pizzas were probably eaten by Greeks and Romans sometime around 1000 B.C. Virgil gave us the first written documentation of large round flat bread with herbs, spices and oils. Pizza with tomatoes didn't hit Italy until after Spanish conquistadors brought tomatoes from the New World to Europe in the 16th century.

In 1889 Queen Margherita was touring her land and sampled pizza, the food of peasants, and loved it. A local baker made a pizza with mozzarella, tomato and fresh basil in her honor and name it Margherita Pizza. The first pizzeria was started in New York City in 1905. Today, pizza is one of the world's most popular foods.

Thai Pizza

1 (12 - 14 inch) pre-baked pizza crust
½ - 1 cup peanut sauce
1½ cups cubed cooked chicken
½ cup shredded carrots
2 tablespoons chopped green onion
¼ cup chopped peanuts
1 cup shredded mozzarella cheese

- Cook one side of pizza crust on oiled grill over medium-hot heat until grill marks appear, about 5 to 10 minutes. Spread peanut sauce on grilled-side of pizza crust and top with chicken, carrots, onion, peanuts and cheese.

- Cook pizza on grill away from direct heat with lid closed for 10 to 15 minutes until cheese melts and pizza is hot throughout. Makes 1 (12 - 14 inch) pizza.

Cilantro Thai Pizza

- Follow instructions for *Thai Pizza (page 76)* and add 2 tablespoons chopped fresh cilantro for an extra flavor boost. Makes 1 (12 - 14 inch) pizza.

Barbecue Chicken Pizza

1 (12 - 14 inch) pre-baked pizza crust
1½ cups cooked, chopped chicken
½ - 1 cup barbecue sauce
¼ cup chopped red onion
2 cups shredded Monterey Jack cheese

- Cook one side of pizza crust on oiled grill over medium heat or away from direct heat and close lid. Cook until grill marks show or crust turns golden brown. Combine chicken and barbecue sauce and mix well. Spread mixture on grilled-side of pizza crust. Add onion and cheese.

- Cook pizza on grill away from direct heat with lid closed for 10 to 15 minutes until cheese melts and pizza is hot throughout. Makes 1 (12 - 14 inch) pizza.

Spicy Barbecue Chicken Pizza

- Follow instructions for *Barbecue Chicken Pizza (page 76)*, but add 1 to 2 teaspoons chili powder, hot sauce or crushed red pepper flakes to chicken-barbecue sauce mixture. Makes 1 (12 - 14 inch) pizza.

Tuna-Capers Pizza

1 (12 - 14 inch) pre-baked pizza crust
½ cup pizza sauce
1 (5 ounce) can chunk tuna, drained
2 tablespoons capers
1½ cups shredded mozzarella cheese

- Cook one side of pizza crust on oiled grill over medium-hot heat until grill marks appear, about 5 to 10 minutes. Spread pizza sauce on grilled-side of pizza crust. Add tuna, capers and cheese.

- Cook pizza on grill away from direct heat with lid closed for 10 to 15 minutes until cheese melts and pizza is hot throughout. Makes 1 (12 - 14 inch) pizza.

Red Pepper Tuna Pizza

- Follow instructions for *Tuna-Capers Pizza (page 77)* and add 1 (7 ounce) jar sliced roasted red peppers. Makes 1 (12 - 14 inch) pizza.

Easy Grilled Pizza Snacks

1 (14 ounce) package English muffins
1 pound bulk sausage, cooked, drained
1½ cups pizza sauce
1 (4 ounce) can sliced mushrooms, drained
1 (8 ounce) package shredded mozzarella cheese

- Split muffins and layer remaining ingredients in order listed on each muffin half, ending with cheese. Cook on oiled, preheated grill over medium heat for about 5 to 7 minutes until cheese melts. Serves 8.

Pizza Snacks with Pepperoni

- Use recipe for *Easy Grilled Pizza Snacks (page 77)* and add pepperoni. Serves 8.

Pizza Snacks with Olives

- Use recipe for *Easy Grilled Pizza Snacks (page 77)* and add sliced green and black olives. Serves 8.

Pizza Snacks with Onion

- Use recipe for *Easy Grilled Pizza Snacks (page 77)* and add sauteed chopped onions. Serves 8.

Pizza Pesto Snacks

- Use recipe for *Easy Grilled Pizza Snacks (page 77)* and replace pizza sauce with prepared pesto sauce. Serves 8.

Alfredo's Pizza Snacks

- Use recipe for *Easy Grilled Pizza Snacks (page 77)* and replace pizza sauce with alfredo sauce. Serves 8.

Real Grilled Cheese Sandwich

1 tablespoon butter, softened
2 slices bread
2 - 3 slices cheddar or American cheese

- Butter 1 side of each bread slice. Place 1 piece of bread (buttered-side down) on oiled grill over medium heat. Add cheese to bread and stack another bread slice buttered side up.

- Grill about 5 minutes until grill marks show and cheese begins to melt. Flatten sandwich slightly with spatula. When bread slices stick together, flip sandwich to brown other side. Serve when cheese melts. Makes 1 sandwich.

Additional Grilled Cheese Combinations:

Try different combinations of cheeses, fruits, vegetables
and breads.

- Queso fresco and thin apple or pear slices

- Monterey jack and diced green chilies

- Shredded parmesan with basil pesto

- Mexican 4-cheese blend cheese, jalapeno slices and Fritos®
  (yes, Fritos®)

- Goat cheese, avocado slices and thin tomato slices

- Cheddar cheese and pulled pork

- American cheese with beer-basted brat slices

- Fontina cheese and grape halves

- Mozzarella, tomato slices, fresh basil and pepper

- Cheddar cheese, red onion and avocado

- Mozzarella cheese, prepared pesto and tomato

- Swiss cheese, Dijon mustard, sliced hard-boiled egg

- Cheddar cheese, tomato, bacon

- Cheddar cheese, pear, bacon, fig jam

- Provolone cheese, spinach and ham or beef slices

- Mozzarella cheese with sliced mushrooms, bell pepper slices
  and black olive pieces

- **Assorted cheeses:** havarti, gouda, bleu, pepper jack, buffalo,
  asiago, longhorn, queso fresco, pepper jack cheese, Colby
  cheese, or Monterey Jack

- **Assorted dressings and spreads:** dijon-style mustard, deli
  mustard, Thousand Island dressing, dijonnaise, salsa or
  barbecue sauce

- **Assorted meats:** smoked turkey, honey ham, chicken breast,
  peppered roast beef, fried bacon or pepperoni

- **Assorted breads:** pumpernickel, rye, whole wheat, sour dough,
  French baguette, Italian bread, focaccia, ciabatta or brown bread

Grilled Pimento Cheese Sandwich

1 (1 pound) package shredded sharp cheddar cheese
3 tablespoons mayonnaise
1 (4 ounce) jar diced pimentos, drained well
8 slices white or whole wheat bread
Butter, softened

- Place cheese in large bowl and add mayonnaise and pimentos. (Make sure pimentos drain well.) If you want it drier, don't use as much mayonnaise. If you want it creamier, add a little more mayonnaise.

- Butter one side of bread, spread layer of pimento cheese about ½ inch thick and top with slice of bread, buttered side on outside. Place sandwich, butter side down, on sprayed, heavy-duty foil on grill over medium heat until bread turns light brown, about 5 minutes.

- When cheese begins to melt, carefully turn sandwich with spatula and grill until sandwiches heat through, about 3 to 5 minutes. Serves 4.

Green Chilies-Pimento Cheese

- Use recipe for *Grilled Pimento Cheese Sandwich (page 80)* and add 1 (5 ounce) can diced green chilies, well drained, and stir into pimento cheese. Serves 4.

Green Onion Grilled Cheese

- Use recipe for *Grilled Pimento Cheese Sandwich (page 80)* and add 2 to 4 chopped fresh green onions with tops. Chop onions and stir into pimento cheese. Add a touch of onion salt, if desired. Serves 4.

Jalapeno Grilled Cheese

- Use recipe for *Grilled Pimento Cheese Sandwich (page 80)* and add about 8 to 10 pickled jalapeno slices, chopped. Stir into pimento cheese. Serves 4.

Three-Cheese Grilled Cheese

- Use recipe for *Grilled Pimento Cheese Sandwich (page 80)*, except divide 2 cups cheese equally among shredded Swiss, 3-cheese Mexican blend, sharp cheddar or cream cheese. Serves 4.

Grilled Cheese-Ham Sandwich

- Use recipe for *Grilled Pimento Cheese Sandwich (page 80)* and add 4 or 5 thin slices of deli ham on top of pimento cheese. Serves 4.

Pepperoni Grilled Cheese

- Use recipe for *Grilled Pimento Cheese Sandwich (page 80)* and add about 8 to 10 pepperoni rounds on top of pimento cheese. Serves 4.

Queso fresco is a popular Mexican cheese made from cow and goat milk. It is soft and great for grilling because it softens substantially, but doesn't melt.

Sandwiches have been around since before Christ, but they rose to prominence with John Montagu, 4th Earl of Sandwich, First Lord of the Admiralty and patron of Captain James Cook. Montagu was an enthusiastic gambler who stayed at the tables for hours without leaving for meals. His valet brought him meat between two slices of bread and a tradition took on an official name.

A Special Grilled Cheese Sandwich

1 small loaf bread, sliced
Butter, softened
1 (12 ounce) bottle chipotle mayonnaise
1 (8 ounce) package shredded Mexican 3-cheese blend
1 - 2 avocados, sliced thin

- For each sandwich, spread softened butter on outside of 2 slices of bread.

- Place 1 slice, butter side down on oiled, preheated grill over medium heat. Top with 1 tablespoon chipotle mayonnaise, plenty of cheese and avocado slices. Top with remaining slice of bread spread with 1 tablespoon chipotle mayonnaise.

- Close grill lid and cook about 5 minutes until grill marks show. Turn sandwich over and cook another 5 minutes until cheese melts completely. Serves 6 to 8.

Hammy Grilled Cheese

- Use *A Special Grilled Cheese Sandwich recipe (page 82)* and add thinly sliced ham to each sandwich. Serves 6 to 8.

Grilled Bacon-Cheese Sandwich

- Use recipe for *A Special Grilled Cheese Sandwich (page 82)* and add cooked bacon to each sandwich. Serves 6 to 8.

Grilled Tomato-Cheese Sandwich

- Use recipe for *A Special Grilled Cheese Sandwich (page 82)* and add thin tomato slices to each sandwich. Serves 6 to 8.

> ***$ave Money!*** *Create a list of grocery prices for the items you buy most often. You can stay on top of bargains and price cycles. This will help you recognize a deal when you see one.*

Favorite Cheese Sandwich

- Use recipe for *A Special Grilled Cheese Sandwich (page 82)* and replace chipotle mayonnaise and 3-cheese blend with olive oil mayonnaise and your favorite cheese (mozzarella, parmesan, sharp cheddar and/or Swiss cheese). Serves 6 to 8.

Red Pepper Grilled Cheese

- Use recipe for *A Special Grilled Cheese Sandwich (page 82)* and add roasted red peppers to each sandwich. Serves 6 to 8.

Seven-Grain Grilled Cheese

- Use recipe for *A Special Grilled Cheese Sandwich (page 82)* and use 7-grain or whole wheat bread. Serves 6 to 8.

Red Pepper Grilled Goat Cheese

1 small loaf bread, sliced
Butter, softened
1 (6 ounce) package goat cheese
1 (12 ounce) jar roasted red peppers
½ cup fresh basil

- For each sandwich, spread softened butter on outside of 2 slices of bread. Place 1 slice, buttered-side down on oiled, preheated grill over medium heat. Top with cheese, roasted red pepper, basil and slice of bread (buttered-side facing up).

- Close grill lid and cook about 5 minutes until grill marks show. Turn sandwich over and cook another 5 minutes until cheese melts completely. Serves 6 to 8.

Grilled Mozzarella Cheese Sandwich

- Use *Red Pepper Grilled Goat Cheese recipe (page 83)* and substitute mozzarella cheese for goat cheese. Serves 6 to 8.

Smoked Carolina Pulled Pork Sandwich

It's a tradition in the South to eat coleslaw right on a pork sandwich. It's great!

1 (3 - 4 pound) pork roast or shoulder
Barbecue Sauce with Mustard (page 326)
Buns
Coleslaw
Dill pickles

- Build hickory, mesquite or pecan wood fire with enough coals to create 250° to 300° heat. Wrap roast in heavy-duty foil to seal in juices.

- Cook roast on grill to one side of medium fire for about 45 minutes to 1 hour. Remove from grill to check internal temperature. Continue to cook until internal temperature reaches 160°.

- When roast cools, pull meat apart with fingers or shred it with fork. Place shredded pork in large saucepan and pour barbecue sauce over it. Cook on medium until sauce is hot. Serve on large buns with coleslaw and dill pickles. Serves 8 to 12.

Grilled Reuben Sandwiches

Butter, softened
8 slices dark rye bread
8 slices Swiss cheese
1 pound thin-sliced corned beef
1 cup well drained sauerkraut
Thousand Island dressing

- Butter bread slices on 1 side. Layer cheese, corned beef and sauerkraut equally on 4 slices. Liberally spread dressing on inside of remaining bread, butter side out, and place on top of sauerkraut.

- Cook on oiled foil or directly on oiled grill over medium heat for about 5 minutes on each side until bread browns on outside. Turn carefully and flatten with spatula. Serves 4.

Grilled Veggie Sandwiches

2 bell peppers, quartered
½ cup sliced red onion
1 teaspoon garlic powder
8 slices sourdough bread
4 tablespoons butter, softened
¼ - ½ cup garlic & herb mayonnaise

- Spray bell peppers and onion with cooking spray and garlic powder. Cook vegetables on oiled grill over medium heat for about 5 to 7 minutes per side until tender and grill marks appear.

- For each slice of bread, spread butter on one side and mayonnaise on other side. Divide and place vegetables on mayonnaise side of 4 bread slices.

- Top with remaining 4 bread slices (buttered-side facing out). Grill sandwiches about 4 minutes per side until bread is toasty. Serves 4.

Deli Veggie Sandwiches

- Use recipe for *Grilled Veggie Sandwiches (page 85)* and add your favorite sliced deli meat. Serves 4.

Garden Fresh Grilled Sandwiches

- Use recipe for *Grilled Veggie Sandwiches (page 85)* and replace bell peppers with any fresh vegetables on hand. Sliced eggplant and squash are great additions. Serves 4.

Add vinegar or a potato if a dish is too salty.

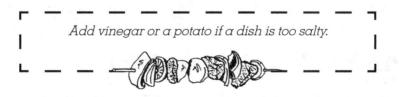

Curried Beef Pitas

⅓ cup plain yogurt
1 small cucumber, peeled, seeded, diced
1 teaspoon lemon juice
1 pound ground beef
¼ cup chopped onion
2 teaspoons curry powder
2 pita pockets, halved

- Combine yogurt, cucumber and lemon juice and refrigerate. Combine beef, onion, curry and ½ teaspoon salt and form into 4 patties.

- Cook on oiled grill over medium-hot fire about 5 to 10 minutes per side until no longer pink in middle and internal temperature is 160°. Place each patty in pita pocket and top with yogurt sauce. Serves 4.

Philly Cheesesteak

This famous regional specialty started in Philadelphia in the 1940's.

1 (1 pound) round, rib-eye, skirt or flank steak
1 onion, sliced
Olive oil
4 premium Italian/Hoagie rolls, split
4 slices American cheese, provolone or Cheez Whiz®

- Season steak with salt and pepper. Cook on oiled grill over medium-high heat for about 10 minutes per side until internal temperature is at least 145°.

- Rub onion with a little olive oil and cook over medium heat for about 5 to 10 minutes per side. Open rolls and lay to one side of fire to toast. Cut meat in thin slices and arrange on rolls with sliced onion and cheese. Place back on grill until cheese melts. Serves 4.

Pizza Philly Cheesesteak

- Use recipe for *Philly Cheesesteak (page 86)* and add pizza sauce. Serves 4.

Pickled Pepper Philly Cheesesteak

- Use recipe for *Philly Cheesesteak (page 86)* and add ketchup and pickled peppers. Serves 4.

Grilled Mushroom Philly Cheesesteak

- Use recipe for *Philly Cheesesteak (page 86)* and add sautéed or grilled mushrooms, sliced. Serves 4.

Grilled Pepper Philly Cheesesteak

- Use recipe for *Philly Cheesesteak (page 86)* and add grilled bell peppers, sliced. Serves 4.

Garlic Philly Cheesesteak

- Use recipe for *Philly Cheesesteak (page 86)* and add ½ cup mayonnaise and 2 teaspoons minced garlic. Serves 4.

After its start-up in 1921, Wonder® Bread brought sliced bread to the national market in 1930. It packaged the bread in a wrapper of colorful circles inspired by the "wonder" of hot air balloons. The popularity of sliced bread was the inspiration for the saying, "The greatest thing since sliced bread".

Grilled Chicken Sandwiches

1 medium onion, minced
1 small green bell pepper, minced
2 tablespoons butter
¾ cup ketchup
2 tablespoons brown sugar
2 tablespoons mustard
1 tablespoon Worcestershire sauce
4 small boneless, skinless chicken breast halves
4 hamburger buns

- Saute onion and bell pepper in butter. Add ketchup, brown sugar, mustard, Worcestershire sauce and 1 teaspoon salt in saucepan and simmer 15 minutes.

- Sprinkle chicken with salt and pepper and cook on oiled grill over hot fire to sear outside of both sides of chicken. Move away from fire, lightly baste with sauce and close lid.

- Cook for about 10 to 13 minutes per side until internal temperature reaches 165°. Several minutes before chicken is ready, baste liberally with sauce and again after you remove it from grill. Place chicken on buns and top with sauce. Serves 4.

Grilled Turkey Sandwich with Marmalade

Butter, softened
8 - 12 slices white or whole wheat bread
1 (8 ounce) package cream cheese, softened
¼ cup orange marmalade
1 pound thinly sliced deli turkey

- Butter one side of each slice of bread. Beat cream cheese and orange marmalade in bowl and spread evenly on 4 to 6 pieces of bread. Place 4 to 5 slices turkey on marmalade mixture and top with bread, buttered side out.

- Cook on oiled foil or directly on oiled grill over medium heat for about 5 minutes on each side until bread browns. Turn carefully with spatula. Serves 4 to 6.

Hot Dagwood Bunwiches

8 slices Swiss cheese
8 slices ham
8 slices deli turkey
8 slices American cheese
4 regular hamburger buns

- Open all 4 buns. On bottom buns, place 2 slices each of Swiss cheese, ham, turkey and American cheese and top with remaining buns.

- Grill on sprayed foil or directly on oiled grate over medium heat for about 5 minutes on each side until bread browns. Turn carefully and flatten with spatula. Serve when cheese melts. Makes 4 sandwiches.

TIP: Make up extra sandwiches and freeze. Wrap each bunwich individually in foil, freeze and thaw in refrigerator before grilling.

Grilled Turkey-Spinach Sandwiches

⅔ cup mayonnaise
2 teaspoons minced garlic
8 slices Oatnut® bread
1 pound deli thin-sliced turkey
8 ounces brie cheese, thick sliced
1 - 2 cups fresh spinach leaves

- Combine mayonnaise and garlic and spread on 1 side of each bread slice. Add turkey, brie and lots of spinach leaves and top with remaining bread.

- Grill on sprayed foil or directly on oiled grate over medium heat for about 5 minutes on each side until bread browns and cheese melts. Turn carefully and flatten with spatula. Serves 4.

$ave Money! Don't go to the grocery store hungry!!

Grilled Ham and Cheese Sandwich Loaf

1 loaf Italian bread
4 tablespoons butter
½ - ⅔ pound cooked ham, sliced thin
3 slices Swiss cheese, cut in half

- Slice about two-thirds the way through loaf and cut 12 slices. On every other slice spread butter and tuck in cheese and ham evenly to create 6 sandwiches. Place loaf in center of large, sprayed, heavy-duty foil and fold closed.

- Grill over medium heat for 15 to 20 minutes until cheese melts; rotate loaf often for even heating. Remove from grill and open foil carefully. Pull apart sandwiches and enjoy! Serves 4 to 6.

Spicy Mustard-Ham Loaf

- Use recipe for *Grilled Ham and Cheese Sandwich Loaf (page 90)* and spread 2 tablespoons spicy brown mustard on loaf before grilling. Serves 4 to 6.

Deli Counter Loaf

- Use recipe for *Grilled Ham and Cheese Sandwich Loaf (page 90)*, but substitute your favorite deli meat (mesquite turkey, rotisserie-style chicken, roast beef) for ham. Serves 4 to 6.

Delicatessens are small shops similar to small grocery stores with a counter and stools for patrons. First operated by Germans in the U.S., delicatessens served cooked meats and prepared dishes. They grew to be a Jewish tradition because they were open on Sundays and served kosher foods. The center of delicatessens is in New York City.

Grilled Open-Face Ham Sandwich

2 cups cooked, ground ham
½ cup drained pickle relish
2 eggs, hard-boiled, chopped
⅓ cup mayonnaise
Butter, softened
4 thick slices bread

- In bowl, combine ground ham, pickle relish, eggs and mayonnaise. Spread butter on 1 side of bread.

- Spread ham mixture on plain side and lay buttered side on preheated, oiled grill or on foil away from direct medium-hot heat. Close lid and cook until bread browns slightly, about 10 minutes. Serves 2 to 4.

Grilled Open-Face Chicken Sandwich

- Use recipe for *Grilled Open-Face Ham Sandwich (page 91)*, but use cooked ground chicken instead of ham. Add chopped onion and black or green olives. Serves 2 to 4.

Chicken breast halves today are almost twice as large as they were several years ago. Breeders are growing bigger chickens with bigger chicken breasts. During processing, they inject breasts with a saline solution or broth to "plump up" the chickens. This is supposed to make the meat easier to cook and keep it from drying out. If you don't like the idea, buy organic or less-processed chicken. They tend to be smaller and may not go through the "plumping" process.

Peanut Butter-Bacon Sandwich

These are some of the best "kid" sandwiches around.

1 tablespoon butter
¼ cup peanut butter
2 - 4 strips bacon, fried crisp
2 slices bread

- Spread one side of bread slices with butter. Spread other side with peanut butter. Top with bacon and second slice of bread, buttered side out.

- Cook on sprayed foil or directly on grill over medium heat for about 5 minutes on each side until bread browns on outside. Makes 1 sandwich.

Honey-Peanut Butter-Bacon Sandwich

- Use recipe for *Peanut Butter-Bacon Sandwich (page 92)* and add 1 tablespoon honey to peanut butter before spreading. Makes 1 sandwich.

Banana-Peanut Butter-Bacon Sandwich

- Use recipe for *Peanut Butter-Bacon Sandwich (page 92)* and add banana slices on top of peanut butter. Makes 1 sandwich.

Peanut Butter-Chocolate Chip Sandwich

- Use recipe for *Peanut Butter-Bacon Sandwich (page 92)*. Instead of bacon, add 1 tablespoon chocolate chips on top of peanut butter. Makes 1 sandwich.

Grilled PBJ Sandwich

- Use recipe for *Peanut Butter-Bacon Sandwich (page 92)*, but omit bacon and add your favorite jelly. Makes 1 sandwich.

Rye Tuna Grill

1 (6 ounce) can white tuna, drained, flaked
½ cup shredded Swiss cheese
1 rib celery, finely chopped
½ cup mayonnaise
8 slices rye bread
Butter, softened

- Combine tuna, cheese, celery, mayonnaise, ½ teaspoon salt and ¼ teaspoon pepper and mix well.

- Spread butter on one side of bread slices. On other side of 4 bread slices, spread tuna mixture and top with remaining bread slices, buttered side out.

- Place on preheated, oiled grill over medium heat with lid closed for about 5 minutes until bread begins to get crispy. Turn carefully with spatula and grill on other side until it is crispy, about 5 minutes. Serves 4.

Tuna Melt Packs

1 (6 ounce) can tuna, drained
2 tablespoons chopped onion
2 tablespoons chopped dill pickles
2 tablespoons mayonnaise
¼ cup shredded cheddar cheese
4 slices bread

- Combine all ingredients except bread. Spread evenly on 2 slices bread and top with remaining slices. Place each sandwich on large, sprayed heavy-duty foil. Fold and seal foil. Cook on grill over medium heat for 15 minutes until heated through, turn once. Serves 2.

Dijon Tuna Melts

- Use recipe for *Tuna Melt Packs (page 93)* and use creamy dijon-style mustard instead of mayonnaise. Serves 2.

Hot Grilled Sandwich Specialties

Hot sandwiches from the grill are more special than regular sandwiches and make meals memorable.

- Combine the following ingredients and cook on oiled medium-hot grill for about 5 to 10 minutes per side until grill marks show and cheeses melt.

Pumpernickel-Corned Beef Sandwich

Pumpernickel bread
Mayonnaise
Deli-sliced corned beef
Swiss cheese slices

Grilled Pastrami on Rye

Light rye bread
Dijon-style mustard
Slices of pastrami
Mozzarella cheese slices
Deli coleslaw

Grilled Turkey-Avocado Crisp

Rye bread
Mozzarella cheese slices
Sliced turkey
Avocado slices

Grilled Turkey-Spinach Melt

Multi-grain bread
Deli turkey breast slices
Havarti cheese slices
Fresh spinach
Garlic Mayonnaise (recipe page 97)

Grilled Turkey with Chutney

French rolls
Thin slices brie cheese
Deli turkey breast slices
Chutney Spread (recipe page 98)
Mayonnaise

Grilled Peppered Beef Sandwich

Marble rye bread
Deli peppered-roast beef
Sweet onion slices
Horseradish Mayonnaise (recipe page 96)

Grilled Corned Beef-Sauerkraut Sandwich

Dark rye bread
2 slices corned beef
2 slices swiss cheese
4 tablespoons sauerkraut
Russian dressing

Grilled Ham-Mozzarella Pockets

Pita bread
Ham slices
Mozzarella cheese slices
Sweet pickle slices
Bean sprouts
Mayonnaise

Grilled Turkey and Cheese

French bread slices
Turkey and beef slices
American cheese slices
Monterey Jack cheese slices
Mayonnaise

$ave Money! *Don't be loyal to brands. Try what's on sale and you may find the less expensive item is just as good as your favorite brand.*

Grilled Beef-Avocado Mix

Pumpernickel bread
Deli roast beef
Fresh spinach
Tomato slices
Quick Guacamole (recipe page 97)

Grilled Tropical Chicken Sandwich

Kaiser rolls
Grilled chicken breasts
Canned pineapple slices
Leaf lettuce
Sesame-Ginger Mayonnaise (recipe page 98)

Grilled Bacon-Remoulade Sandwich

Honey nut bread
Crisp cooked bacon slices
Tomato slices
Bibb lettuce
Remoulade Mayonnaise (recipe page 97)

Special Burger-Sandwich Spreads

Try the following spreads to liven up basic sandwiches. It's fun just to grill a burger or an ordinary sandwich outside, but it's even cooler to put a surprise flavor inside.

Horseradish Mayonnaise

A special zing for any burger.

½ cup mayonnaise
1 tablespoon chopped fresh chives
1 tablespoon horseradish
⅛ teaspoon seasoned salt

- Combine ingredients and spread on toasted bun or bread. Refrigerate remaining mayonnaise. Makes about ½ cup.

Remoulade Mayonnaise

Terrific with brats, fish sandwiches, pork and chicken.

½ cup mayonnaise
2 tablespoons chunky salsa
1 teaspoon sweet pickle relish
1 teaspoon dijon-style mustard

- Combine ingredients and spread on toasted bun or bread. Refrigerate remaining mayonnaise. Makes about ½ cup.

Garlic Mayonnaise

⅔ cup mayonnaise
1 tablespoon chopped roasted garlic
1 teaspoon finely chopped onion
⅛ teaspoon salt

- Combine ingredients and press on toasted bun or bread. Refrigerate leftover mayonnaise. Makes about ⅔ cup.

Quick Guacamole

Great on burgers, fish sandwiches, shrimp wraps, fish tacos, garden burgers or turkey burgers.

1 (1 ounce) packet dry onion soup mix
2 (8 ounce) cartons avocado dip
2 green onions with tops, chopped

- Combine ingredients and spread on toasted bun or bread. Refrigerate remaining mayonnaise. Makes about 2 cups.

> *Mayonnaise is said to have been invented by the personal chef of the duc de Richelieu in honor of the French victory at Mahon in 1756. It was originally named Mahonnaise, but mahonnaise was misspelled in a cookbook in 1841 and has been called mayonnaise ever since. There are also other stories about its origin.*

Chutney Spread

Great when you want a sweet and tart flavor to make people sit up and take notice.

⅓ cup peach preserves
½ cup chopped fresh peaches
2 teaspoons finely chopped green onion
½ teaspoon balsamic vinegar
¼ teaspoon crushed red pepper flake

- Combine ingredients and spread on toasted bun or bread. Refrigerate remaining mayonnaise. Makes about 1 cup.

Sesame-Ginger Mayonnaise

Really nice with a garden burger.

½ cup mayonnaise
1 (1 ounce) packet dry onion soup mix
1 tablespoon honey
1 tablespoon toasted sesame seeds
2 teaspoon grated fresh ginger root

- Combine ingredients and spread on toasted bun or bread. Refrigerate remaining mayonnaise. Makes about ½ cup.

Basic Hamburgers

1 - 1¼ pounds ground beef
1 egg, optional
2 teaspoons Worcestershire sauce
4 to 5 hamburger buns

- Mix ground beef with egg, Worcestershire and about ½ teaspoon each of salt and pepper. Form into 4 or 5 patties about ½-inch thick and about 4 inches in diameter.

- Cook on oiled grill over medium-hot fire for about 6 to 8 minutes on each side until internal temperature is 160°. Spread buns and arrange on grill open side down until heated. Add lettuce, tomatoes, onion, mayonnaise or mustard to burgers and serve. Serves 4 to 5.

Coleslaw-Sunflower Burgers

- Use recipe for *Basic Hamburgers (page 98)* and top with coleslaw and sunflower seeds. Serves 4 to 5.

Nutty Harvest Burgers

- Use recipe for *Basic Hamburgers (page 98)* and top with apple slices, chopped peanuts and brie or goat cheese. Serves 4 to 5.

Farmer-in-the-Dell Burgers

- Use recipe for *Basic Hamburgers (page 98)* and top with thin slices of cucumber, sliced olives and mayonnaise. Serves 4 to 5.

South-of-the-Border Burgers

- Use recipe for *Basic Hamburgers (page 98)* and top with Mexican 4-cheese blend and guacamole. Serves 4 to 5.

Pastrami-Cheese Burgers

- Use recipe for *Basic Hamburgers (page 98)*. With about 5 minutes left before removing from grill, top burgers with slices of pastrami and slices of mozzarella cheese. Serves 4 to 5.

Salami-Swiss Burgers

- Use recipe for *Basic Hamburgers (page 98)*. With about 5 minutes left before removing from grill, top burgers with slices of salami and slices of Swiss cheese. Serves 4 to 5.

Roasted-Pepper Burgers

- Use recipe for *Basic Hamburgers (page 98)* and top with a little horseradish, mayonnaise and several strips roasted red bell peppers. Serves 4 to 5.

Monster Burgers

- Use recipe for *Basic Hamburgers (page 98)*. With about
  5 minutes left to grill, add several slices deli-shaved corned
  beef and 2 slices muenster cheese to each patty. Serves 4 to 5.

Pizza Burgers

- Use recipe for *Basic Hamburgers (page 98)* and add ½ cup pizza
  sauce mixed with 2 scant teaspoons minced garlic and ¼ cup
  thin slices fresh mushrooms to beef before forming patties.
  Serves 4 to 5.

Mushroom Burgers

- Use recipe for *Basic Hamburgers (page 98)* and add 1 chopped
  portobello mushrooms to ground beef and top each patty with
  2 slices provolone cheese. Serves 4 to 5.

Baked Brie Burgers

- Use recipe for *Basic Hamburgers (page 98)*. With about
  5 minutes left to cook, add thin slices brie cheese on top
  of burgers and cook until cheese begins to melt. Top with
  mayonnaise and spinach leaves. Serves 4 to 5.

Nutty Burgers

- Use recipe for *Basic Hamburgers (page 98)* and add ¾ cup
  chopped nuts (pecans, walnuts, cashews) to hamburger meat.
  Serves 4 to 5.

Make-It-Stretch Burgers

- Use recipe for *Basic Hamburgers (page 98)* and add ¾ cup
  mashed potatoes and 1 well-beaten egg to ground beef
  mixture. Serves 4 to 5.

Italian Burgers

- Use recipe for *Basic Hamburgers (page 98)*. With about 5 minutes left to cook, add slices or shredded Italian-blend cheese and pizza sauce. Serves 4 to 5.

Hungarian Burgers

- Use recipe for *Basic Hamburgers (page 98)* and add ⅓ cup chopped carrots and 1 tablespoon Hungarian paprika to meat. Serves 4 to 5.

Herb Burgers

- Use recipe for *Basic Hamburgers (page 98)* and add ¼ teaspoon each of thyme, oregano and rosemary to meat. Serves 4 to 5.

Hurry Curry Burgers

- Use recipe for *Basic Hamburgers (page 98)* and add ⅛ teaspoon curry powder and ⅛ teaspoon coriander to meat. Serves 4 to 5.

Basic Hamburgers with Breadcrumbs

1 - 1½ pounds ground beef
½ cup breadcrumbs
¼ cup chopped onion
4 - 5 hamburger buns

- Combine all ingredients, form into balls and flatten into patties. Salt and pepper both sides of each patty. Cook on oiled grill over medium-hot fire for about 7 to 10 minutes on each side until internal temperature is 160°.

- Spread buns and arrange on grill open side down to toast. Serve with lettuce, tomatoes, onion, mayonnaise or mustard. Serves 4 to 5.

Easy Pork Burgers

- Use recipe for *Basic Hamburgers with Breadcrumbs (page 101)* except use 1 - 1½ pounds ground pork instead of beef and top with red onion slices, tomato slices and romano cheese. Serves 4 to 5.

Grilled Cheeseburgers on Rye

1 pound lean ground beef
4 slices cheddar cheese
8 slices rye bread
¼ cup (½ stick) butter, softened

- Season meat with salt and pepper and form into 4 patties. Cook on oiled grill over medium-high heat for about 8 to 10 minutes per side until pink is almost gone and internal temperature reaches 160°.

- About 5 minutes before removing patties, spread buttered bread on grill away from direct heat to toast.

- Remove patties, place one each on toasted side of bread and top with 1 slice each of cheese and bread. Flatten sandwich with spatula and cook with lid closed until grill marks appear and cheese melts, about 5 minutes. Serves 4.

Green Chile Cheeseburgers

- Use recipe for *Grilled Cheeseburgers on Rye (page 102)* and add 1 (4 ounce) can diced green chilies. Serves 4.

Today, there are disputed claims of who made the first hamburger from Seymour, Wisconsin; Akron, Ohio; Hamburg, New York; Tulsa, Oklahoma; the St. Louis World's Fair; Athens, Texas; and New Haven, Connecticut. It seems the popular hamburger was created all over the U.S. during the late 19th and early 20th centuries. All of us can agree, however, that the hamburger is an American original.

Super Double-Cheeseburgers

1¼ pounds ground chuck
1 egg, optional
2 teaspoons Worcestershire sauce
4 - 5 slices American cheese
4 - 5 slices swiss cheese
4 - 5 slices bacon, cooked, crisp
4 - 5 hamburger buns

- Mix ground chuck with egg, Worcestershire, ½ teaspoon salt and ¼ teaspoon pepper. Form into 4 or 5 patties.

- Cook on oiled grill over medium-hot heat for about 6 to 8 minutes on each side. Internal temperature should be 160°.

- A few minutes before burgers are done, add cheeses and bacon on top. Toast 4 buns and spread with mayonnaise or mustard. Arrange burgers on buns to serve. Serves about 4.

Everyday Cheeseburgers

2 pounds ground beef
8 slices cheese
8 hamburger buns
Lettuce, tomatoes, onion slices, pickle slices
Mustard, mayonnaise or ketchup

- Mix ground beef and a little salt and pepper and form into 6 to 8 patties. Cook on oiled preheated grill over medium-hot fire for about 6 to 10 minutes per side until internal temperature reaches 160°.

- Add cheese slice to each patty. Allow cheese to melt and put meat on warm bun. Add onions, lettuce, tomatoes and pickles. Dress with mustard, mayonnaise and/or ketchup. Serves 6 to 8.

Fatty ground beef is great for the grill because the fat burns off and falls into the fire. Save leaner ground beef for the skillet.

Western Cheeseburgers

- Use recipe for *Everyday Cheeseburgers (page 103)*, but replace onion slices with sautéed onion and sautéed fresh mushrooms. Add chili sauce, hickory sauce or ketchup. Serves 6 to 8.

Southwestern Cheeseburgers

- Use recipe for *Everyday Cheeseburgers (page 103)*, but use green chili salsa and grated Mexican, four-cheese blend. Serves 6 to 8.

Burger Meisters

¼ cup beer or beef broth
2 tablespoons Worcestershire sauce
2 teaspoons chili powder
1 teaspoon onion powder
½ teaspoon crushed red pepper flakes
1 pound lean ground beef
4 hamburger buns, split

- Combine beer, Worcestershire, chili powder, onion powder and red pepper flakes. Crumble beef over mixture, mix well and form into 4 patties.

- Cook on oiled grill over medium-high heat for about 6 to 10 minutes per side until internal temperature reaches 160°. Serve on buns. Serves 4.

> *Barbecue is a noun meaning the meat cooked on a grill or smoker.*
>
> *Barbecue is a noun meaning the apparatus where the fire is to cook the food.*
>
> *Barbecue is a noun meaning the event in the backyard where family and friends gather for a cookout.*
>
> *Barbecue is a verb meaning the act of cooking on a grill or smoker.*
>
> *To summarize, it is fun to go to a barbecue where people barbecue on a barbecue and eat barbecue.*

Colby-Bacon Hamburgers

1 pound ground beef
½ cup shredded Colby cheese
2 tablespoons prepared horseradish
1 egg, beaten
½ teaspoon garlic powder
½ cup real bacon bits
4 hamburger buns
Mayonnaise or mustard

- In bowl, combine beef, cheese, horseradish, egg, garlic powder and bacon bits. Mix well and shape mixture into 4 hamburger patties.

- Place patties on oiled grill over medium heat and cook 5 to 10 minutes on each side until internal temperature is 160°.

- Spread bottom buns with mayonnaise or mustard (or a mixture) and top with patty and bun tops. Serves 4.

Characteristics of Woods Used for Grilling and Smoking

Mesquite	Very hot fire; best for grilling; should always use dried wood, not green
Hickory	Flavorful wood; excellent for extended smoking; milder flavor than mesquite
Pecan	Excellent for extended smoking; milder than hickory; used a lot in the Southwest
Apple	Excellent for smoking; best with pork and game; sweet, mild flavor
Cherry	Fair for pork, but is on the bitter side for some people
Maple	Very good milder flavor; slightly sweet; best with pork, seafood and chicken
Alder	Traditional wood for smoking and grilling salmon; very light flavor; native to the Northwest
Oak	Strong flavor; must be used in moderation; best for beef and lamb

Deluxe Colby-Bacon Burgers

- Use recipe for *Colby-Bacon Hamburgers (page 105)* and add fresh bean sprouts and 1 thin slice tomato to each patty. Serves 4.

Teriyaki Burgers

1 pound ground beef
1 egg, beaten
¼ cup teriyaki marinade sauce
¼ cup finely shredded carrots
1 (3 ounce) can french-fried onions, crushed
4 slices Swiss cheese
4 onion buns, split

- Combine beef, egg, teriyaki marinade, carrots and crushed fried onions and form into 4 patties. Cook on oiled grill over medium-hot heat for about 5 to 10 minutes per side until internal temperature reaches 160°.

- Place cheese slice on each patty about 3 minutes before removing from grill. Serve on onion buns. Serves 4.

Asian Burgers

1 pound lean ground beef
1 tablespoon soy sauce
1 teaspoon minced ginger
1 egg, beaten
3 chopped green onions
1 tablespoon dry breadcrumbs
4 kaiser rolls

- Combine beef, soy sauce, ginger, egg, green onions and breadcrumbs and form into 4 patties.

- Cook over medium heat over oiled grill for about 5 to 10 minutes per side until internal temperature is 160°. Place patties in rolls and spread with your favorite toppings. Serves 4.

Big Stuffed Juicy Burgers

1½ pounds ground beef
1 (10 ounce) bottle steak sauce, divided
2 tablespoon fajita seasoning
2 tablespoons dried minced onion
¼ teaspoon cayenne pepper
8 slices American cheese, divided
1 (7 ounce) can diced green chilies, drained
1 (4 ounce) can sliced ripe olives
4 hamburger buns

- In bowl, combine beef, ¼ cup steak sauce, fajita seasoning, onion and cayenne pepper. Mix well and form into 8 thin patties.

- On 4 patties, place one slice of cheese, some green chilies and ripe olives. Top with remaining 4 patties, press down and seal edges of meat to hold stuffing.

- Cook on oiled grill over medium-high heat for about 10 minutes per side. Once each side is seared, brush tops with remaining steak sauce. Continue grilling and basting with steak sauce until meat cooks through and there is no pink. Internal temperature of meat should be 160°.

- Before meat comes off grill, open buns and place, open side down, on grill away from direct heat. Place remaining 4 slices of cheese on tops of patties to melt. Serve meat with buns. Serves 4.

Never use willow, pine, poplar, cottonwood, lumber scraps, treated lumber, acorns, chili pods or other woods with strong, pungent smells or flavors to cook foods.

Jumbo Hamburgers

Double-thick and doubly good

2 pounds ground beef
Ketchup
1 onion, thinly sliced
5 slices gouda, sliced
Butter, softened
5 hamburger buns

- Divide beef into 10 equal portions, with ⅓ cup measure. Place between sheets of wax paper and flatten to form patties about ½-inch thick, 4 inches across.

- Spread 5 patties with ketchup leaving ½-inch around edge for sealing. Season with salt and pepper and top each with onion and cheese slices. Top with other beef patties and seal edges well to avoid leaks.

- Season with salt and pepper. Cook on oiled grill over medium-hot fire for about 5 to 10 minutes per side until internal temperature of meat is 160°. Just before removing patties, place opened buns away from direct fire to toast. Serves 5.

Jalapeno-Blue Cheeseburgers

2 pounds ground beef
6 jalapeno peppers, seeded, chopped
1 cup crumbled blue cheese
2 tablespoons finely minced onion
2 teaspoons minced garlic
2 tablespoons soy sauce
6 hamburger buns, split
½ cup mayonnaise
¼ cup ketchup
Shredded lettuce

- In bowl, combine beef, jalapeno peppers, blue cheese, onion, garlic, soy sauce and salt to taste. Make about 6 patties. Cook on oiled grill over medium-hot fire for about 5 to 10 minutes per side until pink is almost gone and internal temperature is 160°.

- Combine mayonnaise and ketchup and spread on bottom of each bun. Top with patty and shredded lettuce. Serves 6.

Jalapeno-Provolone Cheeseburgers

- Use recipe for *Jalapeno-Blue Cheeseburgers (page 108)* except use provolone cheese instead of blue cheese. Place provolone cheese on burgers about 5 minutes before removing from grill. Serves 6.

Glazed Bacon Cheeseburgers

3 tablespoons dark packed brown sugar
1½ teaspoons paprika
½ teaspoon garlic powder
½ teaspoon ground cumin
¼ teaspoon chipotle powder
1 pound ground beef
½ cup shredded sharp cheddar cheese
6 slices bacon, cooked, crumbled
4 buns or rolls
Lettuce, tomato slices, avocado slices, optional

- Combine sugar, spices, and a little salt and pepper in small bowl and set aside. Form beef into 8 thin patties.

- Toss cheese and crumbled bacon together and place equal amount on 4 patties. Stack remaining patties on cheese-bacon mixture. Pinch edges of patties to seal.

- Generously pat each burger with spice mixture. Cook on oiled grill over medium-hot heat about 5 - 10 minutes per side until internal temperature is at least 160°.

- Place cooked burgers on individual rolls. Add lettuce, tomato and avocado, as desired. Serves 4.

> **$ave Money!** *Walk or bike to the grocery store if you only need a few items. You'll save on gas and think a lot harder on whether you actually need something when you have to carry it all the way home.*

Tangy Surprise Burgers

1¼ pounds lean ground beef
4 pineapple rings
½ cup hot and spicy ketchup
⅔ cup packed brown sugar
1 tablespoon Dijon-style mustard
4 kaiser rolls
Deli coleslaw

- Divide beef into four portions and form patties around pineapple rings so that none of pineapple is showing. In saucepan, combine hot and spicy ketchup, brown sugar and mustard and heat until sugar dissolves.

- Cook patties on oiled grill over medium-hot fire for about 5 to 10 minutes until internal temperature reaches 160°. Spoon some of brown sugar sauce over burgers several times before serving.

- Place patties on roll and top with 1 heaping tablespoon of coleslaw. Cover with top bun and serve immediately. Serves 4.

Juicy Bacon Burgers

1¼ pounds ground beef
1 small onion, finely chopped
1 egg
⅔ cup breadcrumbs
½ cup chunky salsa
⅓ cup bacon bits
1 teaspoon minced garlic
4 hamburger buns, toasted

- Combine beef, onion, egg, breadcrumbs, salsa, bacon bits, garlic and salt and pepper to taste and form into 4 patties.

- Cook patties on oiled grill over medium-high heat for about 5 to 10 minutes per side until internal temperature reaches 160°. Place patties on buns. Place on top bun and serve immediately. Serves 4.

Firecracker Burgers

1 pound ground beef
2 tablespoons seasoned breadcrumbs
1 egg, beaten
1 cup Pico de Gallo (recipe page 306)
4 hamburger buns

- Combine beef, breadcrumbs and egg and shape into 4 patties. Cook meat patties on oiled, preheated grill over medium-high heat about 5 to 10 minutes per side.

- Continue to cook until internal temperature reaches 160°. Open buns and place on grill away from direct heat to toast. Before serving arrange several tablespoons pico de gallo on top of patties. Serves 4.

French Onion Burgers

1½ pounds ground beef
1 envelope onion soup mix
1 cup French onion dip
⅓ cup breadcrumbs
6 hamburger buns

- Mix beef, soup mix, onion dip and breadcrumbs. Form 6 patties and cook on oiled grill over medium-hot fire about 6 to 10 minutes per side. Internal temperature should be 160°. Place patties on buns. Serves 6.

Kaiser French Onion Burgers

- Use recipe for *French Onion Burgers (page 111)* and replace hamburger buns with toasted Kaiser rolls. Serves 6.

The Loaded French Onion Burger

- Use recipe for *French Onion Burgers (page 111)* and top with lettuce, tomato, onion, pickles and additional French onion dip. Serves 6.

Double Onion Burger

- Use recipe for *French Onion Burgers (page 111)* and top burgers with grilled or sautéed onions. Serves 6.

Grilled Onion Burgers

2 pounds ground beef
1 package dry onion soup mix
½ cup breadcrumbs
1 egg, slightly beaten
Basic Ranchero Sauce (recipe page 317)

- Mix ground beef, onion soup mix, breadcrumbs and egg in large bowl. Form mixture in 8 (¼ pound) balls. Place on wax paper and flatten to ¼ inch larger than size of hamburger bun.

- Cook on oiled, preheated grill for 5 to 10 minutes on each side until internal temperature reaches 160°. Top with Ranchero Sauce and serve as main dish or as burger on buns. Serves 8.

Tomato-Onion Barbecue Burgers

1 (6 ounce) can tomato sauce
½ cup vegetable oil
¼ cup vinegar
¼ cup Worcestershire sauce
1 clove garlic, minced
1 small onion, minced
1 (1 - 2 pound) package ground beef

- In large bowl mix all ingredients, except beef and whisk well. Refrigerate until ready to use. Form 4 patties out of ground beef and season with salt and pepper.

- Cook on oiled grill over hot fire to sear outside of both sides of patties. Move away from fire, baste with sauce thinly and close lid. Cook for 5 minutes per side.

- Several minutes before beef is ready, baste liberally with sauce. Cook for about 5 to 8 minutes per side until internal temperature reaches 160°. Serves 4.

Favorite Saucy Hamburgers

Works well with pork and chicken also.

1 medium onion, minced
1 small green bell pepper, minced
2 tablespoons butter
¾ cup ketchup
2 tablespoons brown sugar
2 tablespoons mustard
1 tablespoon Worcestershire sauce
1 (1 - 2 pound) package ground beef

- Combine onion, bell pepper, butter, ketchup, brown sugar, mustard, Worcestershire sauce and 1 teaspoon salt in pan and simmer 15 minutes. Form ground beef into patties.

- Cook on oiled grill over hot fire to sear outside of both sides of patties. Move patties away from fire, baste with sauce thinly and close lid.

- Cook for about 5 to 10 minutes per side until internal temperature reaches 160°. Several minutes before beef is ready, baste liberally with sauce and again after you remove patties from grill. Serves 4 to 5.

Saucy Turkey Burgers

- Use recipe for *Favorite Saucy Hamburgers (page 113)* but use 1 to 2 pounds ground turkey instead of beef. Internal temperature should be 165°. Serves 4 to 5.

Saucy Pork Burgers

- Use recipe for *Favorite Saucy Hamburgers (page 113)* but use 1 to 2 pounds ground pork instead of beef. Internal temperature should be 160°. Serves 4 to 5.

$ave Money! Use the weekly store circular to plan your week's meals.

Baked Bean and Burger Packs

1 pound ground beef
⅓ cup breadcrumbs
⅓ cup barbecue sauce
1 (16 ounce) can baked beans
1 medium onion, sliced

- Combine beef, breadcrumbs, barbecue sauce, and ½ teaspoon each salt and pepper. Form into 4 patties. Place each patty on large pieces of sprayed heavy-duty foil. Top evenly with beans and onions. Fold foil loosely to allow air to circulate and seal.

- Cook each package on grill over medium-hot heat for about 20 to 30 minutes until internal temperature is 160°. Open packages carefully. Serves 4.

Bacon-Avocado Burgers

1¼ - 1½ pounds ground chuck
1 egg
2 teaspoons Worcestershire sauce
4 - 6 hamburger buns
6 - 8 bacon slices, cooked crisp, drained
3 ripe avocados
4 - 6 tablespoons mayonnaise

- Mix ground chuck with egg, Worcestershire, ½ teaspoon salt and ¼ teaspoon pepper.

- Form into 4 or 6 patties about ¾ inch thick and about 4 inches in diameter.

- Cook on oiled, preheated grill over medium-hot fire for about 7 minutes per side until internal temperature is 160°. Open buns and place buns face down on grill until grill marks appear.

- Place patties on buns and break bacon slices to fit on top of patties. Peel and slice avocados and place on top of bacon. Spread mayonnaise of top bun before adding to burger. Serves 4 to 6.

Chipotle-Bacon Burgers

- Use recipe for *Bacon-Avocado Burgers (page 114)* and substitute chipotle mayonnaise for mayonnaise. Serves 4 to 6.

Spitfire Chipotle Burgers

- Use recipe for *Bacon-Avocado Burgers (page 114)* and add sliced chipotles in adobo sauce for a fiery extra. Serves 4 to 6.

Black Bean Burgers

½ pound ground beef
1 (16 ounce) can black beans, drained
¼ cup crushed saltine crackers
½ - ¾ cup barbecue sauce, divided
1 egg
4 hamburger buns

- Mix beef, beans, cracker crumbs, 3 tablespoons barbecue sauce, egg and ½ teaspoon each salt and pepper. Shape into 4 patties. Cook on oiled grill over moderate heat for about 7 minutes per side and internal temperature is at least 160°. Place on buns and top with additional barbecue sauce. Serves 4.

Northern Bean Burgers

- Use recipe for *Black Bean Burgers (page 115)* and replace black beans with great northern beans. Serves 4.

Pinto Bean Burgers

- Use recipe for *Black Bean Burgers (page 115)* and replace black beans with pinto beans. Serves 4.

Salsa Black Bean Burgers

- Use recipe for *Black Bean Burgers (page 115)* and substitute salsa for barbecue sauce. Serves 4.

Cheesy Black Bean Burgers

- Use recipe for *Black Bean Burgers (page 115)* and top patties with slices of cheddar cheese. Serves 4.

Cajun Burgers

1¼ pounds ground beef
½ teaspoon hot sauce
½ cup diced white onion
2 teaspoons ketchup
1 tablespoon plus 1 teaspoon Cajun seasoning, divided
1 teaspoon Worcestershire sauce
½ cup mayonnaise
4 slices cheddar cheese
4 hamburger buns

- Combine beef, hot sauce, onion, ketchup, 1 tablespoon Cajun seasoning, Worcestershire and salt and pepper to taste. Form into 4 patties.

- Cook on oiled grill over medium-hot heat for about 10 minutes until internal temperature is 160°. While patties are cooking, combine mayonnaise and 1 teaspoon Cajun seasoning.

- During last 4 minutes of cooking, lay slice of cheese on top of each patty. Spread seasoned mayonnaise on inside of buns and top with your favorite ingredients. Serves 4.

Mexicorn Burgers

1¼ pounds ground beef
½ cup breadcrumbs
1 (7 ounce) can Mexicorn®
3 tablespoons salsa
4 slices Monterey Jack cheese
4 hamburger buns

- Mix ground beef, breadcrumbs and ½ teaspoon salt. Form 8 thin patties. Mix corn and salsa and spoon mixture on top of 4 patties. Top with remaining patties; press edges to seal.

- Cook on oiled grill over medium-hot fire for about 10 to 12 minutes per side to cook through and internal temperature is 160°. Top with cheese and serve on buns. Serves 4.

Chipotle Stuffed Burgers

- Use recipe for *Mexicorn Burgers (page 116)* and add 1 tablespoon chopped chipotle chilies in adobo sauce to corn mixture. Serves 4.

Stuffed Turkey Burgers

- Use recipe for *Mexicorn Burgers (page 116)* and replace ground beef with ground turkey. Serves 4.

Queso Fresco Pepper Burgers

1 red bell pepper or green poblano chile, halved, seeded
1 pound lean ground beef
Queso fresco, sliced
Chipotle mayonnaise
4 regular hamburger buns

- Roast peppers over direct medium heat until outside skin chars. Place in plastic bag and seal for 10 minutes. Remove from bag, peel outside skin and cut in thin slices.

- Season ground beef with a little salt and pepper and shape into 4 patties. Cook on oiled grill over medium heat about 5 to 10 minutes per side until meat is no longer pink and internal temperature is at least 160°. At same time, grill buns away from direct heat to toast.

- Place beef patties on bottom buns and top with peppers and cheese. Spread chipotle-mayonnaise on inside of top bun and cover patties. Serves 4.

> *Grilling is defined as cooking meats, vegetables and fruits over the direct heat of a charcoal, natural gas or hardwood fire. It usually means searing the outside of the food to seal in the juices, then cooking the food over low heat.*

Mini Burger Kebabs

1 pound ground beef
½ cup chopped onion
¼ cup breadcrumbs
¼ cup grated parmesan cheese
2 cloves garlic, minced
1 cup tomato sauce

- Combine all ingredients except tomato sauce in bowl. Add ½ teaspoon each salt and pepper and mix well. Form about 12 small patties and thread onto 2 skewers. (Use 2 skewers to keep them from falling off. Also, leave space in between so they will cook thoroughly.)

- Place kebabs on oiled grill and grill over medium heat about 5 to 10 minutes per side and internal temperature is 160°. Serve with warmed tomato sauce. Serves 4.

Turkey Slider Kebabs

- Use recipe for *Mini Burger Kebabs (page 118)*. Substitute ground turkey for ground beef and add 1 tablespoon Italian seasoning to meat. Internal temperature should be 165°. Serves 4.

Tex-Mex Burgers

1¼ - 1½ pounds ground chuck
1 egg
2 teaspoons Worcestershire sauce
1 (8 ounce) package shredded cheddar cheese
4 - 6 hamburger buns
1 (8 ounce) package guacamole
1 (8 ounce) jar jalapeno slices

- Mix ground chuck with egg, Worcestershire, ½ teaspoon salt and ¼ teaspoon pepper. Form into 4 or 6 patties.

- Cook on oiled, preheated grill over medium heat for about 6 to 10 minutes per side until internal temperature is 160°. About 4 minutes before removing patties, sprinkle with shredded cheese and cook until cheese melts.

- Open buns and place face down on grill until grill marks appear. Place patties on buns, spread with guacamole and sprinkle with jalapenos. Serves 4 to 6.

Sloppy Joe Burgers

1 pound ground beef
½ cup ketchup, divided
¼ cup chopped onion
2 tablespoons brown sugar
1 tablespoon cider vinegar
1 tablespoon Worcestershire sauce
4 hamburger buns

- Mix beef, ¼ cup ketchup, onion, brown sugar, vinegar and Worcestershire sauce. Form 4 patties.

- Cook on oiled grill over medium-hot fire for about 6 to 10 minutes per side until internal temperature reaches 160°. Place buns away from direct heat to warm. Place each patty on bun and top with remaining ketchup. Serves 4.

California Cheeseburgers

2 pounds ground turkey
8 slices provolone cheese
8 whole grain buns
2 avocados
1 cup bean sprouts
2 tomatoes, sliced
Mayonnaise or honey-mustard

- Mix ground turkey and a little salt and pepper and form into 8 patties. Cook on oiled, preheated grill over medium-hot fire for about 5 to 10 minutes per side until internal temperature reaches 165°.

- Add cheese slices on top of meat during last minutes of cooking. When cheese melts, place patty on warm bun. Peel and slice avocado. Add avocado slices, bean sprouts and tomato slices to patty. Dress with mayonnaise or honey-mustard dressing. Serves 6 to 8.

$ave Money! *Ask your grocery store for a price match. The worst that can happen is they say "no."*

Turkey-Chipotle Burgers

2 pounds ground turkey
1 (16 ounce) jar hot chipotle salsa, divided
8 slices Monterey Jack cheese
Sesame seed hamburger buns

- Combine ground turkey with 1 cup salsa in large bowl. Mix well and shape into 6 to 8 patties. Cook patties on oiled grill over medium-hot heat for about 5 to 10 minutes per side until internal temperature reaches 165°.

- Top each patty with cheese slice and heat just long enough to melt cheese. Place burgers on buns, spoon heaping tablespoon salsa over cheese and top with remaining half of bun. Serves 6 to 8.

Easy Turkey Burgers

1 pound ground turkey
⅓ cup shredded 3-cheese blend
¼ cup finely grated onion, drained
1 tablespoon Tony Chachere's Original Creole Seasoning*

- Combine ground turkey, cheese, onion and Creole seasoning. Shape into 4 patties and refrigerate about 30 minutes before cooking.

- Cook patties on oiled, preheated grill over medium-hot heat for about for 5 to 10 minutes per side until internal temperature reaches 165°; turn once. Serves 4.

*TIP: If you don't want to buy Creole seasoning just for this recipe, use 1 teaspoon seasoned salt and ¼ teaspoon cayenne pepper.

Place chicken breasts between pieces of wax paper and roll or mash flat. The piece cooks more evenly and looks bigger.

Easy Turkey Wraps

4 fajita-size flour tortillas
2 cups shredded lettuce
⅔ cup prepared guacamole

- Use recipe for *Easy Turkey Burgers (page 120)*, place tortillas on oiled grill away from direct heat and warm. (Be careful not to burn.) Arrange lettuce equally on each tortilla. Place patties on top of lettuce and spread with guacamole. Fold tortilla in half and serve immediately. Serves 4.

Mexi-Wraps

- Use recipe for *Easy Turkey Burgers (page 120)* and substitute taco seasoning for Creole seasoning. Top with salsa. Serves 4.

Italian Turkey Wraps

1 pound ground turkey
⅓ cup shredded Italian cheese blend
¼ cup finely grated onion
1 tablespoon Italian seasoning
4 fajita-size flour tortillas
Sliced tomatoes or fresh basil
⅔ cup prepared pesto

- Combine ground turkey, cheese, onion and Italian seasoning. Shape into 4 patties and refrigerate about 30 minutes before cooking.

- Cook patties on oiled, preheated grill over medium-hot heat for about for 5 to 10 minutes per side until internal temperature reaches 165°; turn once.

- Place tortillas on oiled grill away from direct heat and warm. (Be careful not to burn.) Arrange tomatoes equally on each tortilla. Place patties on top of tomatoes and spread with pesto. Fold tortilla in half and serve immediately. Serves 4.

Green Chile Barbecue Chicken Burgers

1½ pounds ground chicken
⅔ cup barbecue sauce
1 (4.5 ounces) can diced green chilies, drained
6 slices Monterey Jack cheese
6 hamburger buns

- Mix chicken, barbecue sauce and green chilies. Form 6 patties.

- Cook on oiled grill for about 8 minutes per side until chicken reaches 165° internal temperature. Top each patty with slice of cheese and place on hamburger buns. Serves 6.

Green Chile Turkey Burgers

- Use recipe for *Green Chile Barbecue Chicken Burgers (page 122)* and substitute ground turkey for chicken. Serves 6.

Jalapeno Barbecue Chicken Burgers

- Use recipe for *Green Chile Barbecue Chicken Burgers (page 122)* and substitute 2 to 3 fresh chopped jalapenos for green chilies. Serves 6.

Barbecued Brat-Chicken Burgers

4 chicken tender strips
1 (16 ounce) package bratwurst burger patties
1 cup shredded Mexican 3-cheese blend
Whiskey barbecue sauce
4 hamburger buns

- Place chicken strips between 2 pieces of wax paper and roll or mash chicken flat to about ¼-inch thickness. Season with salt and pepper. Cook chicken and brat patties on oiled grill over direct medium heat for about 5 to 10 minutes per side until chicken patties cook through and are 165°.

- Just before removing from grill, place cheese on top of each brat patty and cook until it melts. Place chicken on top of cheese and serve as is or with barbecue sauce on buns. Serves 4.

Brat Burgers

1 (16 ounce) package bratwurst burger patties
4 slices cheddar cheese
Hamburger buns, optional
Pickles
1 onion, sliced

- Cook patties on oiled grill over direct medium heat for about
  6 to 8 minutes per side until patties are at least 160°. Just before
  moving from grill, place cheese slice on each patty and cook
  until it melts. Serve as is or on buns with pickles and sliced
  onions. Serves 4.

Pork Muffin Burger

1½ pounds ground pork
1 teaspoon minced garlic
6 English muffins
2 teaspoons dijon-style mustard
½ cup barbecue sauce
1 cup refrigerated creamy coleslaw

- In bowl, combine ground pork, garlic, 1 teaspoon salt or
  seasoned salt and ¼ teaspoon pepper. Shape into 6 patties
  about ¾-inch thick. Cook patties on oiled, preheated grill over
  medium heat about 5 minutes on each side until thermometer
  reaches 160°.

- Lightly toast each side of English muffins on grill away from
  direct heat and spread with mustard and a little barbecue
  sauce. Place patties on bottoms of muffins and add coleslaw
  and top muffin. Serve extra barbecue sauce on the side.
  Serves 6.

$ave Money! Look for Manager's Specials,
especially in the meat department. Items that are close
to "sell by" dates can usually be purchased at deep
discounts. This is perfect for meals you plan to cook
right away or freeze for later.

Pork Sliders

6 frozen biscuits
1 pound ground pork
1 tablespoon olive oil
1 tablespoon Worcestershire sauce
1 tablespoon Cajun seasoning
Ketchup, optional

- Bake biscuits according to package directions. Cool and set aside. Combine pork, oil, Worcestershire, Cajun seasoning and 1 teaspoon each salt and pepper. Form into 6 patties.

- Cook on oiled grill over medium-high heat for about 5 to 10 minutes per side until meat reaches 160° internal temperature. Make sliders by placing 1 patty inside each biscuit and top with ketchup. Serves 6.

Grilled Reuben Brat Burgers

1 large onion, sliced
1 - 2 tablespoons butter
1 (14 ounce) can sauerkraut, well drained
1 (16 ounce) package bratwurst burger patties
4 slices Swiss cheese
Thousand Island dressing
4 hamburger buns

- Place onion and butter in skillet and saute until onion is translucent. Add sauerkraut and cook until warm.

- Grill brat patties on oiled grill over medium-hot fire for about 5 to 8 minutes per side until patties cook through. Place cheese on patties and cook until it melts.

- Open buns and place face down away from direct heat to toast on grill. Place patties on buns, add onions and sauerkraut and Thousand Island dressing before serving. Serves 4.

$ave Money! *Don't buy non-grocery items at the grocery store. Prices are usually better elsewhere.*

Caribbean Jerk Burgers

1 pound ground pork
1 tablespoon jerk seasoning
1 teaspoon grated lime peel
French bread
Butter

- Mix pork, seasoning and lime peel and form into 4 patties.
  Cook on oiled grill over medium-hot fire for about 7 to
  8 minutes per side until internal temperature is 160° and
  is no longer pink.

- Slice bread about 1-inch thick. Butter slices liberally on 1 side
  and toast on grill away from direct heat until light brown.
  Place patties on bread. Serves 4.

Northwest Salmon Burgers

1 pound fresh cooked salmon
1 egg, slightly beaten
¼ cup lemon juice
⅔ cup seasoned breadcrumbs
4 hamburger buns
Mayonnaise, lettuce, sliced tomatoes

- In bowl, combine salmon, egg, lemon juice, breadcrumbs and
  a little salt and pepper. Form into patties and cook on oiled,
  preheated grill over medium-hot fire for about 5 minutes per
  side until grill marks show.

- Toast buns on grill away from heat. Serve with mayonnaise,
  lettuce and sliced tomatoes. Serves 4.

TIP: If you can't get fresh salmon, use 1 (15 ounce) can salmon with
*   1 tablespoon liquid from can.*

Rosie Salmon Burgers

- Use recipe for *Northwest Salmon Burgers (page 125)*, but add
  ¼ cup fresh rosemary to salmon mixture before grilling.
  Serves 4.

Tart Salmon Burgers

- Use recipe for *Northwest Salmon Burgers (page 125)*, but replace mayonnaise with tartar sauce. Serves 4.

Sauced-Up Salmon Burgers

- Use recipe for *Northwest Salmon Burgers (page 125)* and replace mayonnaise with chipotle mayonnaise or dijon-style mustard. Serves 4.

New Orleans Salmon Burgers

- Use recipe for *Northwest Salmon Burgers (page 125)* and replace mayonnaise with remoulade sauce. Serve on thin-sliced French bread. Serves 4.

Green Goddess Salmon Burgers

- Use recipe for *Northwest Salmon Burgers (page 125)* and replace mayonnaise with Green Goddess salad dressing. Serves 4.

Southern Salmon Burgers

- Use recipe for *Northwest Salmon Burgers (page 125)* and top with prepared coleslaw. Serves 4.

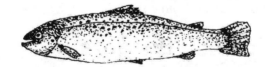

Grilled Portobello Burgers

⅓ cup olive oil, divided
4 large portobello mushroom caps
4 hamburger buns
4 - 8 lettuce leaves
4 - 8 slices tomatoes
4 - 8 onion slices

- Wipe mushrooms with damp paper towel. Sprinkle caps with half the olive oil. Cook on oiled, low-medium heat grill for about 6 minutes. Turn, sprinkle with remaining olive oil and grill until tender, about 6 minutes more.

- Toast hamburger buns away from direct heat. When mushroom caps are ready, place onto toasted bun and add lettuce, tomato slices and onions. If you wish, drizzle with more olive oil. Serves 4.

Balsamic Portobello Burgers

- Use recipe for *Grilled Portobello Burgers (page 127)* but substitute ⅓ cup balsamic vinaigrette for olive oil. Serves 4.

California Portobello Burgers

- Use recipe for *Grilled Portobello Burgers (page 127)* and top with sliced avocado and alfalfa sprouts. Serves 4.

Pesto Portobello Burgers

- Use recipe for *Grilled Portobello Burgers (page 127)*. Generously spread pesto on ciabatta rolls and top mushrooms with sliced mozzarella and tomatoes. Serves 4.

Mama Mia Portobello Burgers

- Use recipe for *Grilled Portobello Burgers (page 127)*. When mushrooms are ready, place onto toasted rolls and generously sprinkle with Italian seasoning. Top with sliced mozzarella and tomatoes. Serves 4.

Hummus Portobello Burgers

- Use recipe for *Grilled Portobello Burgers (page 127)*. Generously spread hummus inside pita pockets. When mushroom caps are ready, place into pita pockets with roasted red peppers. Serves 4.

Garden Burgers

4 vegetarian garden burger patties
2 teaspoons Worcestershire sauce, optional
4 whole wheat hamburger buns or rolls
Lettuce or spinach
Tomato
Mustard or mayonnaise

- Sprinkle patties with Worcestershire, ½ teaspoon salt and ¼ teaspoon pepper. Cook on oiled, preheated grill over low heat for about 5 to 6 minutes on each side.

- Open buns and place face down on grill until grill marks appear. Place patties on buns and add toppings. Serves 4.

Coleslaw Burgers

- Use recipe for *Garden Burgers (page 128)* and replace lettuce and tomatoes with 1 (8.5 ounce) package coleslaw with dressing. Serves 4.

Bean Sprout Burgers

- Use recipe for *Garden Burgers (page 128)* and add bean sprouts and sesame seeds. Serves 4.

Pita Garden Burgers

- Use recipe for *Garden Burgers (page 128)* and replace hamburger buns with pita pockets. Serves 4.

Open-Faced Garden Burgers

- Use recipe for *Garden Burgers (page 128)* and replace hamburger buns with flat bread. Serves 4.

Feta and Dill Garden Burgers

- Use recipe for *Garden Burgers (page 128)* and replace toppings with feta cheese and fresh dill. Serves 4.

Tangy Tomato Garden Burgers

- Use recipe for *Garden Burgers (page 128)* and replace toppings with tomato chutney. Serves 4.

Southwestern Garden Burger

- Use recipe for *Garden Burgers (page 128)* and replace toppings with chipotle mayonnaise and your favorite salsa. Serves 4.

Grilled Onion Garden Burger

- Use recipe for *Garden Burgers (page 128)* and add grilled onion rings. Serves 4.

Cilantro Garden Burger

- Use recipe for *Garden Burgers (page 128)* and replace toppings with avocado slices, cilantro and a splash of lime juice. Serves 4.

$ave Money! *Buy only the quantity you need. Just because an item is "2 for $4" doesn't mean you have to buy 2. You can buy one for $2. (Some specials require a specific quantity so be sure to check the fine print.)*

Burger Spread Specialties

Use these spreads and garnishes to create a different burger and a different dish. Each recipe gives you a new way to enhance hamburger meat and a new flavor surprise.

Creamy Blue Cheese Spread

1 (4 ounce) package cream cheese, softened
¼ cup blue cheese, softened
1 - 2 tablespoons mayonnaise

• Whip all ingredients and spread on buns. Makes about 1 cup.

Spicy Avocado Spread

1 medium avocado, peeled, mashed
1 tablespoon lemon juice
¼ - ½ teaspoon hot sauce

• Mix all ingredients and spread on buns. Makes about ½ cup.

Avocado-Cayenne Cream

2 medium avocados, peeled, mashed
2 tablespoons lime juice
½ teaspoon lime zest
1 - 2 teaspoons cayenne pepper

• Mix all ingredients and spread on buns. Makes about 1 cup.

Nutty Ham Spread

1 (4 ounce) can deviled ham
¾ cup mayonnaise
¾ cup peanuts, chopped
¼ cup sweet pickle relish, drained

• Mix all ingredients and spread on buns. Makes about 2½ cups.

Bacon Whiz Bang

1 cup Cheez Whiz®
6 slices bacon, fried crisp, crumbled

- Mix all ingredients and spread on buns. Makes about 1 cup.

Pine Nut Butter

½ cup (1 stick) butter, softened
½ cup pine nuts

- Whip butter, stir in pine nuts and spread on buns. Makes about 1 cup.

Cheesy Onionnaise

1 (5 ounce) jar Cheez Whiz®
1 tablespoon onion juice or 2 tablespoons onion flakes
2 teaspoons lemon juice

- Mix all ingredients and spread on buns. Makes about ½ to ¾ cup.

Ketchup Crunch

½ cup ketchup
3 - 4 green onions with tops, chopped
½ bell pepper, chopped

- Mix all ingredients and spread on buns. Makes about ¾ cup.

Greek Butter Spread

½ cup feta cheese, softened
½ cup (1 stick) butter, softened

- Whip ingredients and spread on buns. Makes about 1 cup.

Dilly Pickle Relish

¼ cup mayonnaise
3 - 4 baby dill pickles, chopped

- Mix ingredients and spread on buns. Makes about ½ cup.

Barbecue Butter Steak Sauce

½ cup (1 stick) butter, softened
1 cup A1® steak sauce
Dash hot sauce

- Mix ingredients and spread on buns. Makes about 1½ cups.

Tomato-Butter Spread

2 large tomatoes, cored, chopped, drained
1 teaspoon minced basil
¼ cup (½ stick) butter, softened

- Whip ingredients and spread on buns. Makes about 1 cup.

Creamy Italian Spread

1 (4 ounce) package cream cheese, softened
⅛ - ¼ teaspoon oregano
⅛ - ¼ teaspoon rosemary
⅛ - ¼ teaspoon thyme

- Whip ingredients and spread on buns. Makes about ½ cup.

Creamy Onion Spread

1 (4 ounce) package cream cheese, softened
1 small onion, minced
1 - 2 tablespoons mayonnaise

- Whip ingredients and spread on buns. Makes about 1 cup.

Cheese Dip Spread

1 onion, chopped
5 - 6 mushrooms, sliced
¼ cup (½ stick) butter
1 (16 ounce) box Mexican Velveeta® cheese

- Saute onion and mushrooms in butter until translucent. Pour into double boiler with Mexican cheese, melt cheese and mix well. Pour liberally over meat patties. Makes about 2 ½ cups.

Capered Mayonnaise

½ cup mayonnaise
1 tablespoon lemon juice
2 - 3 teaspoons capers, drained

• Whip mayonnaise and lemon juice, add capers and spread on buns. Makes about ½ cup.

Horseradish Kick

¼ cup prepared horseradish
½ cup sour cream
½ teaspoon sugar

• Mix all ingredients and add ½ teaspoon salt. Spread on buns. Makes about ½ cup.

Sticky Spread

¼ cup (½ cup) butter, softened
1 tablespoon molasses
1 tablespoon soy sauce

• Mix all ingredients and spread on buns. Makes about ½ cup.

Hot Dogs

"The noblest of all dogs is the hot dog.
It feeds the hand that bites it."
–Lawrence J. Peter

German immigrants were probably the first to sell their sausages wrapped in bread. Published stories from the 1860's describe German butchers in the Bowery of New York City selling sausages with rolls and sauerkraut.

Great American Hot Dog

All-beef franks
Hot dog buns
Mustard
Shredded cheddar cheese
Chopped onion

Coney Island Hot Dog

Coney Island hot dog refers to ingredients used, not New York City, and is known in much of the North and Midwest. Coney Island does refer to the home of the hot dog.

All-beef franks
Hot dog buns
All-beef chili
Shredded cheese
Chopped onion

Michigan Coney Island Hot Dog

All-beef franks
Hot dog buns
Mustard
All-beef chili, no beans
Chopped onions

Cincinnati Cheese Coney Island Hot Dog

All-beef franks
Hot dog buns
Cincinnati chili
Mustard
Shredded cheese

Chicago-Style Hot Dog

All-beef franks
Poppy seed buns
Mustard
Sweet pickle relish
Dill pickle spear
Chopped onion
Tomato wedges
Sport peppers
Ketchup

According to the National Hot Dog and Sausage Council, Americans eat more than 7 billion hot dogs between Memorial Day and Labor Day.

Washington, D.C. Hot Dog

Spicy sausage franks
Hot dog buns
All-beef chili
Chopped onions
Mustard

Arizona Hot Dogs

All-beef franks
Bacon
Bolillo rolls
Tomatoes, sliced
Chopped onions
Jalapenos
Mustard
Mayonnaise

New York State "Hots"

Hot dogs are called white or red hots depending on the ingredients of the franks. Hots are found in the Rochester, New York area and are the official hot dog of many of the local sports teams.

White hots: mixed uncured, unsmoked pork, veal or beef franks
Red hots: all beef or all pork franks
Hot dog buns
Mustard
Chopped onion
Hot sauce

Slaw Dogs

These are a favorite in the South.

All-beef franks
Hot dog buns
Coleslaw

While many American favorites have one day dedicated to them, the hot dog celebrates the whole month of July as National Hot Dog Month.

Red Snapper Hot Dogs

These are only found in Maine and have this name because of the bright red casings on the franks.

Maine franks
Hot dog buns
Butter

Pizza Dogs

8 all-beef wieners
1 cup pizza sauce
8 hot dog buns
1 cup shredded mozzarella cheese

• Cook hot dogs about 12 minutes on oiled grill over medium-hot fire until outside is bubbly and charred a little. Warm pizza sauce. Place hot dogs in buns and top with pizza sauce and cheese. Serves 8.

Onion Dogs

• Use recipe for *Pizza Dogs (page 136)* and top hot dogs with chopped green onions. Serves 8.

Grilled Fourth of July Brats

1 (6 - 8 count) package bratwurst sausages
Hot dog buns
1 cup marinara sauce
1 (8 ounce) jar roasted peppers
Shredded sharp cheddar or pepper jack cheese slices

• Cook brats on oiled, preheated grill over medium heat for about 5 minutes per side until hot and grill marks show. When brats are just about done, arrange buns away from direct heat and toast for about 3 to 5 minutes.

• Heat marinara sauce and roasted peppers in saucepan. Place brats on toasted buns. Layer roasted peppers, marinara sauce and cheese over bratwurst. Serves 4 to 6.

Bratwurst Heroes with Caramelized Onions and Pepper Strips

1 (6 to 8 count) package bratwurst sausages
2 - 3 onions, thinly sliced
2 red or green bell peppers, seeded, sliced
2 - 4 tablespoons butter
½ teaspoon garlic powder
Hot dog buns

- Cook bratwursts on oiled, preheated grill over medium-hot fire until grill marks show and brats cook thoroughly, about 10 minutes per side; turn frequently.

- Place onions, peppers, butter and garlic powder in center of large piece of foil. Fold into package and cook on grill to one side of direct heat.

- When package begins to sizzle, open foil, stir and move to hottest part of fire. When onions begin to get crusty and caramelize, remove and serve immediately. Before brats are done, toast buns cut side down on grill. Serves 6 to 8.

Grilled Bratwurst with Smoked Peppers

1 (1 - 1½ pound) package bratwurst
1 green, 1 red and 1 yellow bell pepper, halved, cored
Olive oil

- Cook bratwurst on oiled grill over medium-hot fire for about 10 to 15 minutes per side, turn often, until internal temperature is 160°. Slice sausages into ½-inch pieces and set aside.

- Cook oiled bell pepper halves on grill away from direct heat for about 5 minutes per side until skin bubbles on outside. Cut in thin slices and cut in half. Serve with brats. Serves 4 to 6.

Grilled Beer Brats

3 (12 ounce) bottles or cans beer
12 German beef bratwurst
4 onions, sliced thinly
2 green bell peppers, seeded, thinly sliced
2 red bell peppers, seeded, thinly sliced
Oil
Large hot dog buns or sauerkraut and dark bread

- Mix beer and 1 teaspoon pepper in large ovenproof saucepan and heat over medium heat until steaming, but not boiling. Reduce heat to simmer.

- Rub brats and vegetables with a little oil and place on oiled, preheated grill over medium-high heat. Cook until grill marks appear and turn. When brats are done and vegetables are tender, about 15 to 20 minutes, place all in large saucepan with beer mixture.

- Cover and heat on low for about 20 to 30 minutes. Grill hot dog buns cut side down until grill marks show. Place brats and vegetables on buns or serve on plate with sauerkraut and dark bread. Serve immediately with your favorite beer. Serves 8 to 12.

Bratfest

¼ cup (½ stick) butter, melted
1 large onion, sliced
1 (14 ounce) package brats
2 - 3 (12 ounce) cans beer

- Melt butter in large 9 x 13-inch disposable aluminum baking pan on grill over medium-high heat. (If fire is too hot, it will burn butter and you may have to move pan to cooler part of grill.) Saute onion, add brats and cover with beer.

- Cook on grill with lid closed until brats are tender and cooked thoroughly, about 20 minutes, but don't let beer boil or it will be bitter. Drain brats and onions and serve immediately. Serves about 6.

Rainbow Brat Kebabs

4 pork bratwurst
1 (12 ounce) can light beer
1 (8 ounce) package button mushrooms
1 green bell pepper, seeded, quartered
1 red bell pepper, seeded, quartered
1 large sweet onion, peeled, quartered
1 (6 ounce) carton grape or roma tomatoes
1 (16 ounce) bottle Kansas City barbecue sauce

- Cut brats into bite-size pieces and place in large bowl. Pour beer over brats and marinate for 1 hour. Discard marinade. Alternate brat bites with mushrooms, bell peppers and onion on skewers.

- Cook on oiled grill over medium fire for about 5 to 8 minutes per side. Place tomatoes on sprayed foil over grate away from direct heat to cook. Baste brats and veggies frequently with barbecue sauce. Serve immediately. Serves 4.

Cajun Mustard Dip for Brats

1 cup spicy deli mustard
1 teaspoon Cajun seasoning
Hot pepper sauce

- Mix all ingredients. Add hot pepper sauce to taste. Serve with brats. Makes about 1 cup.

Creamy Mustard Sauce for Brats

1 (8 ounce) jar spicy ground mustard
¼ cup sour cream
2 tablespoons prepared horseradish

- Mix all ingredients and serve with brats. Makes about 1¼ cups.

See more dips and sauces to use on brats on pages 305-307.

Beef

Low-cost cuts of beef give you
gourmet tastes on a budget.

Creamy Onion Hamburger Steaks

1 - 1½ pounds ground beef
1 (8 ounce) carton sour cream
1 (1 ounce) packet dry onion soup mix
¾ cup dry breadcrumbs
1 egg, beaten

- Combine beef, sour cream, dry onion soup mix, breadcrumbs, egg and ½ teaspoon black pepper and form into patties.

- Cook on oiled grill over medium-hot fire for about 5 to 7 minutes per side until internal temperature is 160°. Serves 4.

Cheesy Mushroom Hamburger Steaks

1 pound ground beef
1 egg
½ cup chopped onion
1 tablespoon garlic powder
2 tablespoons Heinz® 57® Sauce
1 (4 ounce) can sliced mushrooms, drained
½ cup shredded cheddar cheese

- Combine all ingredients and ½ teaspoon each salt and pepper. Form into 4 patties. Cook on oiled grill over medium-high heat for about 5 to 10 minutes until internal temperature reaches 160°. Serves 4.

Bacon Mushroom Hamburger Steaks

- Use recipe for *Cheesy Mushroom Hamburger Steaks (page 140)*. Wrap bacon strips around each patty and secure with toothpicks before grilling. Serves 4.

Cheesy Veggie Beef Packs

1 pound ground beef
1 cup shredded cheddar cheese
1 tablespoon Worcestershire sauce
1 teaspoon garlic powder
1 teaspoon seasoned pepper
2 small baking potatoes, thinly sliced
1 cup baby carrots

- Combine beef, cheese, Worcestershire sauce, garlic powder, seasoned pepper and 1 teaspoon salt. Form into 4 patties.

- Evenly distribute potatoes on 4 large, sprayed pieces of heavy-duty foil. Top with beef and carrots. Fold loosely to leave room for air to circulate and seal foil.

- Cook on grill over medium-hot fire for about 10 to 20 minutes until internal temperature of meat is 160° and potatoes are tender. Turn several times to reposition packs. Serves 4.

Yukon Veggie Beef Packs

- Use recipe for *Cheesy Veggie Beef Packs (page 141)* and replace baking potatoes with Yukon gold potatoes. Serves 4.

Rainbow Veggie Beef Packs

- Use recipe for *Cheesy Veggie Beef Packs (page 141)* and add cherry tomatoes and chopped green onions before grilling. Serves 4.

Sweet Veggie Beef Packs

- Use recipe for *Cheesy Veggie Beef Packs (page 141)* and substitute sweet potatoes for baking potatoes. Serves 4.

Butternut Beef Packs

- Use recipe for *Cheesy Veggie Beef Packs (page 141)* and add sliced butternut squash instead of baking potatoes. Serves 4.

Taco-Hash Brown Packs

1 pound ground beef
½ cup breadcrumbs
2 tablespoons taco seasoning mix
¼ cup milk
3 cups frozen hash browns
1 cup prepared cheese dip

- Mix ground beef, breadcrumbs, taco seasoning and milk. Form into 4 patties. Mix hash browns and cheese dip. Place 1 patty and equal portions of hash brown mixture on large pieces of heavy-duty foil. Make foil packs large so air can circulate.

- Cook on grill over medium-high heat with lid closed for about 15 to 30 minutes until internal temperature of meat is 160°. Move several times on grill. Serves 4.

Grilled Italian Meatloaf

1 pound ground beef
1 cup shredded Italian blend cheese
½ cup Italian bread crumbs
⅓ cup tomato paste
1 egg

- Combine all ingredients plus 2 teaspoons salt and ½ teaspoon pepper and form into loaf. Place on large piece of sprayed heavy-duty foil. Fold and seal foil loosely for air to circulate.

- Cook on grill over medium-high heat about 40 minutes until internal temperature is 160°; turn frequently. Serves 4 to 6.

Turkey Meatloaf

- Use recipe for *Grilled Italian Meatloaf (page 142)* and substitute ground turkey for ground beef. Internal temperature should be 165°. Serves 4 to 6.

Hamburger Steaks with Onion Sauce

1½ pounds ground beef
½ cup dry, seasoned breadcrumbs
1 large egg
1 tablespoon Worcestershire sauce

- In large bowl, combine ground beef, breadcrumbs, egg and Worcestershire sauce. Shape into 6 patties.

- Cook on oiled grill over medium-hot fire for about 5 to 10 minutes per side. Remove when internal temperature reaches 160°. Top with onion sauce recipe below. Serves 4 to 6.

Onion Sauce

2 onions, thinly sliced
2 tablespoons (¼ stick) butter
1 tablespoon flour
1 (10 ounce) can French onion soup

- Sauté onions in butter until translucent. Stir in flour and mix well. Pour in onion soup and heat. Stir constantly until soup thickens. Pour onion sauce over beef patties.

Peppered Hamburger Steaks

1 - 1½ pounds ground beef
Seasoned salt
1 tablespoon cracked black pepper

- Form meat into 4 to 6 patties and sprinkle with seasoned salt and pepper. Pat black pepper into both sides of each patty. Prepare Blue Cheese Butter recipe below.

- Cook on oiled grill over medium-hot fire for about 5 to 10 minutes per side until internal temperature is 160°. Just before removing from heat, spread Blue Cheese Butter on top and let it melt a little. Serves 4 to 6.

Blue Cheese Butter

½ cup (1 stick) unsalted butter, softened
¼ cup crumbled blue cheese

- Cream all ingredients and ½ teaspoon salt and spread over patties just before serving. Makes about ¾ cup.

Spicy South-of-the-Border Hamburger Steaks

2 pounds ground beef
1 packet taco seasoning mix
1 cup regular or hot chipotle salsa, divided
6 slices hot pepper-jack cheese

- In large mixing bowl, combine beef, taco seasoning and ¼ cup salsa. Shape mixture into 6 patties. Cook on oiled grill over medium-hot fire for about 5 minutes on each side until internal temperature is 160°.

- Place 1 slice of cheese on each ground steak and cook until cheese begins to melt. Remove from grill and pour remaining salsa over top. Serves 6.

Soy Hamburger Steaks

1 pound ground beef
¼ cup soy sauce
¼ cup oil
2 tablespoons ketchup
1 tablespoon vinegar
¼ teaspoon garlic powder

- Form beef into 4 patties and sprinkle with salt and pepper. Combine soy sauce, oil, ketchup, vinegar, garlic powder, and ½ teaspoon each salt and pepper. Pour over patties. Refrigerate for 2 hours; turn once.

- Cook on oiled grill over medium heat for about 10 to 15 minutes per side until internal temperature is 160°. If beef begins to burn, move to lower heat on grill. Serves 4.

Spicy Cajun Rounds

1 pound ground round beef
3 tablespoons seasoned dry breadcrumbs
1 egg
3 green onions, finely chopped
1 tablespoon plus 1 teaspoon Cajun seasoning, divided
1 tablespoon prepared mustard
¼ cup chili sauce
½ teaspoon hot sauce

- In bowl, combine beef, breadcrumbs, egg, onions, 1 tablespoon Cajun seasoning and mustard. Mix well and form into 4 patty rounds. In small bowl, blend chili sauce, remaining 1 teaspoon Cajun seasoning and hot sauce.

- Cook rounds on oiled grill over medium-hot fire for about 5 to 7 minutes per side until internal temperature is 160°. Microwave chili sauce for 30 to 45 seconds and pour over patty rounds before serving. Serves 4.

$ave Money! *Keep a running list of items you need in a convenient place like on your fridge.*

Saucy Hamburger Steaks

1 (15 ounce) can tomato sauce
1 (4 ounce) can sliced mushrooms, drained
½ cup chopped onion
½ cup chopped bell pepper
⅓ cup brown sugar
1 pound ground beef

- Combine all ingredients except beef in saucepan over medium heat for 10 minutes. Keep warm. Form beef into 4 patties and sprinkle generously with salt and pepper.

- Cook on oiled grill over medium-high heat for about 5 to 10 minutes until internal temperature reaches 160°. Pour sauce over hamburger steaks. Serves 4.

Ranch-Seasoned Ground Steaks

1 (1 ounce) packet ranch salad dressing mix
1 pound ground beef
1 cup shredded cheddar cheese

- Combine dressing mix with beef and cheese in bowl. Shape into 4 patties. Cook on oiled grill over medium heat for about 5 to 10 minutes per side. Internal temperature should be 160°. Serves 4.

Mediterranean Ground Rounds

1 pound ground beef
2 tablespoons roasted red pepper, chopped
1 teaspoon dried oregano
½ cup chopped onion
½ cup chopped spinach leaves
1 (8 ounce) bottle Russian dressing

- In bowl, combine beef, roasted red pepper, 1 teaspoon seasoned salt, oregano and onion. Mix well and form into 4 patties.

- Cook on medium-high heat on oiled grill about 5 - 10 minutes per side. Internal temperature should be 160°. Serve on bed of spinach with Russian dressing poured over top. Serves 4.

Smoked Brisket

You'll get as many different opinions about smoking briskets as you will about barbecue. This is one version that's simple and very good.

1 (4 - 5 pound) trimmed beef brisket
Seasoned salt
Cracked black pepper

- Season brisket and leave at room temperature for about 1 hour. Soak mesquite or hickory chips in water for about 1 hour. Start 10 pounds of charcoal in fire box about 45 minutes before cooking. When coals burn down to red hot, add wet mesquite or hickory to fire.

- Place brisket on oiled rack away from fire and close lid. Add wood chips several times to keep smoke circulating. Smoke for about 3 to 4 hours until meat is very tender and internal temperature is at least 145°.

- If you have trouble keeping a consistent temperature, wrap brisket in foil and cook in oven at 275° for about 1 to 2 hours until fork tender. Cool about 30 minutes before slicing. Slice across grain in thin pieces. Serves 8 to 10.

Almost Smoked Brisket

If you don't have time to go through the rigors of smoking a brisket, try this for an easy substitute.

1 (5 - 6 pound) trimmed brisket
1 (6 ounce) bottle liquid smoke
Garlic salt
1 onion, chopped
Worcestershire sauce
1 (6 ounce) bottle barbecue sauce

- Place brisket in roasting pan. Pour liquid smoke over beef. Sprinkle with garlic salt and pepper and top with onion. Cover and refrigerate overnight.

- Before cooking, pour off liquid smoke and douse with Worcestershire sauce. When ready to cook, preheat oven to 300°.

- Cover and bake for 5 hours. Uncover and pour barbecue sauce over brisket and bake for additional 1 hour. Serves 10 to 12.

Brisket with Barbecue Sauce

1 (4 - 5 pound) trimmed brisket
2 tablespoons Worcestershire sauce
Garlic powder

- Place brisket in shallow baking pan and pour Worcestershire over brisket. Sprinkle with garlic powder and salt and pepper to taste. Leave at room temperature for about 1 hour.

- Soak mesquite or hickory chips in water for about 1 hour. Start 10 pounds of charcoal in fire box about 45 minutes before cooking. When coals burn down to red hot, add wet mesquite or hickory to fire.

- Place brisket on oiled rack away from direct fire and close lid. Add wood chips several times to make sure enough smoke is circulating. Smoke for about 3 to 4 hours until internal temperature reaches at least 145° and meat is very tender.

- Let brisket cool for about 30 minutes before slicing. Slice across grain in thin pieces.

Brisket Barbecue Sauce:

1 cup ketchup
⅓ cup Worcestershire sauce
¾ cup packed brown sugar
1 tablespoon lemon juice

- Combine ingredients in saucepan and simmer for 10 minutes until sugar dissolves; stir frequently. Serve sauce with brisket. Serves 8 to 10.

In Texas beef brisket is synonymous with the word barbecue. In other words, when one says barbecue it means brisket. Texans don't barbecue on weekends or use the barbecue to cook on. In Texas barbecue is not a verb or an adjective. It is a noun with only one meaning and that meaning is brisket.

Smoked Short Ribs Texas-Style

Texas-style means there is no tomato-based sauce that covers up the full flavor of beef.

8 - 10 beef short ribs
Oil
Lawry's® seasoned salt
Sugar

- Cut ribs apart and remove fat and silver sheath on top of ribs. Coat with a little olive oil and sprinkle with seasoned salt, black pepper and a pinch of sugar and leave at room temperature for about 1 hour.

Cooking Plan A (When you can control temperature):

- Soak mesquite or hickory chunks in water for about 1 hour. Start 10 to 15 pounds of charcoal in fire box or vertical water smoker about 45 minutes before cooking. When coals burn down to red hot, add wet mesquite or hickory to perimeter of fire.

- Set water pan in vertical smoker and place oiled grill on shelf. Optimum temperature inside smoker is 225° to 250°. Place ribs, bone side down, on rack away from fire and close lid. (You don't need to turn ribs.)

- Add wood chunks several times to make sure enough smoke is circulating and heat is consistent at 225°. For ribs 1 to 2 inches thick, cook about 3 to 4 hours. Serve about 2 to 3 ribs per person.

Cooking Plan B (When you cannot maintain consistent temperature):

- If you can't maintain even temperature, smoke for about 1 to 1½ hours. Remove from smoker and cook in covered, roasting pan with about ½ cup water at 250° for about 2 to 3 hours until fork tender.

- Check water to make sure pan and ribs do not dry out. Remove from oven and cool for about 1 hour before serving. Serve about 2 to 3 ribs per person.

So-Cal Marinated Tri-Tip Roast

2 cloves garlic, minced
⅔ cup soy sauce
¼ cup canola or virgin olive oil
¼ cup packed light brown sugar
2 tablespoons red wine vinegar
1 (2 - 3 pound) tri-tip roast

- Mix garlic, soy sauce, oil, brown sugar and vinegar in bowl. Pour into resealable plastic bag with tri-tip. Marinate in refrigerator overnight.

- Turn plastic bag several times to rotate meat. Cook slowly on oiled, preheated grill to one side of medium heat until meat is tender and internal temperature is at least 145°, about 1 hour. Let meat rest 10 minutes and cut in thin slices across grain. Serves 6.

Grilled Tri-Tip and Potatoes

1 (2 pound) beef tri-tip roast
1 tablespoon coarsely ground black pepper
3 cloves garlic, minced
4 large baking potatoes, sliced lengthwise about ½ inch thick
Olive oil
½ cup sour cream
¼ cup basil pesto sauce

- Season tri-tip with black pepper and garlic and rub into meat. Cook over medium hot, oiled grill for about 10 to 15 minutes per side until internal temperature is at least 145°.

- At same time rub potatoes with olive oil and salt and pepper, wrap in heavy-duty foil and cook on grill until brown on outside and tender on inside, about 20 minutes.

- Wrap tri-tip loosely in foil for several minutes. Mix sour cream and pesto sauce in bowl and dabble over potatoes. Cut thin slices of tri-tip and arrange potatoes on side. Serves 4 to 6.

Sam Adams Flat Iron Steak

1 (2 - 3 pound) flat iron steak, trimmed
2 (12 ounce) bottles Samuel Adams Boston Lager®
2 teaspoons canola oil
2 cloves garlic, minced
1 tablespoon lemon pepper
1 teaspoon seasoned salt

- Place steak in glass baking dish and pour enough beer over steak to cover. Marinate in refrigerator for 2 to 3 hours. Remove steak, pat dry and rub oil on both sides of steak. Discard marinade. Sprinkle garlic, lemon pepper and seasoned salt on both sides of steak and rub in.

- Place steak on oiled grill over medium-hot fire and sear both sides. Reduce heat and cook over medium-low heat until internal temperature is at least 145°. Remove from grill and let rest 10 minutes. Cut in thin slices across grain. Serve immediately. Serves 4 to 6.

South Seas Flat Iron Steak

½ cup soy sauce
½ cup pineapple juice
1 (2 pound) flat iron steak

- Pour soy sauce and pineapple juice in shallow baking dish. Lay steak in mixture and turn to coat both sides. Marinate for 1 hour and turn every 15 minutes.

- Remove from marinade and discard marinade. Cook on oiled grill over medium heat for 10 minutes, turn and cook additional 10 minutes. Continue to cook slowly until internal temperature is at least 145°. Serves 4.

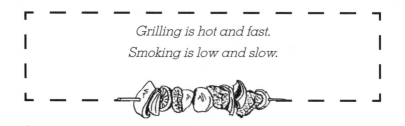

Grilling is hot and fast.
Smoking is low and slow.

Grilled Flat Iron Steak

1 (1½ pound) flat iron steak
½ cup beer
¼ cup teriyaki sauce
¼ cup packed brown sugar
Cracked black pepper
¼ cup extra-virgin olive oil
2 tablespoons balsamic vinegar
1 tablespoon cracked black pepper
1 red bell pepper, seeded, sliced
1 green bell pepper, seeded, sliced
6 - 8 small onions
4 medium tomatoes, quartered

- Season flat iron steak with a little salt and pepper and place in baking dish. Mix beer, teriyaki sauce, brown sugar and cracked black pepper in bowl. Pour over steak, cover with plastic wrap and refrigerate for about 1 hour. Turn frequently.

- Mix olive oil and vinegar and pour over vegetables.

- Place steak on oiled grill over low fire and cook slowly until internal temperature is at least 145°, about 20 to 30 minutes. (Cooking too fast and too long will make steak tough.) Add bell pepper and onions next to steak and cook until grill marks appear on both sides, about 10 minutes per side. Place on top of steak to keep warm.

- About 5 minutes before taking steak off grill, place tomatoes on grill to cook. When tomatoes are tender, remove steak and vegetables from grill and let rest 10 minutes. Thinly slice steak at angle across grain. Serve meat with vegetables on top. Serves 4 to 6.

Flat-iron, flank steak, skirt steak and tri-tip roasts are great cooked on the grill, but they must be seared on the outside and grilled slowly over low to medium heat. In addition, these cuts should be cut in thin slices across the grain when serving.

Grilled Beef Strips with Garlic-Mustard Sauce

⅓ cup apple juice
2 tablespoons dijon-style mustard
1 tablespoon minced garlic
4 (1 inch) thick boneless beef strip steaks

- Combine apple juice, mustard, garlic and 1 teaspoon pepper in bowl and mix well. Set aside ¼ cup sauce for basting. Brush steaks with remaining sauce. Cook steaks on oiled, preheated grill over medium hot fire for about 5 minutes.

- Turn and grill about 5 more minutes until internal temperature is at least 145°. Baste occasionally with remaining sauce. Serves 4.

Marinated New York Strip Steaks

4 (6 - 8 ounce) New York strip steaks, 1-inch thick
⅓ cup Worcestershire sauce
2 teaspoons minced garlic
1 tablespoon vinegar
1 teaspoon sugar

- Place steaks in large sealable plastic bag. Combine all remaining ingredients plus 1½ teaspoons each of salt and pepper and pour in plastic bag. Turn to coat well; refrigerate 1 hour, turning occasionally.

- Cook steaks on sprayed, preheated grill over medium heat for about 5 to 7 minutes, then turn. Steak is done when it is slightly pink inside and internal temperature is at least 145°. Let steaks rest 5 minutes before serving. Serves 4.

Flat-iron steak, boneless blade, petite steak, top blade and patio steaks are all less expensive cuts that work on the grill. They should be cooked medium rare and never well done. For the best results, less tender cuts of beef should be cut in thin slices across the grain and at a 45° angle when serving.

Easy Grilled Rib-Eye Steaks

4 (½ pound) rib-eye steaks
2 (12 ounce) cans beer
1 tablespoon seasoned salt
2 tablespoons lemon pepper

- Place steaks in large bowl with lid. Gently pour beer over steaks and then sprinkle steaks with seasoned salt and lemon pepper. Cover and marinate in refrigerator for 2 hours. Discard marinade.

- Cook steaks on oiled, preheated grill over medium fire for about 5 minutes per side. Check inside and cook additional 5 minutes if it is too pink. For medium rare, internal temperature should be 145°. Serves 4 to 6.

Marinated Brown Beer Steaks

¼ cup dark beer
¼ cup teriyaki sauce
2 tablespoons brown sugar
2 (16 ounce) sirloin steaks
½ teaspoon seasoned salt
½ teaspoon garlic powder

- Mix beer, teriyaki sauce and brown sugar in bowl. Place steaks in flat dish and sprinkle with a little salt and pepper on both sides. Pour beer mixture over steaks and marinate at room temperature for about 10 minutes.

- Discard marinade. Season steaks with seasoned salt, garlic powder and pepper and let rest for about 10 minutes. Place steaks on grill over medium-hot fire and sear both sides. Reduce heat to medium-low and cook until internal temperature is at least 145°. Serves 4.

Petite tender medallions is a butcher's cut from the tender part of the shoulder and tastes similar to sirloin, but is less expensive.

Sam Adams Beer Steak

1 (2 - 2½ pound) sirloin steak
1 (12 ounce) bottle Sam Adams Boston Lager®
Lemon pepper

- Place steak (whole or cut into 4 portions) in sealable plastic bag, pour lager over steak and seal. Refrigerate for about 1 to 2 hours, turning several times, and set aside on counter to come to room temperature.

- Drain beer, season steak with lemon pepper and ½ teaspoon salt on both sides. Cook on oiled grill over medium-hot fire for about 5 minutes per side. Continue cooking until internal temperature is at least 145°. Serves 4.

Sirloin-Spring Greens Salad

1 (½ - ¾ pound) sirloin, trimmed
1 large sweet onion, sliced
1 (8 ounce) bag spring greens salad
Italian dressing

- Season sirloin with a little salt and pepper. Cook on oiled grill over medium-hot fire for about 7 to 9 minutes per side until internal temperature is at least 145°. Cool steak about 10 minutes before slicing. Cut in thin slices across grain.

- Grill onions with a little oil or butter on sprayed foil over grill away from direct heat while steak cooks. Remove onions when they are tender and slightly charred; drain well.

- Toss spring greens with desired amount of dressing and divide equally among 4 plates. Arrange sirloin slices and grilled onions on top. Serves 4.

> *Cooking by indirect heat keeps more moisture in foods than grilling with direct heat.*

Greatest Easy Steak

Learning about dale's steak seasoning may be the best tip you will learn in this cookbook. It is absolutely terrific with everything and makes grilling as easy as it can be!

1 (2 - 2½ pound) sirloin steak
1 (16 ounce) bottle dale's steak seasoning sauce
Garlic salt
Cracked black pepper
1 onion, minced

- Place sirloin in glass baking dish and pour dale's seasoning over steak until sauce is about ¼-inch deep in bottom of pan. Sprinkle garlic salt, pepper and onion over top and marinate for about 15 minutes. Turn and sprinkle with garlic salt and pepper. Marinate for 15 minutes more.

- Cook on oiled grill over medium-hot fire for about 5 minutes per side until internal temperature is at least 145°. Baste while grilling with remaining dale's seasoning. Serves 4 to 6.

Beef-Vegetable Kebabs

1 (2 pound) sirloin steak
4 - 5 green bell peppers, seeded, quartered
3 - 5 onions, peeled, quartered
¼ cup (½ stick) butter, melted

- Slice sirloin into large bite-size pieces. Sprinkle steaks and vegetables liberally with salt and pepper or your favorite seasonings. Put like items on skewers together for more controlled cooking.

- Place skewers on oiled, preheated grill over medium-hot fire about 4 to 5 inches from heat. Baste with melted butter while cooking. Turn after grill marks appear. Cook about 10 to 15 minutes per side until meat's internal temperature is at least 145° and vegetables are tender. Serves 6 to 8.

> The longer meat is cooked, the firmer it becomes. Identify rare, medium and well done steaks by pressing your finger against the meat. A very firm steak is well done. A very soft steak is rare. With practice, you will be able to grill to perfection.

Beef Kebabs with Red Wine Marinade

You will not believe how good this is and how impressive it looks. It is a real treat!

2 - 2½ pounds sirloin steak
1 bell pepper, seeded, cut into chunks
1 (8 ounce) carton button mushrooms
1 (8 ounce) carton cherry tomatoes

Red Wine Marinade:

1 cup red wine
2 teaspoons Worcestershire sauce
2 teaspoons garlic powder
1 cup canola oil
¼ cup ketchup
2 teaspoons sugar
2 tablespoons vinegar
1 teaspoon marjoram
1 teaspoon rosemary
½ teaspoon seasoned pepper

- Cut meat into 1½ to 2-inch pieces. Mix all marinade ingredients and 1 teaspoon salt in bowl and stir well. Marinate steak 3 to 4 hours in marinade. Discard marinade. Place same items on each skewer (all meat, all mushrooms, all bell peppers on each skewer, etc.).

- Place steak on oiled, preheated grill over medium-hot fire and cook about 7 to 10 minutes per side. Cook steak until internal temperature is at least 145°.

- Add mushrooms, peppers and onion skewers on grill and cook about 5 to 7 minutes per side. Place tomatoes on grill during last few minutes of cooking. Cook all vegetables until grill marks show and vegetables are tender. Serves 8.

Creole Pepper Steak

2 cloves garlic, crushed
1 teaspoon thyme
1 teaspoon red pepper
1 pound (1 inch) thick beef top round steak

- Combine garlic, thyme and red pepper. Press evenly into both sides of steak. Cook slowly on oiled, preheated grill over low-medium fire for 5 to 8 minutes per side.

- Turn and cook until internal temperature is 145° for medium rare. (Do not cook fast over hot fire because it will be tough.) Let meat rest for about 10 minutes and cut diagonally into thin slices to serve. Serves 4.

Celebration Steaks

4 (8 ounce) T-bone steaks
⅓ cup Worcestershire sauce
2 teaspoons minced garlic
1 tablespoon vinegar
1 teaspoon sugar

- Place steaks in large resealable plastic bag. Combine all marinade ingredients and pour in plastic bag. Turn to coat well. Refrigerate 1 hour and turn occasionally.

- Cook steaks on oiled, preheated grill over medium fire for about 5 minutes per side. Check center and continue to cook until internal temperature is at least 145°. Serves 4.

Texas Beef Fajitas

If you want a shortcut, substitute Italian dressing for
the marinade.

Marinade:

1 cup prepared salsa or fresh salsa
1 cup bottled Italian dressing
2 tablespoons lemon juice
2 tablespoons chopped green onions
1 teaspoon garlic powder
1 teaspoon celery salt

Fajitas:

2 pounds skirt steak
Flour tortillas

Accompaniments:

Prepared salsa or salsa fresca
Guacamole
Grilled onions
Grilled bell peppers
Chopped tomatoes
Shredded cheese
Sour cream

- Mix 1 teaspoon pepper and all marinade ingredients in large
  bowl and mix well. Add steak and marinate for several hours.
  Grill skirt steak on oiled grill over medium-hot heat for about
  5 to 8 minutes per side and internal temperature is at least 145°.

- Let meat rest 10 minutes and slice into ½ inch wide strips.
  Place on tortillas with selected accompaniments. Serves 6.

Never eat more than you can lift.

–Miss Piggy

Old El Paso Fajitas

El Paso claims to be the home of the first fajitas.

1 (1 pound) skirt steak
1 (12 ounce) bottle or can beer
⅓ cup freshly squeezed lime juice
3 onions, sliced
2 green bell peppers, seeded, thick sliced
1 red bell pepper, seeded, thick sliced
1 teaspoon garlic salt
1 teaspoon lemon pepper
1 teaspoon onion powder
Flour tortillas
Sour cream, shredded cheese, guacamole, pico de gallo

- Tenderize skirt steak to about ¼-inch thick and place in glass baking dish. Mix beer, lime juice, onions and bell peppers and pour over steaks.

- Cover with plastic wrap and refrigerate for about 2 hours. Turn several times while marinating.

- Remove steaks and discard marinade liquid, keeping onions and bell peppers. Sprinkle both sides of steak with garlic salt, lemon pepper and onion powder.

- Cook steak, onions and bell peppers on oiled grill over medium heat until done. Steak is ready when internal temperature is at least 145°, about 8 minutes per side. Let steak rest about 10 minutes and slice across grain into thin strips. Serve with flour tortillas, sour cream, shredded cheese, guacamole and pico de gallo as desired. Serves 4.

Fajitas are original to Texas and probably have their roots in the Texas cattle drives. Traditionally, fajitas are strips of skirt steak, marinated, grilled and cut in strips about 3 inches long and ½ inch wide. These are served with flour tortillas and a variety of vegetables. Fajitas are amazing not only for their flavor, but also because such an inexpensive cut of beef is so delicious.

Quick Fajitas on the Grill

1½ pounds flank steak, tenderized
2 bell peppers, cut in strips
2 onions, halved, sliced
1 (2 ounce) packet fajita marinade
¼ cup olive oil
Juice of 1 lime
1 (10 count) package flour tortillas

- Place tenderized steak, bell pepper and onion into sealable plastic bag with fajita marinade, olive oil, lime juice and 2 tablespoons water.

- Seal bag and turn to coat meat and vegetables. Refrigerate 30 minutes or longer for extra flavor.

- Drain marinade and discard. Wrap bell pepper and onion in 2 large squares of foil. Wrap tortillas in foil with a few drops of water and seal.

- Place flank steak, vegetable packets and tortillas on oiled, preheated grill over medium-low heat. (Place tortillas at side of heat.)

- Grill steak about 6 to 8 minutes per side until internal temperature is 145° for medium rare. Rotate vegetable packages to be sure they cook evenly. Flip tortilla package. Remove all from grill and cover to keep warm.

- Cut meat into thin slices. Serves 4 to 6.

Peppered Flank Steaks

1 (1 - 1½ pound) flank steak
Seasoned salt
¼ cup fresh cracked black pepper

- Sprinkle meat with seasoned salt. Pat black pepper into both sides of steak.

- Cook on oiled grill over medium-hot fire for about 5 to 8 minutes per side until internal temperature is at least 145°. Serves 4.

Slow-Grilled Flank or Skirt Steak

Juice of 1 lemon
½ cup soy sauce
3 tablespoons oil
2 tablespoons Worcestershire sauce
1 clove garlic, minced
2 chopped green onions
2 pounds flank or skirt steak

- Mix all ingredients except steak and pour over steak. Refrigerate for 4 to 12 hours and turn occasionally. Discard marinade.

- Cook on oiled grill over low heat for about 10 minutes, turn and cook additional 10 minutes. If fire is low enough, you may need to cook additional 10 to 20 minutes. Flank steak is ready when internal temperature is at least 145°. Serves 4.

Husband's Favorite Flank Steak

2 pounds flank steak
¼ cup soy sauce
¼ cup Worcestershire sauce

- Score flank steak with sharp knife and place in glass baking dish. Combine soy sauce and Worcestershire sauce and pour over steak. Marinate steak in refrigerator for 2 to 4 hours. Turn steak several times.

- Remove steak from marinade and discard marinade. Cook on oiled grill over medium heat for about 5 to 7 minutes per side until internal temperature is at least 145°. Set aside for 10 minutes before slicing. Serves 4.

Meats should be at room temperature before placing on grill or in smoker.

Easy Marinated Flank Steak

1 cup red wine
½ cup vegetable oil
½ cup teriyaki sauce
4 cloves garlic, pressed or minced
1 large onion, chopped
1 (1 - 2 pound) flank steak
1 (12 ounce) carton mushrooms
1 (12 ounce) cherry tomatoes

- Mix wine, oil, teriyaki, garlic, onion and ½ teaspoon black pepper in large sealable bag. Place steak in bag and marinate in refrigerator for about 8 hours and turn several times. Let stand about 30 minutes before cooking.

- Clean mushrooms, remove stems and wash tomatoes. Cook steak on oiled grill over medium fire and mushrooms and tomatoes away from direct heat.

- Cook steak for about 5 to 10 minutes per side until internal temperature is at least 145°. Cook mushrooms and tomatoes at same time and turn as needed. Serves 4.

On-the-Border Steak

½ teaspoon dry mustard
2 tablespoons fajita seasoning
1 teaspoon minced garlic
1½ pounds flank steak
Canola oil
1 cup chunky salsa, heated
Rice, cooked

- Combine ½ teaspoon pepper, dry mustard, fajita seasoning and garlic in bowl. Rub flank steak with a little oil, sprinkle seasonings over steak and refrigerate for 4 to 6 hours.

- Grill steak on each side on covered, oiled grill for 6 to 8 minutes on medium heat. Cool about 10 minutes. Cut steak diagonally across grain into thin strips. Serve over rice with hot salsa. Serves 4.

Red Wine Marinated Flat Iron Steak

1½ pounds flat iron, skirt or flank steak
1 cup red wine
1 cup chili sauce
½ cup red wine vinegar
¼ cup vegetable oil
2 tablespoons Worcestershire sauce
1 tablespoon prepared mustard
1 teaspoon onion powder
½ teaspoon garlic salt

- Place steak in sealable bag. Mix all remaining ingredients and pour over steak. Seal and refrigerate for about 12 hours in refrigerator. Let stand at room temperature for about 15 minutes before cooking.

- Cook on oiled grill over medium-hot fire for about 5 minutes per side until internal temperature is at least 145°. Do not overcook. Let meat rest 10 minutes and cut across grain in ¼-inch thick slices. Serves 4.

Grilled Flank Steak

2 pounds flank steak
¼ cup soy sauce
⅓ cup honey
2 tablespoons cider vinegar
1½ teaspoons garlic salt
¾ cup vegetable oil
1 small onion, finely minced

- Score steak about ¼ inch deep on each side and remove visible fat. Combine soy sauce, honey, vinegar, garlic salt, oil and onion in shallow bowl. Marinate steak overnight in refrigerator.

- Remove steak from marinade and discard marinade. Cook on oiled, preheated grill over medium fire for about 10 minutes on each side until internal temperature is at least 145°. Let rest 10 minutes and carve diagonally into thin slices. Serves 4 to 6.

Stuffed Flank Steak Medley

2 (1 pound) flank steaks
1 (1 pound) can peeled, seeded tomatoes, drained
2 cloves garlic, pressed
1 small onion, minced
1 (4 ounce) can diced green chilies, drained
1 teaspoon sugar
½ teaspoon vinegar
Louisiana Red Sauce (recipe page 318)

- Pound or roll flank steak out flat and thin and set aside. Mix all remaining ingredients well. Place equal amounts of mixture on each flank steak and roll up tightly. Secure with toothpicks or several skewers.

- Sprinkle outside of rolls with salt and pepper. Place each roll on large oiled heavy-duty foil, fold and seal to allow for air expansion. (It's all right if skewers stick out.)

- Cook on grill away from direct, medium-hot fire about 20 minutes. Turn and rotate and cook about 10 to 15 minutes more until steak is tender and internal temperature is at least 145°. Pour Louisiana Red Sauce over steak before serving. Serves 4 to 6.

Carne Asada

There are several cuts of beef that are great in this recipe: skirt, sirloin, rump and round.

1 pound skirt steak
Lime

- Pound steak thin to about half its original thickness. Season with lime juice and salt and pepper.

- Cook on oiled grill over medium fire about 5 minutes per side until the internal temperature is at least 145°. Let stand about 10 minutes and then slice across grain in ¼-inch cuts. Serve with salsa, hot sauce, jalapenos, pico de gallo, guacamole, rice or beans. Serves about 4.

Carne Asada Tacos

- Cook meat just as in recipe for *Carne Asada (page 165)*. Chop meat after it cooks and serve with soft corn tortillas and pico de gallo. Makes about 4 to 6 tacos.

Carne Asada with Cheese

1 (1½ pound) sirloin steak
1 lime
6 flour tortillas
¾ cup Mexican blend shredded cheese
Salsa

- Rub both sides of sirloin with salt, pepper and juice of lime. Refrigerate about 45 minutes, remove from refrigerator and let stand about 15 minutes.

- Cook sirloin on oiled grill over medium fire about 5 to 10 minutes per side until internal temperature is at least 145°.

- During last 5 minutes, wrap tortillas in foil and place away from direct heat to warm. Remove all from grill and sprinkle cheese over steak. Let steak rest 10 minutes and slice into strips. Serve in tortillas with salsa. Serves 6.

Oregano Marinated Steak

2 pounds (1 inch) thick London broil steak
Marinade:
½ cup bottled Greek vinaigrette dressing
1 tablespoon dried oregano
1 teaspoon lemon juice

- Dry steak with paper towels before placing in marinade. Mix vinaigrette, oregano, lemon juice and ½ teaspoon pepper in large resealable plastic bag. Add steak and press air out of bag; seal and turn several times to distribute marinade well. Refrigerate for 1 hour before grilling.

- Remove steak from marinade and discard marinade. Cook on oiled grill over medium-hot heat for 5 to 10 minutes per side until internal temperature is at least 145°. Before slicing, let steak rest for about 10 minutes. Slice steak against the grain. Serves 4 to 6.

Stuffed Steak Rolls

2 (1 pound) flank steaks
½ - ¾ pound ground beef
1 tablespoon onion flakes
1 tablespoon dried parsley
1 cup soft breadcrumbs
1 package dry onion soup mix

- Pound or roll flank steak out flat and thin and set aside. Brown ground meat in skillet just until most of pink is gone. Drain well. Add onion flakes, parsley and breadcrumbs and mix.

- Place equal amounts of mixture on each flank steak and roll up tightly. Secure with toothpicks or several skewers to keep roll together. Rub outside of rolls with dry onion soup mix. Place each roll in large piece of sprayed heavy-duty foil; fold and seal packets. (It's all right if skewers stick out.)

- Cook on grill away from direct, medium-hot fire for about 20 minutes. Turn and rotate and cook about 10 to 15 minutes more until steak is tender and internal temperature is at least 145°. Serves 6 to 8.

Ginger Grilled Steak

1½ pounds flank steak
¼ cup low-sodium soy sauce, divided
¼ cup sugar
¼ cup ketchup
3 tablespoons cider vinegar
1 tablespoon bottled ground fresh ginger

- Place flank-steak in large resealable plastic bag and pour half soy sauce over steak. Marinate steak about 30 minutes.

- In bowl, combine remaining soy sauce, sugar, ketchup, vinegar, ginger and ¼ teaspoon pepper. Cook steak on oiled, preheated grill over medium-high heat for about 5 to 6 minutes per side. Baste several times with sauce.

- Steak is done when internal temperature is at least 145°. Let steak rest 10 minutes and cut diagonally across grain in thin slices; drizzle with remaining sauce mixture. Serves 4.

Grilling London Broil Cuts

London Broil cuts are usually chuck shoulder, top round
and bottom round cuts that are usually large and relatively
inexpensive. They are great when slow-cooked in the oven, but
are a more difficult challenge when cooked on the grill. Here
are several helpful suggestions that make grilling London Broils
better on the grill.

1. Rub both sides of meat with kosher salt, place in plastic bag,
   push out air and seal. Refrigerate for about 3 hours.

2. Remove from refrigerator and leave at room temperature for
   about 30 minutes. Rinse meat in warm water and pat dry.

3. Rub oil on meat and sprinkle with black pepper. Or choose
   from these seasonings:

   - lemon pepper and garlic salt
   - pressed garlic cloves
   - oregano and basil
   - rosemary
   - garlic salt, ground ginger and onion flakes

4. Cook on oiled grill over medium heat and turn meat frequently.
   (This keeps fibers from contracting which helps tenderness.)
   Cook until internal temperature reaches at least 145°. If meat
   gets hotter than this, meat will be tougher and drier.

5. Remove from heat and cool for about 10 minutes. Slice at a
   45° angle in ¼-inch thick slices.

*To make cleanup extra easy, use non-stick cooking
spray or vegetable oil on grill. After you sear outside of
meat, place sheet of heavy-duty foil over grate before
adding sauces or basting meat to avoid extra cleaning.*

Garlic-Seasoned London Broil

3 cloves garlic
3 tablespoons olive oil
3 teaspoons soy sauce
Dash Worcestershire sauce
1 (1½ - 2 pound) London broil

- Chop garlic and let stand in olive oil for 30 minutes. Remove garlic; add soy sauce, Worcestershire sauce and a little salt and pepper. Pour over steak and marinate for 1 to 2 hours. Let stand at room temperature for about 15 minutes

- Cook on oiled grill over medium fire for about 10 minutes, turn and continue to cook with lid closed for about 10 to 15 minutes more until internal temperature is at least 145°. Serves 4.

TIP: Cook thick cuts slowly at a consistent temperature. If that's not practical, grill to get smoked flavor and finish cooking in oven at 300° until internal temperature is at least 145°.

London Broil

1 - 1½ pounds London broil beef cut
Garlic powder, optional
½ cup steak sauce
1 tablespoon Worcestershire sauce
1 lemon

- Season London broil with salt, pepper and garlic powder. Mix steak sauce, Worcestershire and juice of lemon in large sealable plastic bag and add steak. Refrigerate for about 1 hour. Let stand at room temperature for about 15 minutes.

- Cook on oiled grill over medium-hot fire for about 5 to 7 minutes per side until internal temperature is at least 145°. Serves 4.

A sop or basting mixture flavors the outside of meats while they cook.

Easy London Broil

1 (12 ounce) can cola
1 (10 ounce) bottle teriyaki sauce
1 (3 pound) London broil

- Combine cola, teriyaki sauce and 1 teaspoon black pepper in large sealable plastic bag. Add steak and marinate in refrigerator for 1 to 2 hours and turn occasionally. Remove London broil from marinade and discard marinade.

- Cook slowly on oiled grill over low fire for about 8 to 10 minutes, turn and cook additional 6 to 8 minutes until internal temperature is at least 145°. (Do not cook fast over hot fire.) Let stand for about 10 minutes before slicing diagonally across grain. Serves 6 to 8.

Smoked Chuck Roast

1 (3 - 4 pound/3 inch thick) blade or chuck roast
1 (5 ounce) bottle soy sauce
1 lemon
½ cup bourbon
⅓ cup packed brown sugar
1 tablespoon Worcestershire sauce

- Place roast in sealable plastic bag. Mix all remaining ingredients and pour over roast. Marinate in refrigerator for 8 to 12 hours and turn several times. Let stand at room temperature for about 30 minutes.

- Smoke on oiled grill away from medium-hot fire (300°) for about 2 hours per side. Turn several times and smoke until internal temperature reaches 145° for medium rare. Serves 6 to 8.

Marinades are mixtures of oil and an acid-based ingredient usually wine, vinegar or citrus juice, and herbs and seasonings. (The oil lubricates and the acid tenderizes the meat.) Soak meat in the marinade overnight or for several hours so it absorbs the flavors.

Green Chile-Stuffed Tenderloin

2 cloves garlic, minced
1 medium onion, chopped
1 tablespoon virgin olive oil
1 (4 ounce) can diced green chilies, drained
½ cup shredded Mexican 4-cheese blend
½ cup seasoned breadcrumbs
4 (2-inch thick) beef tenderloin fillets

- Cook garlic and onion in oil in large skillet until they are translucent. Add green chilies, cheese and breadcrumbs. Stir several times and remove from heat.

- Make horizontal slice three-quarters through fillets. Place green chilies mixture in middle of fillets, fold and seal with toothpicks to hold mixture in place.

- Grill on oiled grate over medium-hot fire for about 5 to 10 minutes per side until internal temperature is at least 145°. Serves 4.

Seasoned Beef Tenderloin

3 tablespoons dijon-style mustard
2 tablespoons prepared horseradish
1 (3 pound) center-cut beef tenderloin
½ cup seasoned breadcrumbs

- Combine mustard and horseradish in bowl and spread over beef tenderloin. Press breadcrumbs into horseradish-mustard mixture and wrap in sprayed foil. Refrigerate for about 12 hours.

- Remove foil and sear outside of tenderloin on preheated oiled grill over hot fire to seal in juices. Wrap in sprayed heavy-duty foil and cook over medium-hot fire for 8 to 10 minutes per side until internal temperature is at least 145°. Serves 6.

Use sealing plastic bags or non-corrosive containers to marinate meats. Marinades with acid-based marinades or sauces react to aluminum foil and create unpleasant flavors.

Rosemary-Thyme Beef Tenderloin

¼ cup red wine vinegar
½ cup extra-virgin olive oil
½ cup teriyaki sauce
4 large cloves garlic, crushed
2 tablespoons rosemary
2 tablespoons thyme
1 (5 pound) beef tenderloin, trimmed

- In glass baking dish, mix together vinegar, oil, teriyaki sauce, garlic, rosemary and thyme. Whisk thoroughly to mix, add tenderloin and turn to coat. Marinate in refrigerator several hours. Remove and let stand about 30 minutes before cooking.

- Apply ample amount of cracked black pepper to tenderloin several times before cooking. Grill over medium-hot fire for about 10 to 15 minutes per side and continue cooking until internal temperature is at least 145°. Serves 10.

Grilled Filet Mignon

4 (6 - 8 ounce) thick filets mignons
Seasoned pepper
Garlic salt

- Season filets on both sides with pepper and garlic salt and let come to room temperature. Cook on oiled, preheated grill over medium fire with red to white coals for about 5 to 7 minutes per side until internal temperature is at least 145°. Serve immediately. Serves 4.

Internal temperature for medium rare steak is 145°, 160° for medium and 170° for well done.

Smoked Beef Jerky

An electric smoker is really great for this recipe because you can set it on a temperature and forget it.

2 - 4 pounds round, flank, skirt or flat iron steak
Salt or seasoned salt
Freshly ground black pepper

- Preheat electric smoker to 175°. Slice beef across grain in very thin slices about ¼ inch thick. Place on baking sheet and sprinkle both sides lightly with salt and a lot of freshly ground black pepper.

- Cook until beef gets very dense, dark brown, flexible, but not burned, about 3 to 4 hours. Check it after 2 hours. Store in airtight bags.

Teriyaki Beef Jerky

- Sprinkle beef slices with a few drops of teriyaki sauce on each side and rub into beef.

Lemon-Pepper Beef Jerky

- Sprinkle beef slices with lemon-pepper seasoning on each side and rub into beef.

Spicy Beef Jerky

- Sprinkle beef slices with a few drops of Worcestershire sauce and hot sauce. Rub into beef.

Cracked Pepper Beef Jerky

½ cup teriyaki sauce
¼ cup liquid smoke
¼ cup Worcestershire sauce
2 to 3 tablespoons fresh cracked black pepper
2 tablespoons light brown sugar
1 teaspoon garlic salt

- Mix all ingredients with 1 teaspoon salt. Marinate beef strips in mixture overnight in refrigerator.

Chicken and Turkey

You'll never get bored with these simple recipes that are flavor-packed.

Herb-Seasoned Smoked Chicken

1 (2 - 3 pound) whole chicken fryer
¼ cup minced green onion with tops
¼ cup diced celery
2 - 3 cloves garlic, pressed
1 lemon, halved

- Season chicken with a little salt and pepper. Combine onion, celery, garlic and several teaspoons lemon juice and rub most of it on outside of chicken breasts. Place remaining seasonings and lemon halves in cavity.

- Soak hickory, pecan, oak or cherry wood chips for about 1 hour. Build wood fire or wood-charcoal fire in firebox, spread coals and place soaked wood chips around outside of fire.

- Place chickens on oiled grill away from direct heat with lid closed. Cook at 250° to 300° for about 30 to 45 minutes per side until juices are clear and internal temperature is 165°. Serves 4 to 6.

- If using a gas grill, preheat both sides of grill. Turn one side off. Place soaked wood chips in disposable aluminum pan with a little water on top of burners not on.

- Place chicken on oiled grill away from direct heat and directly over wood chips. Continue to follow instructions for Herb-Seasoned Smoked Chicken.

Rosemary-Herbed Smoked Chicken

1 (2 - 3 pound) whole chicken fryer
¼ cup fresh snipped parsley
2 tablespoons fresh rosemary
2 tablespoons fresh chopped basil
2 tablespoons oil

- Season chicken with a little salt and pepper. Mix fresh herbs with oil and rub into chicken. Follow cooking instructions in *Herb-Seasoned Smoked Chicken (page 174)*. Serves 4 to 6.

Butterflied Grilled Chicken

1 (2 - 3 pound) whole chicken, rinsed
Olive oil

- Cut chicken down backbone and lay out flat. Tuck wings under and stick leg under skin at top of breast. Rub with olive oil and salt and pepper on both sides.

- Cook on oiled grill away from direct medium-hot heat for about 20 to 30 minutes per side with lid closed until juices are clear. Internal temperature should be 165°. Cut in pieces and serve. Serves 4 to 6.

Butterflied Bacon-Covered Chicken

1 (2 - 3 pound) whole chicken, rinsed
Olive oil
4 - 5 slices bacon, cut up

- Use recipe for *Butterflied Grilled Chicken (page 175)*, but stuff bacon under skin in as many places as possible. Serves 4 to 6.

$ave Money! *Have a budget and stick to it!*

Lemon-Buttered Chicken Splits

2 (2 pound) whole chickens
1½ (3 sticks) cups unsalted butter, softened
2 cloves garlic, pressed
2 - 4 lemons
Freshly ground black pepper

- Wash and pat dry chickens. Split chickens in half lengthwise and press flat. In bowl, combine butter, garlic, 1 teaspoon salt and ½ teaspoon pepper.

- Cut lemons in half and squeeze ¼ cup juice into butter mixture. Scrape off about 1 teaspoon lemon zest and stir into butter.

- Spread mixture on chickens and let flavors penetrate for several hours in refrigerator. Allow chicken to reach room temperature before cooking.

- Cook on oiled, preheated grill, hollow side down, to one side of medium-hot fire. Position drip pan with several cups water below area for chicken. Close lid on grill.

- Cook for 20 to 25 minutes per side. Cook until chicken is tender, juices are clear and internal temperature is 165°. Serves 6 to 8.

Quick and Easy Grilled Chicken

1 (3 - 3½ pound) chicken, quartered
3 tablespoons olive oil
⅔ cup prepared barbecue sauce

- Brush chicken quarters with olive oil and sprinkle on a little salt and pepper. Cook on oiled grill over medium-hot fire for 10 to 15 minutes per side until juices are clear and internal temperature is 165°.

- Brush with barbecue sauce during the last 5 to 10 minutes of grilling. Serves 4 to 6.

> **$ave Money!** Remember, the biggest package isn't always the cheapest. The only way you can be sure is to use a calculator to figure out the cost per unit. Many store displays also show cost per unit.

Chicken with Wine Sauce

1 (2 - 3 pound) whole chicken, quartered
1 (12 ounce) carton button mushrooms, sliced
2 tablespoons butter
¾ cup white wine
1 cup sour cream

- Cook chicken on oiled grill over medium-high heat for about 10 to 13 minutes per side until juices are clear and internal temperature is 165°.

- Saute mushrooms in butter over medium heat for about 5 minutes. Add wine and cook for about 20 minutes on low. Remove from heat and stir in sour cream. Pour over cooked chicken before serving. Serves 4.

Smoked Standing Chicken

1 (3 pound) chicken
1 (12 ounce) can beer, divided
1 (8 ounce) jar dijon-style mustard
1 (8 ounce) bottle Italian salad dressing

- Soak hickory, mesquite or pecan wood chunks in water for about 1 hour. Start wood fire about the same time.

- Remove any fat in cavity of chicken and dry. Mix half beer with mustard and spread over chicken. Spread mustard mixture generously in cavity.

- Pour Italian dressing in remaining ½ can beer. Place on sturdy baking sheet and position chicken with beer can inside cavity. (Chicken will be sitting up at attention.)

- After fire is glowing, but not flaming, add wood chunks, drip pan and chicken. Close lid and cook for about 50 minutes to 1 hour. Continue cooking, covered, until internal temperature is 165° and juices are clear. Serves 4 to 6.

Beer-in-the-Butt Chicken

2 - 3 pound whole chicken
2 tablespoons vegetable oil
3 - 4 tablespoons seasoned salt
Garlic powder
1 (12 ounce) can high quality beer

- Remove neck and giblets from chicken and discard. Rinse chicken well and pat dry with paper towels. Rub chicken lightly with oil and seasonings and set aside.

- Place open beer ¾ full on small baking pan with sides. Place rear cavity of chicken over beer and position chicken to sit upright. Transfer pan with chicken to middle of preheated grill.

- Cook over medium-high indirect heat with grill covered, for about 1¼ to 1½ hours until internal temperature reaches 165° in thickest area and juices are clear. Remove from grill and let stand for 10 minutes before carving. Serves 4.

Spicy Barbecued Chicken

¼ cup ketchup
¼ cup cider vinegar
1 - 2 tablespoons prepared horseradish
1 tablespoon brown sugar
2 cloves garlic, pressed
1 whole chicken, quartered
Seasoned salt

- Mix ketchup, vinegar, horseradish, brown sugar and garlic in small saucepan and bring to a light boil. Reduce heat to simmer and cook for about 5 minutes to thicken.

- Cook chicken on oiled grill over medium fire for about 8 to 10 minutes and turn. Baste chicken with sauce on both sides and continue cooking for about 10 minutes until juices are clear and internal temperature is 165°. Serves 4.

Borracho Pollo

Borracho pollo means drunk chicken in Spanish.

1 (12 ounce) can Mexican lager
1 - 2 chipotle peppers
1 teaspoon finely chopped cilantro
¼ teaspoon cumin
1 lime
½ cup (1 stick) unsalted butter, melted
1 (2 - 3 pound) whole chicken

- Blend half of beer with chipotle, cilantro, cumin, 1 teaspoon salt, juice from lime and melted butter. Fill marinating syringe and inject thickest parts of bird thoroughly.

- Place in refrigerator for about 1 hour, remove and let stand for about 15 minutes. Place chicken on top of remaining beer can so it is inside chicken.

- Place all on baking sheet and place on grill over medium-hot fire with lid closed for about 30 to 50 minutes. Turn and continue cooking until there is no pink and juices are clear. Internal temperature should be 165°. Serves 4 to 6.

Smoked Citrus Chicken

1 (.5 ounce) package Baja Citrus Marinade seasoning mix
¼ cup orange juice
¼ cup oil
1 teaspoon honey
1 (2 - 3 pound) chicken, quartered

- Mix marinade seasoning mix, orange juice, oil and honey and pour into large sealable bag. Place chicken quarters in bag and coat with seasonings. Marinate for about 30 to 45 minutes. Discard marinade.

- Cook chicken on oiled grill away from direct heat for about 2 hours at about 250° to 300°. Continue to cook until juices are clear and internal temperature is 165°. Serves 4 to 6.

Grilled Chicken with Mustard Barbecue Sauce

4 chicken quarters
1 - 2 tablespoons hot sauce
½ cup ketchup
¼ cup butter (½ stick), melted
2 tablespoons sugar
1 tablespoon mustard
½ teaspoon minced garlic
¼ cup lemon juice
¼ cup white vinegar
¼ cup Worcestershire sauce

- Rub chicken with thin coat of hot sauce. Sprinkle with salt and pepper. Combine all remaining ingredients in bowl.

- Pour over chicken and marinate, covered, in refrigerator for 1 hour. Cook on oiled, preheated grill away from direct medium-hot fire for about 10 minutes.

- Turn and continue to cook until juices are clear and internal temperature reaches 165°. Serves 4.

Campground Happy Meals

This is great for not washing dishes. Serve on heavy paper plates.

4 chicken quarters
1 (8 ounce) bottle Italian dressing
2 large sweet onions, sliced
4 roma tomatoes, halved
1 - 2 cloves garlic, pressed

- Marinate chicken in Italian dressing in refrigerator for at least 1 hour. Wrap each quarter in sprayed heavy-duty foil with equal amounts of onions, tomatoes, garlic and a little salt and pepper. Seal foil so juices won't leak and there's room for air to circulate.

- Cook on preheated grill over medium fire for about 15 minutes, reposition and continue cooking for 10 minutes until juices of chicken are clear and its internal temperature is 165°. Serves 4.

Special Delivery Chicken

6 chicken quarters
1 sweet potato, peeled
1 green bell pepper, seeded
1 (15 ounce) can pineapple chunks, drained
½ cup (1 stick) butter

- Place 6 pieces of sprayed heavy-duty foil large enough to cover and to seal chicken on counter. Cut sweet potato into 6 slices. Cut bell pepper into 6 slices.

- Place one slice of each on top of chicken quarter. Top with pineapple, 1 tablespoon butter, ¼ teaspoon salt and dash of pepper for each package.

- Fold foil over food so air will circulate and seal edges to make airtight package. Cook on preheated grill over medium heat for about 40 to 50 minutes until juices are clear and internal temperature is 165°; turn once or twice. Serves 4 to 6.

Homer's Best Smoked Chickens

This recipe is a terrific, fresh-tasting sop.

2 whole chickens, halved or quartered
Seasoned pepper
½ cup (1 stick) butter
2 teaspoons Worcestershire sauce
2 dashes hot sauce
2 tablespoons lemon juice
½ teaspoon garlic salt
1 (8 ounce) can 7UP®

- Soak hickory, pecan, oak or cherry wood chips for about 1 hour. Build all wood fire or wood-charcoal fire in firebox, spread coals and place soaked wood chips around outside of fire.

- Sprinkle chickens with seasoned pepper and leave at room temperature for 30 minutes. Melt butter in small saucepan and add remaining ingredients.

- Cook chicken for about 30 minutes per side with lid closed at about 250°, but baste liberally with 7UP® mixture. Remove from grill when juices are clear and internal temperature is 165°. (After smoking subsides or heat drops, you can finish cooking in covered dish in oven at 300° until done.) Serves 8 to 10.

Chicken with Lemon Sauce

¼ cup minced onion
2 cloves garlic, crushed gently
¼ cup extra virgin olive oil
¼ cup lemon juice
1 (2 - 3 pound) whole chicken, quartered

- Saute onion and garlic in olive oil until onion is translucent and discard garlic. Add lemon juice and ½ teaspoon salt. Pour over cooked chicken before serving or use as basting sauce.

- Cook chicken on oiled grill over medium-hot fire for about 10 to 13 minutes per side until juices are clear and internal temperature is 165°. Serves 4.

Lemon-Dijon Chicken

4 - 6 skinless chicken quarters
Olive oil
Lemon pepper

- Rub chicken quarters with olive oil, lemon pepper and a little salt. Cook on oiled grill over medium-hot fire for about 7 to 10 minutes per side until juices are clear and internal temperature is 165°.

- Just before removing from heat, arrange several pats of Lemon-Dijon Butter (recipe below) on top and melt before serving. Serves 4 to 6.

Lemon-Dijon Butter

½ cup (1 stick) unsalted butter, softened
3 tablespoons dijon-style mustard
1 teaspoon lemon juice
1 teaspoon grated lemon zest

- Cream all ingredients and spread over chicken before serving.

Mesquite-Smoked Chicken

1 (.5 ounce) package Mesquite Marinade seasoning mix
1 medium onion, chopped
½ cup ketchup
1 (2 - 3 pound) chicken, quartered

- Mix marinade seasoning mix, onion and ketchup and pour into large sealable bag. Place chicken quarters in bag and coat with seasonings. Marinate for about 30 minutes. Discard marinade.

- Cook chicken on oiled grill away from direct heat for about 2 hours at about 250° to 300°. Continue to cook until juices are clear and internal temperature is 165°. Serves 4 to 6.

$ave Money! *Only go to the grocery store when you have to. You'll avoid tempting impulse buys and save time and gas.*

Grilled Chicken with Raspberry Sauce

1 (2½ - 3 pound) chicken, quartered
Seasoned salt
Seasoned pepper
Raspberry Barbecue Sauce (recipe page 315), divided

- Season chicken quarters liberally with seasoned salt and pepper. Cook chicken on oiled grill over medium heat with lid closed for about 8 to 10 minutes per side until juices are clear and internal temperature is 165°. Baste chicken with Raspberry Barbecue Sauce during last minutes of cooking. Spread additional sauce on chicken before serving. Serves 4 to 6.

Chipotle Smoked Chicken

This is also great using pork.

1 (.5 ounce) package Chipotle Pepper Marinade seasoning mix
½ cup (1 stick) butter, melted
1 (2 - 3 pound) chicken, quartered

- Mix marinade seasoning mix and butter and pour into large sealable bag. Place chicken quarters in bag and coat with seasonings. Marinate for about 30 to 45 minutes. Discard marinade.

- Cook chicken on oiled grill away from direct heat with lid closed for about 2 hours at about 250° to 300°. Continue to cook until juices are clear and internal temperature is 165°. Serves 4 to 6.

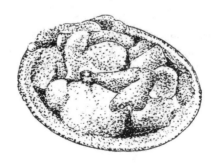

Grilled Chicken Special

1 (12 ounce) bottle or can beer
½ cup (1 stick) butter
2 cloves garlic, minced
1 tablespoon seasoned salt
4 chicken quarters
Garlic powder

- Mix beer, butter, garlic, seasoned salt and a little pepper in small saucepan over low heat until butter melts and seasonings combine.

- Place chicken quarters on hot grill over medium-high heat and sear both sides. Reduce heat and baste chicken with beer mixture frequently. Sprinkle garlic powder over coals several times and cook until chicken internal temperature is 165° and juices are clear. Serves 4.

Smoke-Gets-in-Your-Eyes Chicken

4 cups mesquite wood chips
2 (12 ounce) bottles or cans beer
6 chicken-leg quarters, skinned
1 (10 ounce) bottle barbecue sauce

- Soak mesquite wood chips in beer for about 1 hour. Heat grill for medium fire. Add wood chips around edges and some on top of charcoal fire or gas grill that is medium-hot.

- Place leg quarters on oiled grill and cook for about 5 to 8 minutes until grill marks show. Turn chicken and cook other side for about 5 to 8 minutes until grill marks show. (Make sure fire is not too hot or chicken will cook too fast and dry out.)

- Remove chicken and place each piece on enough foil to completely cover leg quarter. Coat chicken with barbecue sauce on both sides. Wrap and seal edges of foil.

- Add more mesquite chips around edges. Make sure fire is medium low and place foil packages on grill. Cook for about 20 to 25 minutes until internal temperature of chicken is 165° and juices are clear. Serves 4 to 6.

Honey-Glazed Chicken

1 (10 ounce) bottle Heinz® 57® Sauce
½ cup honey
1 (2 pound) package chicken pieces

- Combine Heinz® 57® Sauce and honey; set aside. Sprinkle chicken with salt and pepper.

- Cook on oiled grill over medium-high heat for about 10 minutes per side. Cook until internal temperature reaches 165° and juices are clear. Baste chicken liberally with sauce on both sides. Serves 4.

Teriyaki Chicken

1½ - 2 pounds chicken pieces, skinned
½ cup soy sauce
¼ cup dry sherry
2 tablespoons sugar
2 tablespoons grated fresh ginger root
4 cloves garlic, crushed
2 tablespoons oil

- Rinse chicken, pat dry and arrange in baking dish. Combine soy sauce, sherry, sugar, ginger root, garlic and oil. Pour over chicken and toss to coat.

- Cover and marinate in refrigerator 6 hours, turning occasionally. Drain.

- Pat chicken dry and place on hot oiled grill over medium heat for about 30 minutes, turn occasionally, until internal temperature is 165° and juices are clear. Serves 4.

Prime is the best grade of beef and the most expensive. Choice is next and Select is third. The American Heart Association logo sometimes appears on the leanest cuts of beef. The exact same cut without the American Heart Association logo will cost less than the one with the logo.

Chicken Legs with Beer Sop

½ (12 ounce) can or bottle beer
1 onion, chopped
1 tablespoon prepared mustard
½ teaspoon garlic salt
2 - 3 pounds chicken legs, skinned

- Combine beer, onions, mustard and garlic salt in sealable plastic bag. Add chicken and refrigerate for 1 to 2 hours.

- Cook chicken legs on oiled grill over medium fire for about 10 minutes per side until juices are clear and internal temperature is 165°. Serves 4.

Parmesan Ranch Chicken

½ cup shredded parmesan cheese
1 (.4 ounce) packet dry ranch salad dressing mix
2 pounds chicken drumsticks

- Combine cheese and dressing mix in bowl. Rub into chicken and refrigerate for 30 minutes. Remove and leave chicken at room temperature for about 10 minutes.

- Cook on oiled, preheated grill away from direct medium-high fire with closed lid for about 30 to 40 minutes until juices are clear and internal temperature is 165°; turn several times. (Do not touch bone with thermometer.) Serves 4.

Chicken is done when juices are clear and meat is white, not pinkish. Remove chicken to check temperature with a meat thermometer (should be 165°). You can also check color of meat near bones or joints before you think it is done so you won't overcook it, but this will release juices. Put it back on the grill just enough to cook it properly.

Chili Sauce Chicken

¾ cup chili sauce
¾ cup packed brown sugar
1 (1 ounce) packet onion soup mix
⅛ teaspoon cayenne pepper
2 pounds chicken thighs

- Combine chili sauce, brown sugar, onion soup mix, cayenne pepper and ¼ cup water in bowl. Season chicken with a little salt and pepper and cook on oiled grill over medium-hot fire. Sear outside of chicken for about 5 minutes on each side and brush on chili sauce.

- Cook about 5 to 10 more minutes more per side. Continue basting with chili sauce. Don't let sauce burn. Serve when internal temperature is 165° and juices are clear. Serves 4.

Special Sauce Barbecued Chicken

½ (12 ounce) bottle or can beer
1 onion, diced
½ cup ketchup
1 tablespoon molasses
2 cloves garlic, minced
1 teaspoon seasoned salt
4 boneless, skinless chicken breast halves

- Mix beer, onion, ketchup, molasses, garlic, seasoned salt and a little pepper in bowl. Sprinkle salt and pepper generously over chicken. Place on oiled, hot grill over medium-high heat and sear outside of chicken.

- Reduce heat a little and baste chicken on both sides. Cook slowly and baste for about 10 to 15 minutes per side until internal temperature is 165° and juices chicken are clear. Serves 4.

$ave Money! When items you use frequently are on sale, stock up.

Grilled Chicken with Homemade Barbecue Sauce

6 boneless, skinless chicken breast halves or quarters
3 cups ketchup
½ cup packed brown sugar
¼ cup Worcestershire sauce
2 tablespoons vinegar
1 teaspoon hot sauce

- Wash chicken breasts and dry with paper towels. Combine remaining ingredients in saucepan, add a little salt and pepper and mix well. Bring to a boil, reduce heat to low and simmer for 15 minutes.

- Sear chicken on oiled grill over medium-high heat, then move to indirect heat and baste liberally. Grill for about 8 minutes per side until juices are clear and internal temperature is 165°. Serves 4 to 6.

Chicken Cutlets with Dijon Sauce

4 - 6 boneless, skinless chicken breast halves
3 tablespoons butter
2 tablespoons olive oil
1 bunch green onions with tops, chopped
1 red bell pepper, seeded, minced
2 ribs celery, chopped
2 tablespoons dijon-style mustard

- Cut each piece of chicken in half lengthwise and place between 2 sheets of wax paper. Pound each piece to about ¼ inch thick. Season chicken with a little salt and pepper.

- Cook on oiled grill over medium fire for about 5 to 10 minutes per side until internal temperature reaches 165° and juices are clear. Keep chicken warm.

- Melt butter in skillet. Add oil, onions, bell pepper, celery and mustard and cook just until onions are translucent. (Add extra butter if needed.) Pour over chicken to serve. Serves 4 to 6.

Easy Drunk Chicken

1 cup beer
1 cup soy sauce
2 cloves garlic, minced
4 boneless, skinless chicken breast halves

- Combine beer, soy sauce, garlic and 1 cup water in baking dish. Place chicken breast halves in dish and spoon sauce over top. Season with a little salt and pepper.

- Seal with plastic wrap and refrigerate overnight. Turn once and reseal.

- Discard marinade and cook chicken on oiled, preheated grill over medium-low heat for about 10 minutes per side until internal temperature reaches 165° and juices are clear. Do not overcook. Serves 4.

Basic Grilled Chicken

4 - 6 boneless, skinless chicken breast halves
Oil
Thyme
Garlic powder
Pinch brown sugar

- Rub chicken breasts with oil and sprinkle with seasonings and a little salt. Refrigerate for 15 to 20 minutes. Cook on oiled grill over medium-hot fire for about 10 to 20 minutes per side until juices are clear and internal temperature is 165°. Serves 4 to 6.

Meat with a bone in it will take longer to cook than meat without a bone. A boneless chicken breast will take about 15 to 18 minutes to cook. A breast with bone will take about 25 to 30 minutes.

Beer-Sop Grilled Chicken

1 cup (2 sticks) butter
1 (12 ounce) bottle or can beer
1 tablespoon lemon-pepper seasoning
1½ teaspoons seasoned salt
6 - 8 boneless, skinless chicken breast halves
2 bell peppers, seeded, sliced

- Mix butter, beer, seasonings and about ½ teaspoon pepper in small skillet over medium-low heat until butter melts and seasonings combine.

- Place chicken on oiled, preheated grill over medium-high heat and sear outside of chicken. Reduce heat, spread chicken with sop and baste frequently. Cook until juices run clear and internal temperature is 165°. Serves 6 to 8.

Beer-Basted Chicken

1 (12 ounce) bottle beer
½ cup (1 stick) butter, melted
1 (2 - 3 pound) chicken, quartered
Lemon pepper

- Mix beer and melted butter. (Do not heat beer.) Season all sides of chicken liberally with lemon pepper. Cook chicken on oiled grill over medium-hot heat for about 15 minutes per side.

- Baste liberally with beer-butter. Chicken is ready to serve when juices are clear and internal temperature is 165°. Serves 4 to 6.

One of the tricks of excellent grilling and smoking is the fire you build: how long it stays hot, how long it smokes and what the temperature is. Trial and error is the best teacher to create your own method, style and flavors. It's all part of the fun and challenge.

Marinated Beer Chicken

1 cup (2 sticks) butter
1½ teaspoons seasoned salt
1 (12 ounce) bottle or can beer
6 - 8 boneless, skinless chicken breast halves

- Stir butter, seasoned salt and about ½ teaspoon pepper in skillet over medium-low heat until butter melts. Remove from heat and add beer.

- Place chicken on oiled, preheated grill over medium-high heat and sear outside of chicken to hold in juices. Reduce heat or move away from direct heat.

- Baste frequently with butter sop for about 5 to 10 minutes until juices are clear and internal temperature is 165°. Serves 6 to 8.

Italian Chicken with Beer Chaser

4 skinless, boneless chicken breast halves
1 cup Italian-style salad dressing
1 (12 ounce) can beer

- Place chicken in glass dish or bowl. Pour dressing over chicken and turn to coat. Cover dish, refrigerate and marinate for 3 hours.

- Cook chicken on oiled grill over medium heat for about 7 to 10 minutes per side. Cook until internal temperature reaches 165° and juices are clear.

- Place chicken in deep dish and pour beer over top. Cover and refrigerate overnight. Warm on low heat before serving. Serves 4.

Use a meat thermometer to be certain of the doneness of meat. Chicken should have an internal temperature of 165° in its thickest part and juices should be clear. Beef and pork should be at least 145° for medium rare. Ground meats should be 160°. Seafood should be opaque or flake easily with fork. Game should be 160° to 165°.

Island Packets with Soy Sauce Glaze

This is great picnic fare. Make packets at home and serve on paper plates. Clean-up is a breeze.

2 large, boneless, skinless chicken breast halves, sliced
1 Texas 1015 SuperSweet or Vidalia® onion, sliced
2 red bell peppers, cored, sliced
1 (20 ounce) can pineapple chunks, drained
Soy Sauce Glaze (recipe follows)

- Spray 4 large sheets of heavy-duty foil large enough to hold all ingredients. Divide chicken, onions, bell peppers and pineapple equally among packages.

- Season with a little salt and pepper. Pour soy sauce glaze over contents, fold foil so air will circulate and seal to hold juices.

- Cook packets on preheated grill over medium-hot fire with lid closed for about 10 to 20 minutes; rotate once. Open packets and continue to cook until juices of chicken are clear, internal temperature is 165° and meat is no longer pink. Serves 4.

Soy Sauce Glaze

Use with Island Packets, chicken or pork.

1 (8 ounce) can crushed pineapple
2 tablespoons brown sugar
2 tablespoons soy sauce
½ teaspoon red pepper flakes

- Combine all ingredients and pour into Island Packets. Makes about 1 cup.

To cook with indirect heat on a gas grill, light both sides of grill and preheat. Turn one side off and place food above "off" burners. Close lid.

Marinated Ginger Chicken

1 (12 ounce) bottle sweet wheat beer, flat
½ cup olive oil
2 tablespoons peeled, finely minced ginger
2 cloves garlic, minced
¼ cup orange zest
6 boneless, skinless chicken breast halves

- Combine all ingredients (except chicken) in large bowl. Place chicken in marinade and make sure marinade covers. Cover and refrigerate for at least 4 hours or overnight.

- Turn chicken several times while in refrigerator. Remove chicken from marinade and discard marinade. Cook on oiled grill over medium fire for about 10 to 15 minutes per side.

- Chicken is done when internal temperature is 165° and juices are clear. Serves 6.

Easy Mustard Chicken

4 chicken breast halves
¾ cup prepared mustard
1 tablespoon dry mustard
¾ cup (1½ sticks) butter
1½ teaspoons onion salt
½ teaspoon celery salt
1½ teaspoons dry mustard

- Brush chicken with blend of prepared mustard and dry mustard; cover and refrigerate for several hours or overnight.

- Mix remaining ingredients with ¼ teaspoon salt and ½ teaspoon pepper. Baste with mixture while grilling over medium heat about 10 to 15 minutes per side until internal temperature is 165°. Serves 4.

Thousand Island and Italian dressings are great inexpensive marinades for chicken or pork.

Basted Chicken with Asian Ginger Sauce

¼ cup soy sauce
¼ cup honey
1 teaspoon ground ginger
1 clove garlic, pressed
1 teaspoon grated lemon peel
¼ - ½ teaspoon crushed red pepper flakes

- Mix all ingredients for sauce in glass baking dish or sealable plastic bag.

Chicken and Vegetables

3 - 4 boneless, skinless chicken breast halves
1 (12 ounce) carton button mushrooms, stemmed
1 - 2 green bell peppers, quartered, seeded

- Cut chicken into bite-size pieces and marinate in Asian Ginger Sauce for about 1 hour. Discard marinade. Place chicken on skewers and vegetables on different skewers.

- Cook on oiled, medium-hot grill for about 5 to 10 minutes per side for chicken and about 5 to 8 minutes for vegetables. Chicken is done when juices are clear and internal temperature is 165°. Serves 4.

Grilled Catalina Chicken

4 boneless, skinless chicken breast halves
½ cup Catalina dressing

- Trim all visible fat from chicken. Combine dressing and ½ teaspoon black pepper. Pour into oblong dish, add chicken and turn to coat. Marinate chicken 4 to 6 hours or overnight in refrigerator. Discard marinade.

- Cook on oiled grill over medium heat for about 5 to 10 minutes per side until internal temperature is 165° and juices are clear. Don't overcook. Serves 4.

Roasted Teriyaki Chicken

¾ cup roasted garlic-teriyaki marinade
2 tablespoons packed brown sugar
2 tablespoons oil
4 boneless, skinless chicken breast halves

- In bowl, combine marinade, brown sugar and oil. Pour into large, sealable plastic bag and add chicken breasts. Press air out of bag, close securely and refrigerate for 2 to 4 hours. Turn bag several times to coat chicken well.

- Remove chicken from bag and discard marinade. Grill chicken over medium hot fire for about 8 to 10 minutes per side. Continue cooking until internal temperature is 165°. Serves 4.

South-of-the-Border Chicken

1 (12 ounce) bottle pale ale
2 limes, divided
1 teaspoon honey
¼ cup chopped cilantro
4 - 5 boneless, skinless chicken breast halves

- Mix beer, juice of 1 lime, honey and cilantro in sprayed baking dish and place chicken breast halves in dish. Cover with plastic wrap and refrigerate for 30 minutes; turn once.

- Discard marinade and season chicken with salt and pepper. Cook on oiled grill over medium heat for about 7 to 10 minutes per side. Squeeze remaining lime juice over chicken and cook until juices run clear and internal temperature is 165°. Serves 4.

> *Buying whole chickens and whole wings instead of trimmed, skinless or boneless chicken, is a good way to save money. Grilling a whole chicken or cutting it into quarters is less expensive and adds variety.*

Tarragon Chicken

¾ cup olive oil
¾ cup lemon juice
3 cloves garlic, minced
8 - 10 boneless, skinless chicken breast halves
1 tablespoon fresh tarragon or 1 teaspoon dried tarragon

- Mix olive oil, lemon juice and garlic in bowl. Pour into sealable plastic bag. Add chicken to marinade in plastic bag and refrigerate for at least 1 hour. Discard marinade and season chicken breasts with tarragon, salt and pepper.

- Cook on oiled grill over medium fire for about 10 to 15 minutes per side until internal temperature is 165° and juices are clear. Serves 8 to 10.

Grilled Chicken with Apple Salsa

¼ cup dry white wine
¼ cup apple juice
½ teaspoon grated lime peel
4 medium boneless, skinless chicken breast halves
Apple Salsa (recipe follows)

- Combine wine, apple juice and lime peel and pour over chicken. Cover and marinate 30 minutes in refrigerator. Discard marinade.

- Cook on oiled grill over medium coals for about 10 to 15 minutes per side until internal temperature is 165° and juices are clear. Pour apple salsa on top of chicken before serving. Serves 4.

Apple Salsa

2 cups chopped gala apples
¾ cup Anaheim chile pepper, seeded, chopped
½ cup chopped onion
¼ cup lime juice

- Combine ingredients in large bowl and mix well. Refrigerate 30 minutes before serving. Makes 3½ cups.

Apricot-Glazed Chicken

½ cup teriyaki baste-and-glaze sauce
½ teaspoon dried ginger
1 cup apricot preserves
4 boneless, skinless chicken breast halves

- In small bowl, combine teriyaki glaze, ginger and apricot preserves. Mix well and set aside. Salt and pepper chicken breast halves and place on oiled, preheated grill over medium heat.

- Grill 10 to 15 minutes per side until internal temperature is 165° and juices are clear.

- When chicken has 5 minutes remaining in cooking time, brush liberally with teriyaki-apricot mixture. Serves 4.

Grilled Chicken with Apricot Sauce

6 boneless, skinless chicken breast halves
1 cup apricot preserves
1 (8 ounce) bottle Catalina dressing
1 (1 ounce) packet onion soup mix

- Season chicken with a little salt and pepper. Cook on oiled, preheated grill over medium-hot fire and sear outside of chicken. Move to medium fire or away from high heat and cook for about 10 to 20 minutes per side, depending on size of breasts.

- Combine apricot preserves, dressing and soup mix in small saucepan. Just before chicken is done, brush some of apricot sauce over chicken, but do not burn. Chicken is done when juices are clear and internal temperature is 165°. Pour remaining sauce over chicken before serving. Serves 6.

$ave Money! Take advantage of the bulk bins of cereal, baking ingredients and spices. You'll avoid waste by buying just the amount you need.

Grilled Chicken with Russian Dressing

- Use recipe for *Grilled Chicken with Apricot Sauce (page 198)*, but use Russian dressing instead of Catalina. Serves 6

Grilled Lemon Chicken

2 teaspoons garlic salt
1 tablespoon freshly grated lemon peel
2 teaspoons dried thyme leaves
6 boneless, skinless chicken breast halves

- Combine garlic salt, lemon peel, thyme leaves in bowl with a little pepper. Sprinkle seasoning mixture over chicken breasts.

- Cook on oiled, preheated grill over medium fire for about 10 to 15 minutes per side until juices are clear and internal temperature is 165°. Turn once during cooking. Serves 6.

Citrus Chicken

4 - 6 boneless, skinless chicken breast halves
½ cup orange juice
½ cup lemon juice
3 cloves garlic, pressed

- Place chicken breasts in sealable plastic bag. Mix remaining ingredients and ½ teaspoon each salt and pepper in bowl and pour over chicken. Marinate in refrigerator for about 3 hours; turn several times.

- Remove chicken and drain for about 10 minutes at room temperature. Cook on oiled grill over medium heat for about 10 to 15 minutes per side. Chicken is done when juices are clear and internal temperature is 165° in thickest part. Serves 4 to 6.

Salsa-Grilled Chicken

4 - 5 boneless, skinless chicken beast halves
1 cup thick-and-chunky salsa
¼ cup packed dark brown sugar
1 tablespoon dijon-style mustard

• Pound chicken to about ½-inch thick. Combine remaining ingredients in large bowl. Add chicken to bowl, coat with marinade and marinate for 3 to 4 hours in refrigerator; turn several times.

• Cook on oiled grill over medium fire until juices run clear and internal temperature is 165°. Serve with additional salsa. Serves 4 to 5.

Chicken Piccata

This dish is usually breaded and pan-fried, but the recipe works well with grilled chicken too.

4 large boneless, skinless chicken breast halves
½ cup (1 stick) butter
2 tablespoons flour
2 tablespoons capers
1 cup dry white wine
1 - 2 lemons

• Butterfly and flatten breasts to about ¼-inch thickness, season with salt and pepper and set aside.

• Melt butter over low heat and sprinkle flour over top. Stir well to remove lumps and add capers.

• Pour in wine and bring sauce to a low boil. Cook until sauce thickens. Remove from heat and add 3 tablespoons lemon juice. Set aside and keep warm.

• Cook chicken on oiled grill over moderate fire for about 10 to 12 minutes per side until juices and internal temperature is 165°. Remove from grill, plate each breast and pour sauce over each. Serves 4.

Marinated Chicken Fajitas

Marinade:

1 cup salsa
1 cup Italian vinaigrette
2 tablespoons lemon juice
2 tablespoons chopped green onions
1 teaspoon garlic powder

- Combine all marinade ingredients and 1 teaspoon pepper in bowl and mix well.

Chicken:

6 - 8 boneless, skinless chicken breast halves
Flour tortillas

- Remove any fat from meat, wipe dry with paper towels and place meat in shallow baking dish. Pour marinade over meat and marinate overnight for at least 6 hours in refrigerator.

Accompaniments for Fajitas:

Salsa
Guacamole
Grilled onions
Grilled bell peppers
Chopped tomatoes
Shredded cheese
Sour cream

- Cook chicken on oiled grill over medium heat for about 10 minutes per side until juices are clear and internal temperature is 165°. Cut meat diagonally. Place a few strips on warmed flour tortilla, select accompaniments and roll to eat. Serves 8 to 10.

Grilling specialists prefer real woods, such as hickory, oak, mesquite, cherry, pecan, maple, and indirect heating for grilling purposes.

Tequila-Lime Chicken

½ cup lime juice
¼ cup tequila
1½ teaspoons chili powder
1½ teaspoons minced garlic
6 boneless, chicken breast halves with skins

- In large plastic bag that seals, combine all ingredients except chicken and mix well. Add chicken breasts, seal bag and turn to coat. Refrigerate about 10 hours or overnight. Remove breasts from marinade and sprinkle chicken with a little salt and pepper. Discard marinade.

- Cook on oiled grill over medium fire for about 7 to 10 minutes per side. Cook until juices are clear and internal temperature is 165°. Remove to platter, cover and let stand for 5 minutes before serving. Serves 6.

Honey-Mustard Grilled Chicken

½ teaspoon lemon pepper
¾ cup mayonnaise
2 tablespoons country dijon-style mustard
¼ cup honey
4 - 5 boneless, skinless chicken breast halves

- In bowl, combine lemon pepper, mayonnaise, mustard and honey and mix well. Divide honey-mustard mixture equally into 2 bowls.

- Cook on oiled grill over medium heat until internal temperature is 165° and juices are clear, about 10 minutes per side; baste chicken while grilling with 1 bowl of honey-mustard mixture. Serve with remaining honey-mustard mixture. Serves 4.

$ave Money! *Hit the local farmers' market – especially near closing time. Vendors will be more willing to negotiate prices so they don't have to carry the produce back home.*

Pineapple-Glazed Chicken

This is wonderful served with cooked rice.

1 (15 ounce) can pineapple chunks with juice
1 cup honey-mustard grill-and-glaze sauce
1 bell pepper, seeded, chopped
4 boneless, skinless chicken breast halves

- Combine pineapple chunks, honey-mustard sauce and bell pepper in saucepan. Bring to a boil, reduce heat to low and simmer for 10 to 15 minutes until sauce thickens slightly. Divide into 2 bowls.

- Season chicken with a little salt and pepper. Cook on oiled grill over medium fire for about 8 minutes, turn and continue cooking for additional 5 minutes.

- Brush half honey-mustard sauce on both sides and continue cooking until internal temperature is 165° and juices are clear. To serve, pour remaining warmed sauce over each breast. Serves 4.

Jerk Chicken Kebabs

1 bottle, Caribbean jerk marinade
2 pounds boneless, skinless chicken breasts, cubed
Olive oil
1 large onion, quartered
20 whole mushrooms
1 large red bell pepper, cubed

- In large bowl, pour marinade over chicken pieces. Cover and refrigerate at least 30 minutes. Prepare grill to medium heat (or when heat makes you pull your hand away in 4 seconds.) Discard marinade.

- Sprinkle vegetables with olive oil. Thread skewers, alternating 1 piece of chicken, 1 piece onion, 1 mushroom and 1 piece pepper, ending with chicken.

- Cook on oiled grill for about 15 to 20 minutes and turn after grill marks appear. Grill until juices are clear and internal temperature of chicken is 165°. Serves 4.

Grilled Chicken Cordon Bleu

6 boneless, skinless chicken breast halves
6 slices Swiss cheese
6 thin slices deli ham
3 tablespoons canola oil
1 cup seasoned breadcrumbs

- Butterfly and flatten chicken to ¼-inch thick and place 1 slice cheese and ham on each piece of chicken to within ¼-inch of edges. Fold in half and secure with toothpicks.

- Brush chicken with oil and roll in breadcrumbs. Cook, covered, on oiled grill over medium heat for 15 to 18 minutes until juices run clear and internal temperature is 165°. Serves 6.

Bacon-Wrapped Chicken Rolls

6 boneless, skinless chicken breast halves
1 (8 ounce) queso fresco or cream cheese
3 tablespoons butter
6 bacon strips

- Flatten chicken to ⅓ to ½-inch thick. Spread 2 to 3 tablespoons cheese over each piece. Dot with butter and a little salt, roll up and fold ends like envelope. Wrap each tightly with 1 bacon strip and secure with toothpick, if needed.

- Cook on sprayed heavy-duty foil or on oiled grill over medium heat until bacon is crisp and internal temperature is 165°. Serves 6.

TIP: Queso fresco is a popular Mexican cheese that softens when grilled, but does not melt. It is usually in the refrigerated section next to sausage and lunch meat.

$ave Money! *Organize your grocery list by store layout to avoid wandering the aisles and being tempted by impulse buys. This is also a great time saver.*

Barbecued Chicken Salad

Dressing:

¾ cup ranch dressing
3 tablespoons barbecue sauce
2 tablespoons salsa

• Combine all dressing ingredients in bowl. Refrigerate.

Salad:

3 boneless, skinless chicken breast halves
1 (9 ounce) package romaine lettuce
1 (15 ounce) can seasoned black beans, drained
12 - 15 cherry tomatoes

• Sprinkle chicken with a little salt and pepper. Cook chicken
breasts on oiled, preheated grill over medium fire about 6 to
7 minutes per side until inside temperature is 165° and juices
are clear.

• Let chicken rest 10 minutes and cut in thin strips. Place
chicken strips on top of cut-up romaine, black beans and cherry
tomatoes. Toss enough dressing with salad to lightly coat.
Serves 6.

TIP: *Grill some extra chicken breasts and freeze them. This will
make another meal easier and faster.*

*Gas grills are best when attached to the main gas line
to the house. Tanks of propane or natural gas may run
empty while cooking a meal. Gas grill lids should be
open when started and left open for several minutes.
Close lid after all gas in the air is gone.*

Grilled Chicken Pasta

6 boneless, skinless chicken breast halves
Creole seasoning
1 (12 ounce) package rotini (short spirals) pasta
1 (12 ounce) package cubed mozzarella cheese
1 red onion, chopped
1 yellow bell pepper, seeded, chopped
1 (10 ounce) package frozen baby green peas, thawed
1 - 1½ cups honey-mustard dressing

- Season chicken with Creole seasoning. Cook chicken on oiled, preheated grill over medium heat for 6 to 10 minutes on each side until juices are clear and internal temperature is 165°.

- Remove from heat and place on plate to cool. When chicken is cool enough, cut into strips. Refrigerate.

- Cook pasta in saucepan according to package directions, drain and rinse in cold water; set aside.

- Mix cheese, onion, bell pepper and peas in large bowl. Add chicken and pasta to vegetable mixture and toss.

- Pour in 1 cup honey-mustard dressing and toss again. Add more dressing, if needed. Refrigerate until time to serve. Serves 6 to 8.

Grilled Chicken Pasta Salad

- Use recipe for *Grilled Chicken Pasta (page 206)* and add 1 head romaine lettuce, torn in pieces, before tossing with dressing. Serves 6 to 8.

> *There are two kinds of charcoal: briquettes and hardwood charcoal. Briquettes come in a standard dense briquette and a fast-burning briquette. Fast-burning briquettes are good for cooking hot dogs or hamburgers, but they will not last long enough for grilling most other meats.*

Szechuan Chicken Salad

1 pound boneless, skinless chicken breasts
½ cup teriyaki marinade
2 tablespoons creamy peanut butter
2 tablespoons soy sauce
¼ cup rice wine vinegar
2 teaspoons sugar
Cayenne pepper or hot chili paste
1 head iceberg lettuce, torn or chopped into bite-size pieces
1 bunch green onions, thinly sliced
2 tablespoons chopped fresh cilantro
Fried rice noodles, optional

- Remove fat from chicken breasts. Place in resealable plastic bag with teriyaki marinade. Refrigerate and marinade for at least 1 hour or up to overnight.

- Cook chicken on oiled grill over medium heat for about 10 minutes per side until internal temperature is 165° and juices are clear. Let rest at least 5 minutes before thinly slicing.

- Put peanut butter, soy sauce, rice wine vinegar and sugar in blender. Mix until ingredients blend well and add a little cayenne pepper.

- Place lettuce in bowl and combine with green onions, cilantro and chicken. Toss with dressing and optional noodles. Serve immediately. Serves 4 to 6.

TIP: For quicker version of this dish, buy pre-cooked boneless skinless breasts and slice them thinly.

Fire for Steaks and Burgers

Coals for the fire should be red with white ash on top. You should be able to hold your hand over the fire for two seconds. This is a good fire for searing.

Grilled Chicken Caesar Salad

4 boneless, skinless chicken breast halves
1 (10 ounce) package romaine salad greens
½ cup shredded parmesan cheese
1 cup seasoned croutons
¾ cup Caesar dressing

- Season chicken with a little salt and pepper. Cook on oiled, preheated grill over medium heat for about 8 to 10 minutes per side until juices are clear and internal temperature is 165°.

- Combine salad greens, cheese and croutons in large bowl. When ready to serve, toss with dressing. Cut chicken breasts into strips and place chicken strips on top. Serves 4 to 6.

Grilled Cornish Game Hens

4 - 8 sprigs fresh thyme
4 Cornish game hens
Olive oil
1 tablespoon fresh thyme leaves or 2 teaspoons dried
    thyme leaves
2 dried bay leaves, crushed
½ teaspoon dried rosemary

- Soak sprigs of fresh thyme in water for about 20 to 30 minutes. Rub hens with olive oil. Sprinkle with thyme leaves, bay leaves, rosemary, and 1 teaspoon each of salt and cracked black pepper; rub into birds. Place fresh sprigs in cavities.

- Cook on oiled grill over medium fire for about 10 to 15 minutes per side until skin is crispy and juices are clear. Internal temperature of thickest part of meat is 165°. Serves 4.

Water-soaked wood chips or flavored briquettes provide smoky flavors for gas grills, but wood is always best.

Smoked Turkey Legs

The biggest challenge is cooking turkey legs so they are not tough. So, cook long and slow.

4 - 6 turkey legs
Seasonings

- Marinate legs in favorite seasonings for about 1 to 2 hours. Cook on oiled grill with indirect medium heat for about 30 to 45 minutes with lid closed.

- If you lose fire before legs are done, finish cooking in oven at 250° for about 1 to 3 hours. Legs are done when juices are clear and internal temperature is 165°.

- Before serving, remove splinter bones at bottom of meat. (They should pull out easily.) Serves 4 to 6.

Jerk Turkey

Turkey tenderloins are wonderful. You will be glad you cooked them!

2 tablespoons jerk seasoning
1 (1½ - 2 pound) package turkey or chicken tenderloins
1 tablespoon fresh chopped rosemary
1½ cups raspberry-chipotle sauce, divided

- Rub jerk seasoning evenly over tenderloins, sprinkle with rosemary and press into meat. Cover and refrigerate for 1 to 2 hours.

- Cook tenderloins on oiled grill over medium heat for 5 to 10 minutes per side. Baste with half raspberry-chipotle sauce. Turkey is done when juices are clear and internal temperature is 165°.

- Let tenderloins stand 10 minutes before slicing and serve with remaining raspberry-chipotle sauce. Serves 4.

TIP: *There are so many wonderful prepared meat sauces in the grocery stores that it makes it easy to be a genius cook.*

Holiday Smoked Turkey

1 (10 - 14 pound) butter-basted turkey
Poultry seasoning
1 onion, peeled, halved
2 - 3 small ribs celery
2 - 3 strips bacon
Butter or oil

- Thaw turkey in refrigerator for 3 to 4 days. Soak hickory or pecan chips in water for about 1 hour before cooking. When charcoal is flaming slightly and coals are white, place chips around perimeter. Fill pan with water and place in position.

- Remove giblets, neck and neck skin from turkey. Tie wings to bird to keep them from drying out. Place washed, dried turkey, breast-side up, in heavy, disposable foil roasting pan.

- Rub poultry seasoning, salt and pepper on turkey inside and out and insert onion and celery in cavity of turkey. Lay strips of bacon across top of turkey.

- Pour a little water in turkey pan and place on grill. Close grill cover and cook for 20 to 30 minutes per pound with smoker temperature about 250° to 275°.

- Baste occasionally during cooking time with butter or oil and replenish fire as needed. (Don't open lid unless necessary to maintain heat.)

- Turkey is done when juices are clear and internal temperature of breast away from bone reaches 165°.

- Remove from smoker, wrap tightly in foil. Allow turkey to stand for about 15 to 20 minutes before carving.

- Use pan drippings in turkey pan to make gravy. Discard onion and celery. Throw away turkey pan. Serves 10 to 18.

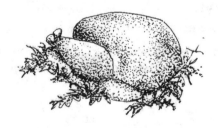

Foolproof Smoked Turkey

This recipe gives you the smoked flavor without the hassles of temperature control and replenishing the fire on a smoker.

- Use recipe for *Holiday Smoked Turkey (page 210)*, but only smoke turkey for about 1 to 1½ hours at 275° to 325°.

- Remove from smoker, wrap tightly in foil and cook in preheated oven at 250° for about 10 to 20 minutes per pound. Baste with melted butter. If turkey is not brown on outside, cook without foil until brown.

- Turkey is done when juices are clear and internal temperature of breast away from bone reaches 165°. Allow turkey to stand for about 15 to 20 minutes wrapped tightly before carving. Serves 10 to 18.

Seasoned Smoked Turkey Legs

6 - 8 frozen turkey legs, thawed
Seasoned salt
Seasoned pepper

- Sprinkle seasoned salt and pepper liberally over legs. Soak about 10 chunks of hickory, pecan, cherry or alder wood in water for at least 1 hour.

- Start about 10 pounds of charcoal in vertical water smoker or a wood fire. When fire is red hot with small flames, place wood chunks around outside of fire. Place water pan on rack and fill with water.

- Place turkey legs on oiled grate and close lid. About half way through cooking, quickly wrap foil around bottom of legs. Smoke turkey legs about 3 to 5 hours at 250°.

- If heat does not last long enough for turkey to reach internal temperature of 165°, finish cooking in oven at 300°. Serves 6 to 8.

Pork

Terrific pork recipes make grilling more
rewarding when friends and family chow down.

Smoked Cherry-Pineapple Ham

1 (6 - 8 pound) fully cooked, shank or butt ham with bone
Whole cloves
½ cup packed brown sugar
1 (8 ounce) can sliced pineapple with juice
5 - 6 maraschino cherries

- Score surface with shallow diagonal cuts making diamond
  shapes and insert cloves into diamonds. Soak about 10 chunks
  hickory, pecan, cherry or alder in water for at least 1 hour. Start
  about 10 pounds of charcoal in vertical water smoker.

- When fire is red hot with small flames, place wood chunks
  around outside of fire. Place water pan on rack and fill with
  water. Place ham on oiled grate and close lid. Do not open.
  Cook according to manufacturer's recommended times.

- Combine brown sugar and juice from pineapple in bowl
  and mix. Dabble on ham and arrange pineapple slices
  and cherries with toothpicks. Cook additional 15 minutes.
  Serves 10 to 12.

Ham with Orange Sauce

1 cup orange juice
2 tablespoons brown sugar
1½ tablespoons cornstarch
⅓ cup white raisins
1 (½ inch) thick slice fully cooked ham

- Combine orange juice, brown sugar, cornstarch and raisins in saucepan. Bring to a boil, stirring constantly, until mixture thickens.

- Cook ham on oiled, preheated grill over medium-hot fire about 5 to 7 minutes per side. Place ham slice in shallow baking dish. Pour orange sauce over slice before serving. Serves 3 to 4.

Honeyed Ham Slices

Menfolk say it's mouth-watering to watch ham sizzling on a grill.

6 slices pre-cooked lean ham, about ½-inch thick
¾ cup honey glaze (recipe follows)

- When coals are white with ashes, place heavy-duty metal foil, on top of grill. Lay ham slices on sprayed foil; grill on one side, about 20 minutes.

- Turn ham; grill on other side about 10 minutes. Brush generously with Honey Glaze and grill until ham looks shiny. Serves 6 to 8.

Honey Glaze:

½ cup honey
½ cup packed brown sugar
2 tablespoons flour
Pineapple juice, orange juice or apricot nectar

- Combine honey, brown sugar, flour and enough juice (about 2 tablespoons) to make smooth paste. Makes 1 cup.

Mustard Ham Slices

- Use recipe for *Honeyed Ham Slices (page 213),* but rub ham slices with Mustard Glaze (recipe below) before grilling instead of basting with Honey Glaze during grilling. Serves 6 to 8.

Mustard Glaze:

½ cup packed brown sugar
2 tablespoons flour
1 teaspoon dry mustard

- Combine all ingredients and rub into both sides of ham slices before grilling.

Grilled Ham with Marmalade Apples

½ cup orange marmalade
2 tablespoons butter
¼ teaspoon ground ginger
2 (½ inch thick) ham slices
2 apples, cored, quartered

- Combine marmalade, butter and ginger. Microwave on HIGH for 1 minute until mixture melts and stir once.

- Cook ham on oiled, preheated grill over medium fire (about 300°) for about 8 to 10 minutes. Turn and spread marmalade sauce on top of ham. Place apple quarters on grill, but away from direct heat. Cook for about 5 to 8 minutes.

- Turn again, spread remaining marmalade sauce on top and place apple on top of sauce. Ham is done when internal temperature is at least 145°. Serves 4 to 6.

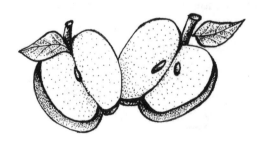

Honey-Basted Ham Steaks

2 tablespoons ketchup
2 tablespoon honey
1 teaspoon lemon juice
2 (½ inch thick) ham steaks

- Combine ketchup, honey and lemon juice and baste ham
  steaks while cooking. Cook on oiled grill over medium-hot
  fire for about 4 to 5 minutes per side until internal temperature
  reaches 145°. Serves 4 to 6.

Sweet Pineapple Ham Slices

1 (15 ounce) can pineapple chunks with juice
1 cup pineapple preserves
1¼ cups packed brown sugar
¼ teaspoon ground cinnamon
1 - 2 (2 pound) ready-cooked ham slices

- Combine pineapple, preserves, brown sugar and cinnamon in
  saucepan and heat to mix well. Cook ham slices on oiled grill
  over medium-hot fire for about 5 to 7 minutes per side.

- When internal temperature is 145°, place on platter. Pour
  pineapple sauce over top and serve immediately. Serves 4.

Easiest Lemon Pork Chops

4 (1 inch) thick center-cut pork chops
2 - 3 tablespoons olive oil
1 - 2 lemons

- Dry pork chops with paper towel, let stand to reach room
  temperature and season with olive oil, a little lemon juice and
  a lot of salt and pepper.

- Cook on oiled, preheated grill over medium fire for about 5 to
  8 minutes, turn and continue cooking about 5 to 8 minutes until
  internal temperature reaches 145°. Remove chops from grill,
  drizzle with a little more lemon juice and serve immediately.
  Serves 4.

Lemon-Rosemary Pork Chops

½ cup lemon juice
1 teaspoon dried rosemary
1 teaspoon garlic powder
3 tablespoons olive oil
4 - 5 (1 inch) thick pork chops

- In large plastic bag, combine lemon juice, rosemary, garlic and olive oil. Place pork chops in bag and marinate at least 3 hours or overnight, turning occasionally

- Cook on oiled grill over medium heat about 8 minutes on each side and cook until internal temperature reaches at least 145°. Serves 4 to 5.

Orange-Dijon Chops

1 cup orange marmalade
3 tablespoons dijon-style mustard
3 tablespoons soy sauce
4 - 6 pork chops

- In small saucepan over low heat, stir marmalade, dijon-style mustard and soy sauce until preserves melt. When ready to grill, sprinkle both sides of pork chops with salt and pepper.

- Place chops on oiled grill about 5 inches from medium-hot heat. Cook until internal temperature is 145°. Turn once during cooking and brush with preserves mixture last 2 minutes of cooking time.

- When ready to serve, heat remaining preserves mixture to boiling and serve hot with pork chops. Serves 4 to 6.

$ave Money! Leave the kids at home when you grocery shop. You'll avoid caving in to temptations and save time.

Orange-Glazed Pork Chops

6 - 8 medium thick pork chops
Lemon pepper
Seasoned salt
1 (6 ounce) can frozen orange juice concentrate, thawed

- Season pork chops with lemon pepper and seasoned salt. Cook on oiled, preheated grill over medium fire for about 5 to 10 minutes per side. Just before chops are done, brush on orange juice and grill until internal temperature is 145°. Serves 6 to 8.

Marinated Pork Chops

½ cup oil
¼ cup lemon juice
3 cloves garlic, crushed
1 teaspoon paprika
6 bay leaves
6 (1 inch thick) pork chops

- Combine ½ teaspoon each of salt and pepper with all ingredients except chops in shallow baking dish; mix well. Add meat, cover and marinate overnight in refrigerator.

- Discard marinade and cook chops on oiled grill over low heat for about 10 minutes per side. Pork is done when internal temperature is 145°. Serves 6.

Pork Chops with Pineapple Sauce

4 - 6 thin-cut pork chops
Seasoned salt
Pineapple Sauce (recipe page 323)

- Season pork chops and cook on oiled grill over medium heat for about 5 to 7 minutes per side, turn and cook additional 2 to 3 minutes until internal temperature is 145°. Serve with Pineapple Sauce. Serves 4 to 6.

Honey-Pineapple Pork Chops

1 (6 ounce) can frozen pineapple juice concentrate, thawed
¼ cup packed brown sugar
⅓ cup wine or tarragon vinegar
⅓ cup honey
6 - 8 thick, boneless pork chops

- Combine pineapple juice, brown sugar, vinegar and honey in bowl. Pour over pork chops. Marinate in refrigerate for about 1 hour.

- Cook on oiled, preheated grill over indirect medium heat with lid closed for about 20 minutes on both sides. Pork is done when juices are clear and internal temperature is at least 145°. Serves 6 to 8.

Glazed Grilled Pork Chops

1 cup mayonnaise
2 tablespoons lime juice
2 tablespoons chopped fresh cilantro
1 teaspoon chili powder
4 (½-inch) thick pork chops

- Combine mayonnaise, lime juice, cilantro and chili powder and blend well. Reserve ½ cup glaze to brush over pork chops while grilling. Spread remaining glaze over pork chops and refrigerate for about 30 minutes.

- Cook chops on oiled grill over medium fire for about 5 to 7 minutes per side until internal temperature is at least 145°. Baste liberally while cooking. Serves 4.

Along the east coast of North Carolina, barbecued meat is chopped or sliced pork with a peppery vinegar sauce. Side dishes include coleslaw and hush puppies. West of Raleigh, the sauce is made of vinegar and tomatoes. Side dishes include bread and sometimes a stew.

Pork Chops with Maple Syrup Marinade

⅓ cup red-wine vinegar
⅓ cup maple syrup
¼ cup soy sauce
¼ cup olive oil
½ teaspoon ground ginger
4 to 6 (1-inch thick) center-cut pork chops

- Combine all ingredients except chops and mix well in 9 x 13-inch glass dish. Place chops in dish and turn several times to coat. Marinate overnight or at least 6 hours in refrigerator; turn occasionally.

- Discard marinade and cook chops on oiled, preheated grill over medium heat about 5 to 8 minutes on each side until internal temperature is at least 145°. Serves 4 to 6.

Sweet Worcestershire Pork Chops

¼ cup Worcestershire sauce
¼ cup ketchup
⅓ cup honey
4 - 6 (½ inch) thick pork chops

- Combine Worcestershire sauce, ketchup and honey in small saucepan and simmer while pork chops cook. Cook pork chops on oiled, preheated grill over medium-low until grill marks show on both sides, about 8 minutes per side.

- Spread 1 tablespoon sauce on both sides of each chop during last few minutes of cooking. Remove from grill when internal temperature is at least 145°. Cover chops with remaining sauce and serve. Serves 4 to 6.

Barbecue is Kansas City's claim to fame. The barbecue sauce is tomato-based with molasses, sugar, pepper, vinegar and secret spices.

Sweet Chops

This sauce is also great with hamburgers or chicken.

1 small onion, chopped
2 - 3 cloves garlic, pressed
1 tablespoon butter
1 (6 ounce) bottle chili sauce
½ cup packed brown sugar
1 tablespoon Worcestershire sauce
1 lemon
6 - 8 center-cut pork chops

- Saute onion and garlic in butter in saucepan. Add chili sauce, brown sugar and Worcestershire, cook on medium for several minutes and stir well. Add juice of ½ lemon. Reduce heat to low and cook for about 15 minutes. Remove from heat and let stand for about 30 minutes.

- Salt and pepper pork chops and cook on oiled grill over medium-hot fire to sear outside of both sides. Baste with sauce and cook for about 5 minutes per side over medium-low heat until internal temperature is at least 145°. Serves 6 to 8.

Grilled Honey-Maple Pork Chops

¼ cup honey
¼ cup maple syrup
¼ teaspoon allspice
6 (6 ounce, ¾-inch thick) pork loin chops

- In bowl, combine honey, syrup and allspice and mix well. Sprinkle pork chops with a little salt and pepper. When ready to grill, brush pork chops heavily with honey mixture.

- Cook on oiled grill over medium heat for about 7 minutes per side until internal temperature is at least 145°. Turn and brush occasionally with honey mixture. Serves 6.

Barbecued Pork Chops

1 tablespoon chili powder
1 teaspoon paprika
¼ cup packed brown sugar
½ cup vinegar
1 (10 ounce) can tomato soup
6 thin-cut pork chops

- Combine all ingredients except pork chops in bowl. Cook over oiled, preheated grill over medium fire for 4 to 5 minutes per side until internal temperature is at least 145°. Spread sauce over pork the last few minutes of cooking. Serves 4 to 6.

Grilled Sweet Pork Chops

1 cup ketchup
1 cup cola
½ cup packed brown sugar
4 - 6 thick-cut pork chops

- Combine ketchup, cola and brown sugar. Cook pork on oiled grill over medium fire for about 4 to 6 minutes per side until internal temperature is at least 145°. During last few minutes of cooking, baste with ketchup sauce until crusty on outside. Serves 4 to 6.

In Tennessee, Memphis claims to be the Barbecue Cooking Capital of the World. Pork, specifically ribs, is the dominant meat and is served "wet" with sauce or "dry" with a rub of secret seasonings. Coleslaw goes on a barbecue sandwich, not on the side.

Grilled Teriyaki Chops

3 ounces lager
⅔ cup teriyaki sauce
¼ cup cider vinegar
¼ cup sweet sherry
⅓ cup packed brown sugar
2 tablespoons chopped, fresh ginger root
6 (1-inch thick) butterfly-cut pork chops

- Pour beer, teriyaki sauce, vinegar, sherry, brown sugar and ginger root into medium saucepan. Cook on medium-high heat and stir mixture until brown sugar dissolves and sauce reduces to about 1⅓ cups.

- Place pork chops in sprayed 9 x 13-inch baking dish and pour sauce over chops. Cover with plastic wrap and refrigerate overnight. Turn chops several times to coat both sides of pork.

- When ready to grill, allow chops to get to room temperature. Discard marinade. Place chops on oiled grill and cook over medium heat until brown, about 4 to 5 minutes on each side. Cook until internal temperature is at least 145°. Serves 6.

Grilled Pork Chops
with Balsamic Marinade

⅓ cup Worcestershire sauce
¼ cup balsamic vinegar
¼ cup olive oil
1 clove garlic, pressed
4 boneless (1 inch thick) pork chops

- In large plastic bag, combine all marinade ingredients and add pork chops. Seal bag and turn to coat chops; refrigerate overnight or for at least 8 hours.

- Cook on oiled, preheated grill over medium fire for about 8 minutes. Turn and cook for about 5 minutes until internal temperature is at least 145° and juices are clear. Serves 4.

Grilled Pork Loin

½ teaspoon garlic powder
¼ teaspoon celery salt
½ teaspoon onion salt
2 tablespoons lemon juice
1 (4 - 5 pound) pork loin

- Combine garlic powder, celery salt, onion salt and lemon juice in bowl. Rub mixture into loin and place in covered glass dish. Refrigerate for at least 8 hours or overnight.

- Cook pork on oiled, preheated grill over medium fire for about 30 minutes, turn and cook additional 30 until internal temperature is at least 145°. Check frequently to avoid overcooking. Set aside for at least 10 minutes before cutting. Serves 8 to 10.

Smoked Pork Loin

1 (4 - 5 pound) boneless pork loin roast
½ cup orange juice
⅓ cup peanut butter
¼ teaspoon cayenne pepper

- Build wood fire with mesquite, hickory, oak or cherry large enough for about 3 inches of coals in fire box. When coals have formed and fire has short flames, place roast on oiled grill, cover and cook for about 30 to 45 minutes.

- Combine orange juice, peanut butter and cayenne pepper in small bowl and whisk until mixture is smooth. Brush roast with peanut butter sauce and grill for additional 20 to 30 minutes; brush frequently with remaining sauce. Roast is done when internal temperature is at least 145°. Serves 8 to 10.

In South Carolina and Georgia, barbecued meat is chopped or sliced with a yellow mustard-based sauce. In Georgia, side dishes include coleslaw, light bread and hash (a stew-like dish).

Award-Winning Pork Tenderloin

⅔ cup soy sauce
⅔ cup canola oil
2 tablespoons crystallized ginger, finely chopped
2 tablespoons real lime juice
1 teaspoon garlic powder
2 tablespoons minced onion
1 pork tenderloin

- Combine all marinade ingredients in bowl and pour over pork tenderloin. Marinate for 24 to 36 hours in refrigerator and turn multiple times.

- Cook on oiled, preheated grill over medium heat for about 30 to 45 minutes until internal temperature is at least 145°. Serves 6.

Peppered Pork Tenderloin

3 (12 ounce) bottles ale
2 tablespoons whole peppercorns
1 teaspoon sage
½ cup packed brown sugar
1 orange, peeled, halved
1 lemon, peeled, halved
2 (2 - 3 pound) pork tenderloins

- Combine all ingredients except pork in large soup pot. Pour in ¼ cup salt and bring to a boil. Reduce heat and simmer until salt and sugar dissolve. Simmer for about 50 to 60 minutes.

- Transfer brine to container and refrigerate. When brine cools, add tenderloins and put plate on top to keep pork submerged. Marinate for 2 days.

- Remove from marinade, wash and pat dry. Cook tenderloins on oiled grill over medium heat for about 30 to 45 minutes, turn frequently and cook until internal temperature is at least 145°. Set aside for about 10 minutes slicing. Serves 8.

Barbecued Pork Loin

Serve this as a main dish or cubed with toothpicks as an hors d'oeuvre.

½ cup soy sauce
1 tablespoon honey
2 tablespoons sherry wine
2 garlic cloves, minced
¼ cup sugar
¼ cup chicken broth
1 tablespoon oyster sauce
Dash fresh ground pepper
1 (2 - 2½ pound) boneless pork loin

- In shallow pan, combine all ingredients, except pork, and stir well; marinate pork loin for 2 to 3 hours at room temperature or preferably overnight in refrigerator. Turn occasionally. Discard marinade.

- Cook meat on oiled, preheated grill over medium-hot fire for 10 minutes per side.

- Turn and continue to grill for 20 to 30 minutes over medium-low heat until internal temperature is at least 145°.

- Cool about 10 minutes before slicing. Cut pork loin into thin slices against grain for main dish or cut into bite-size pieces as appetizers. Serves 4 to 6 as main dish and about 10 to 12 as appetizers.

Grilled Balsamic Pork Tenderloin

⅓ cup balsamic vinegar
2 teaspoons minced garlic
½ teaspoon cayenne pepper
1 (2 to 2½ pound) pork tenderloin

- In large sealable plastic bag, combine vinegar, garlic, pepper and 1 teaspoon salt. Place tenderloin in bag, seal and marinate for 8 hours or overnight. Turn occasionally.

- Cook on oiled, preheated grill with lid closed away from direct high heat for about 10 to 20 minutes on each side until meat is no longer pink and internal temperature is at least 145°. Do not overcook. Let stand about 10 minutes before slicing. Serves 4 to 6.

Seared Pork Tenderloin

½ cup barbecue sauce
½ cup teriyaki sauce
¼ cup olive oil
1 (2½ - 3 pound) pork tenderloin
½ cup applesauce

- Mix barbecue sauce, teriyaki sauce and olive oil in saucepan and set aside.

- Season tenderloin with a little salt and pepper. Place on oiled, preheated grill over hot fire and sear on all sides to seal in juices. Cook away from direct heat for about 20 to 30 minutes per side.

- Preheat oven to 350°. Transfer tenderloin to sprayed baking dish. Brush with barbecue-teriyaki-oil mixture. Liberally spread applesauce over pork and bake for 10 to 30 minutes until juices are clear and internal temperature is at least 145°. Serves 6.

Grilled Pork Tenderloin with Rice

2 (1 pound) pork tenderloins
1 tablespoon canola oil
2 tablespoons jerk seasoning

- Rub tenderloins with oil and sprinkle with jerk seasoning. Cook on oiled grill over medium heat for about 25 minutes, brown on both sides and cook until internal temperature is at least 145°.

Rice and Beans:

1 (6 ounce) package chicken-flavored rice
1 (15 ounce) can black beans, drained, rinsed
½ cup roasted red bell pepper, sliced
2 tablespoons chopped cilantro

- Cook rice according to package directions and add beans, bell pepper, cilantro and a little salt and pepper. Spoon on serving platter. Slice tenderloin and arrange on top of rice-bean mixture. Serves 6 to 8.

Pork Tenderloin with Red Pepper Sauce

2 (1 pound each) pork tenderloins
1 teaspoon garlic salt

- Sprinkle tenderloins with garlic salt and 1 teaspoon pepper. Cook on oiled grill over medium fire for about 5 to 10 minutes per side. Pork is done when internal temperature is at least 145°. Let rest 10 minutes and slice. Serve with Red Pepper Sauce. Serves 4 to 6.

Red Pepper Sauce:

1 onion, chopped
Oil
1 (10 ounce) jar roasted red peppers, rinsed
1 (8 ounce) carton sour cream
1 (1 ounce) packet ranch-style dressing mix

- Sauté onion in a little oil until translucent. Stir in red peppers and heat thoroughly. Remove from heat and stir in sour cream and dressing. Transfer to food processor and puree until smooth. Serve warm over sliced tenderloins. Makes about 1½ cups.

Garlic-Herb Pork Tenderloin

2 (1 pound) pork tenderloins
1 (12 ounce) bottle roasted garlic and herb marinade, divided
1 (8 ounce) package medium egg noodles
¼ cup (½ stick) butter

- Butterfly pork lengthwise, being careful not to cut all the way through. Press open to flatten and place in large plastic bag with seal.

- Pour ¾ cup marinade into bag and close top securely. Marinate for 25 minutes and turn several times.

- Cook on oiled grill over medium fire for about 10 to 15 minutes and turn. Cook additional 5 minutes; cook until internal temperature is at least 145°. Cook noodles according to package directions and stir in butter. Serve sliced tenderloin over noodles. Serves 4.

Marinated Seasoned Pork Loin

1 (4 pound) boneless pork loin roast
1 (8 ounce) bottle Italian salad dressing
1 cup dry white wine
3 cloves garlic, minced
10 black peppercorns

- Pierce roast at 1-inch intervals with fork and place roast in large, resealable plastic bag. Combine salad dressing, white wine, garlic and peppercorns in bowl. Reserve ½ cup mixture for basting while grilling.

- Pour marinade over roast and refrigerate for 8 hours; turn occasionally. Remove roast from marinade and discard marinade. Place roast on rack in oiled grill. Cook with lid closed away from direct medium-high heat for about 30 minutes.

- Turn, baste liberally and continue grilling for about 15 to 20 minutes. Baste again. When internal temperature is at least 145° in thickest part, remove roast. Let roast stand about 10 minutes before slicing. Serves 6 to 8.

Grilled Sweet-and-Sour Pork Bites with Rice

2 tablespoons cornstarch
1 (14 ounce) can beef broth
2 tablespoons soy sauce
2 tablespoons brown sugar
¼ teaspoon ground ginger
1 pound boneless pork tenderloin, cut into 2-inch pieces
4 cups hot cooked rice

- Mix cornstarch, broth, soy sauce, brown sugar and ginger in saucepan. Cook on medium-high heat and stir until mixture boils and thickens a little; reduce heat to simmer.

- Season pork with a little salt and pepper and place on sprayed foil over grate. Cook on grill over medium heat, turning frequently, for about 10 to 15 minutes until internal temperature is at least 145°. Brush sauce on pieces for about last 5 minutes. Place pork on rice and pour remaining sauce over top. Serves 4.

Pork Tenderloin with
Green Chile Rajas

The flavor of pork works well with green chilies, roasted and cut
in strips called rajas.

2 - 3 New Mexico green chilies
2 cloves garlic, minced
1 (2 pound) pork tenderloin
Seasoned salt

- Place chilies on oiled, preheated grill over medium-hot grill
  until they char on outside. Remove and place in sealed plastic
  bag for about 10 minutes. Remove, peel off skin and slice into
  ¼-inch strips. Season with garlic and a little salt and pepper
  and refrigerate for several hours.

- Sprinkle seasoned salt and black pepper liberally over pork
  tenderloin. Cook on oiled, preheated grill over medium heat
  about 10 to 20 minutes per side until internal temperature is
  at least 145°. Warm chilies on grill and serve over tenderloin.
  Serves 4 to 6.

*In Texas barbecued meat is always beef (except for
pork ribs) and is sliced or chopped with or without
a thin tomato-based sauce added to the meat. Side
dishes include coleslaw, white bread, pinto beans,
onions, dill pickle slices and jalapenos.*

Tenderloin Kebabs

1 (1 pound) pork tenderloin
2 tablespoons chili powder
2 tablespoons snipped cilantro
2 teaspoons brown sugar
1 teaspoon garlic salt
2 bell peppers, cored, seeded, quartered
1 pint cherry tomatoes

- Cut tenderloin in 1 - 2-inch cubes and place in large sealable plastic bag. Mix chili powder, cilantro, brown sugar, garlic salt and ½ teaspoon black pepper in small bowl and pour into bag. Move pieces around to coat with seasonings. Let stand for about 15 minutes.

- Place peppers and tomatoes on skewers. (Use 2 skewers through vegetables to keep them from turning.) Place vegetables on oiled grill around edge of fire and cook about 5 to 10 minutes per side until tender.

- Place pork on skewer. Cook on oiled grill over medium fire for about 5 to 7 minutes per side until internal temperature is at least 145°. Serves 2 to 4.

Incredible Slow-Cooked Ribs

2 slabs ribs
1 (8 ounce) bottle Italian salad dressing
1 - 2 tablespoons seasoned salt

- Place ribs, bone down, in bottom layer of sprayed foil and "paint" ribs with dressing. Sprinkle with seasoning and cover with foil. Place wrapped ribs on grill away from direct medium-hot charcoal fire and medium heat for gas grill.

- Cook for about 2 to 3 hours with lid closed and turn ribs every 30 to 45 minutes. Dab dressing over meaty portions. Continue to cook with low heat until meat falls off bone.

- For "wet" ribs, coat with your favorite barbecue sauce during last 30 or 45 minutes with lid closed and foil open. Serves 4 to 5.

Sweet Rack of Pork

Rack(s) pork ribs
Maple syrup
Montreal Steak seasoning
Butter

- Fill marinade syringe several times with maple syrup and inject into ribs thoroughly. Pour syrup over top and bottom of ribs, sprinkle all sides with steak seasoning and marinate for about 2 hours.

- Cook on oiled grilled over medium fire for about 10 minutes, turn and cook for about 15 minutes with lid closed. (Move pork away from fire if it starts to flame.) Preheat oven to 250°. Remove ribs to glass baking dish and arrange pats of butter over top of ribs.

- Cook in oven for about 20 minutes until internal temperature is at least 145° and meat falls off bones. Let meat rest for about 10 before cutting. Serve about 3 to 4 ribs per person.

Tailgate Ribs

10 pounds pork ribs
Garlic powder
Creole seasoning
1 cup Worcestershire sauce
1 (12 ounce) can beer
Barbecue sauce

- Prepare ribs the day before the game. Place ribs in an aluminum tray. Season with salt, pepper, garlic powder and Creole seasoning. Add Worcestershire sauce and beer to tray. Cover and refrigerate overnight.

- On game day, prepare grill to medium-low heat. Place ribs on oiled grill and close lid. Turn ribs often and baste with barbecue sauce several times until ribs cook through, about 30 to 40 minutes. Serves 6 to 10.

TIP: For better pork ribs, turn each section over. Lift white membrane (paper-thin) with butter knife. Pull, using paper towel, until completely removed. This will allow seasoning to enter meat from both sides. The ribs will be twice as tender too.

Tex-Mex Ribs

1 cup barbecue sauce
2 tablespoons chili powder
1 teaspoon ground cumin
4 pounds pork ribs

- In a small bowl, combine barbecue sauce, chili powder and cumin. Place pork ribs on oiled grill over medium heat with lid closed for about 10 minutes.

- Remove cover; baste ribs with sauce and continue to grill for 20 minutes until ribs cook through. Turn ribs frequently while grilling. Serves 4.

Spunky Smoked Spareribs

5 - 6 pounds spareribs
1 (6 ounce) can frozen orange juice concentrate, thawed
2 teaspoons Worcestershire sauce
1 teaspoon garlic powder

- Season spareribs with a little salt and pepper. Soak about 10 hickory, pecan or cherry chunks in water for at least 1 hour. Cook on vertical water smoker.

- Start fire with about 6 to 10 pounds charcoal or build wood fire to equal same amount of coals. When coals are red hot, but not flaming, place wood chunks on outside of fire.

- Place water pan on rack and fill with water. Place spareribs on oiled grill and close lid. Do not open for about 2 hours.

- Combine orange juice, Worcestershire and garlic powder in bowl and brush mixture on both sides of ribs. Baste ribs with orange juice mixture. Continue to cook covered for another 1 to 2 hours until internal temperature away from bone is at least 145°. Serves 6.

Always remove the membrane on the back of ribs before cooking. It will make it easier to get the meat off pork or beef ribs.

Hangover Ribs

2 - 3 (2 pound) racks pork spareribs
2 (12 ounce) bottles lager
1½ cups honey
½ cup barbecue sauce
1 tablespoon prepared mustard
2 teaspoons seasoned salt
¼ cup lemon juice

- Cut ribs in small sections and place in large piece of sprayed heavy-duty foil or larger glass baking dish. Combine remaining ingredients with a little salt and pepper in large bowl and pour over ribs. Cover and refrigerate overnight. Turn several times to cover all ribs.

- When ready to cook, discard marinade. Place on oiled grill with medium-low heat and cook for about 45 minutes to 1 hour. Turn often and cook slowly. Cook until internal temperature is at least 145° and meat falls off bones. Serves 6 to 8.

Backyard Country Ribs

1 cup tomato sauce
1 cup red wine vinegar
½ cup vegetable oil
2 tablespoons seasoned salt
2 tablespoons chili powder
2 teaspoons lemon pepper
2 teaspoons ground cumin
2 racks country pork ribs

- Mix tomato sauce, vinegar and vegetable oil with all seasonings. Cut ribs into several sections and place in sealable plastic bags. Pour one-half marinade over ribs in bags and set other half in refrigerator for basting later. Marinate for about 2 to 3 hours and turn several times.

- Cook on oiled grill over medium-low fire for about 1 hour. Turn and baste with fresh marinade frequently.

- Wrap in foil and cook on edges around fire or in oven at 250° for 1 to 2 hours until meat falls off bone. Serves about 4 to 6.

Barbecued Ribs

There are as many dry rubs and barbecue sauces as there
are cooks. Any one of these recipes will be great with pork ribs.

Ribs:

4 - 5 pounds pork baby back ribs or country-style ribs

- Choose one of the following three recipes for rub or sauces.

Grilling:

- Cook ribs on oiled, preheated grill over medium fire, about
  275° to 300°. Add drip pan half full of water away from fire and
  under grate, if possible. Sear outside of ribs, turn and cook
  over drip pan for about 1 hour 30 minutes to 2 hours 30 minutes.

- Ribs are done when internal temperature is at least 145° and
  meat falls off bone.

Roasting:

- If you have a hard time controlling heat at a consistent 275° to
  300°, grill as directed above for about 1 hour and remove from
  grill. Wrap in foil and continue to cook in oven at 275° for about
  1 to 2 hours until ribs fall off bone. Serves 6.

Dry Seasoning Rub:

¼ cup paprika
2 tablespoons chili powder
1 tablespoon dry mustard
1 teaspoon basil, minced
½ teaspoon cayenne pepper
½ teaspoon onion salt
½ teaspoon garlic salt

- Combine all ingredients in medium bowl and mix thoroughly.
  Rub onto ribs and let set for 1 hour before cooking.

Continued next page...

*Cook ribs in large slabs instead of individual ribs to
keep them moist and juicy.*

Continued from previous page...

Barbecue Sauce:

1 cup chopped onion
½ cup oil
1 cup ketchup
⅓ cup fresh lemon juice
3 tablespoons sugar
3 tablespoons Worcestershire sauce
2 tablespoons prepared mustard

• Saute onion in oil until soft and clear. Add remaining
  ingredients, 1 cup water, 2 teaspoons salt and 1 teaspoon
  pepper. Simmer for 30 minutes. Baste ribs with sauce during
  the last hour of cooking. Serve remaining sauce with ribs.
  Makes about 2 cups.

Teriyaki Sauce:

½ cup teriyaki sauce or soy sauce
½ cup white wine
2 cloves garlic, minced
¼ cup packed brown sugar
¼ cup Worcestershire sauce

• Combine all ingredients and divide into 2 bowls. Marinate ribs
  with half sauce. Discard marinade. Baste ribs with remaining
  sauce during last hour of cooking. Makes about 1 cup.

*The story goes that at one time pigs roamed wild on
Manhattan Island and residents built a long wall on the
northern edge of what is now lower Manhattan. The
road beside the wall turned into a street named Wall
Street. Today it represents one of the greatest financial
markets in the world.*

Smoked Country Spareribs

4 - 5 pounds pork spareribs
¾ cup ketchup
¼ cup lemon juice
⅓ cup packed brown sugar
1 tablespoon Worcestershire sauce
1½ teaspoons garlic powder
1 teaspoon minced green onion

- Place ribs in sprayed 9 x 13-inch baking dish. Mix remaining ingredients and 1 teaspoon each of salt and pepper in bowl and pour half over ribs. Save remaining half to baste ribs. Cover and refrigerate for 24 hours.

- Cook on oiled, preheated grill, covered, to one side of medium fire at about 300° to 350° for about 1 hour. Baste several times with sauce, after about 30 minutes turn and baste again. Continue to cook away from fire about 300° for 2 or 3 hours until meat falls off bone.

- If you cannot maintain heat, remove from grill, wrap ribs in sprayed foil and seal so juices do not leak. Continue to cook in preheated oven at 300° for 2 hours until ribs pull apart easily. Serves 6.

Tender Grilled Spareribs

1 cup beer
2 tablespoons lemon juice
2 tablespoons chili powder
½ teaspoon dijon-style mustard
⅔ cup honey
1 (3 pound) rack pork spareribs

- Combine ½ teaspoon pepper with all ingredients except ribs in bowl and mix well. Place spareribs in large shallow baking pan and spoon marinade over ribs. Bake for 1 hour at 350° in oven and baste every 15 minutes.

- Remove ribs from baking pan and grill over high heat with meaty-side down, for about 6 to 8 minutes on each side; baste several times. Ribs cook through when internal temperature of meat away from bone is at least 145°. Cut ribs between the bones. Serves 6.

Sassy Ribs with Apricot Sauce

2 racks baby back ribs, cut into individual ribs

Apricot Sauce:

¼ cup hoisin sauce
¼ cup wine vinegar
2 tablespoons soy sauce
⅓ cup apricot preserves

- Line large shallow baking pan with sprayed foil and place ribs, meaty side down, close together, but not touching. In small bowl, combine all sauce ingredients and mix well.

- Sprinkle salt and pepper on ribs and cook on oiled grill over medium heat for about 5 to 10 minutes per side.

- Baste liberally with one-third of sauce to brown ribs on outside several minutes before cooking is finished. Spoon remaining sauce on ribs just before serving. Serves 4 to 6.

Slow-Cooked Pork Ribs

4 pounds baby back pork ribs
1 (16 ounce) bottle barbecue sauce
2 - 4 dashes hot sauce
1 (12 ounce) bottle porter, room temperature
Pinch sugar

- Sprinkle ribs with sugar and 1 tablespoon pepper. Sear outside of ribs on oiled, preheated grill over high heat. Cook until grill marks show on both sides. Remove ribs from grill and place in sprayed slow cooker.

- Pour barbecue sauce, hot sauce, beer and sugar in saucepan and heat on low just long enough for flavors to mix. (Do not boil.)

- Pour sauce over ribs, cover and cook on LOW for about 5 to 6 hours until meat falls off bones. Serves 4 to 6.

Smoked Baby Back Ribs with Lemon Pepper Rub

2 tablespoons brown sugar
1 teaspoon lemon pepper
1 teaspoon paprika
2 racks baby back ribs

- Combine brown sugar, lemon pepper, paprika with 1 to 2 teaspoons salt and 1 to 2 teaspoons pepper. Rub on ribs about 30 to 45 minutes before grilling. Let stand at room temperature.

- Cook on oiled grill at about 250° away from direct medium-low fire for about 45 minutes per side until ribs are tender and internal temperature is at least 145°. Serves 4.

Smoked Dijon Baby-Back Ribs

6 - 8 pounds baby-back pork ribs
2 (12 ounce) bottles dijon-honey marinade with lemon juice,
    divided

- Slather about half dijon-honey marinade over ribs in large baking dish, cover and refrigerate overnight.

- Before cooking in vertical water smoker, charcoal or wood smoker, soak about 10 15 chunks of hickory, pecan, cherry or alder in water for at least 1 hour. Start about 10 pounds of charcoal in vertical water smoker.

- When fire is red hot with small flames, place wood chunks around outside of fire. Place water pan on rack and fill with water.

- Place ribs on oiled grate and close lid. (Use rib racks on grate.) Do not open. Cook according to manufacturer's recommended times. Before removing from grill baste ribs with remaining marinade until hot and slightly charred. Ribs are done when meaty parts reach 145°. Serves 6 to 8.

Sweet and Spicy Baby Back Ribs

1 rack baby back ribs
¼ cup balsamic vinegar
2½ cups packed brown sugar
1½ tablespoons ground ginger
2 tablespoons - ¼ cup Louisiana crawfish seasoning
1 teaspoon paprika

- Rinse ribs and dry with paper towels. Marinate in balsamic vinegar for about 30 minutes. Mix brown sugar, ginger, crawfish seasoning and paprika. Rub half seasoning mixture over meat liberally.

- Cook on oiled grill over medium-low fire for 45 minutes to 1 hour and turn frequently. Sprinkle ribs with remaining seasoning mixture while grilling.

- Wrap ribs in foil and place at edge of fire with lid closed or in oven at 250° for about 2 hours until meat falls off bones. Serves about 2.

Molasses Rib Feast

1 rack baby back ribs
Seasoned salt
½ cup barbecue sauce with molasses
¼ cup red wine vinegar
¼ cup kosher dill pickle juice
1 teaspoon coarse black pepper
1 teaspoon soy sauce
1 teaspoon Worcestershire sauce
½ teaspoon lime juice

- Rub ribs with seasoned salt. Combine remaining ingredients, pour over ribs and marinate for about 1 hour.

- Cook on oiled grill over medium-low heat for about 1 to 2 hours. Turn several times and remove from grill when internal temperature is at least 145°. Serves 2.

$ave Money! *Be on the lookout for "double coupon" days at your grocery store.*

Smoked Baby Back or Country-Style Ribs

The simplicity of this is unbelievable and the flavor is outstanding!

4 - 6 racks baby back or country-style ribs
Salt, pepper, sugar

- Lay out racks of ribs on baking sheets. Sprinkle with 3 times as much salt and pepper as sugar. Rub in seasonings and set aside for about 30 minutes.

- Use charcoal with water-soaked, mesquite or hickory wood chips or mesquite, hickory or oak wood fire and burn to red hot coals without strong flame.

- Place ribs on oiled grill away from direct fire, close lid and cook for about 4 to 5 hours. Add wood chips every hour or so. Outside of ribs will caramelize and get crusty, but ribs should be moist. Ribs are done when the internal temperature reaches at least 145° and meat is tender. Serves 8 to 12.

TIP: *Use barbecue sauce if you particularly like sauce, but this simple combination of salt, pepper and sugar surpasses the sweet, spicy, gooey taste of barbecue sauce.*

Easy One-Hour Smoked Baby Back Ribs

You don't have to add wood every hour for this recipe.

- Use recipe for *Smoked Baby Back or Country-Style Ribs (page 240)*, but smoke for 1 hour. Remove ribs from smoker or grill and wrap in foil so juices do not leak.

- Roast in preheated oven at 300° for about 2 to 3 hours until ribs pull apart easily. Serves 8 to 12.

Sauerkraut and Kielbasa

2 (16 ounce) cans sauerkraut
2 (12 ounce) cans beer
1 tablespoon light brown sugar
1 (1 pound) package kielbasa sausage

- Wash sauerkraut thoroughly and drain in colander. Place in large saucepan and pour beer over top. (Make sure beer more than covers sauerkraut.) Add brown sugar and stir. Simmer for about 1 hour 15 minutes. (Do not boil beer.)

- Cook sausage on oiled, preheated grill over medium fire for about 10 minutes per side until crispy brown on outside and cooked thoroughly. Slice sausage, drain sauerkraut and add sausage to sauerkraut. Serves 4.

Camp-Style Eggs in a Bucket

Whether playing make-believe with the kids in a backyard tent or firing up a campsite grill, this is a tasty dish.

½ pound bulk pork sausage
1 (16 ounce) can cream-style corn
6 eggs

- Brown sausage in cast-iron skillet over hot fire and drain fat. Add corn and stir. Beat eggs and pour into corn-sausage mixture.

- Cook dish just like scrambled eggs and serve when mixture is firm. Serves 4.

TIP: Substitute ¼ pound bacon, chopped for the sausage. Vary color and flavor by adding ¼ cup minced onion or scallions and 3 tablespoons finely chopped red or orange bell pepper.

Don't poke holes in brats before grilling. It lets out all the moisture in the brats.

Steaming Fresh Pork Tamales

This sounds too simple to be good, but it's a big hit. Men will eat a bunch, so get ready.

12 - 24 fresh pork tamales with husks (not paper wrappers)
Salsa

- Place tamales with husks on preheated grill over medium fire with lid closed for about 5 minutes. Turn tamales and cook until grill marks show and tamales are hot inside. Serve with salsa. Serves 6 to 12.

Seafood

Not only extra healthy, but extra
delicious seafood recipes are sure winners.

Basic Grilled Fish

Use this any time you need a fast and easy way to grill fish.

2 - 4 tablespoons butter, melted
1 - 2 tablespoons lemon juice
1 tablespoon parsley flakes
2 (4 - 6 ounce) fish fillets

- Combine butter, lemon juice and parsley flakes and pour over fillets. Add a little salt and pepper to both sides of fillets. Cook on oiled grill or on foil over medium-hot fire for about 3 to 5 minutes per side until fish flakes easily with fork and meat is white. Serves 2.

Grilled Whitefish

2 pounds whitefish fillets
Olive oil
1 lemon, halved

- Brush both sides of fillets with oil and season with salt and pepper. Drizzle juice of ½ lemon over both sides of fish and set aside for about 20 minutes.

- Place fish on heavy-duty sprayed foil on grill over medium fire. Cook for about 5 minutes on 1 side, turn and cook until fish flakes. (Do not turn more than once or fillets will fall apart.) Slice remaining half of lemon and serve with fish. Serves 4.

Grilled Fish with Mango Salsa

4 fish fillets
Extra-virgin olive oil
1 lime, halved
Garlic salt
Mango Salsa (recipe follows)

- Rinse and dry fillets. Rub with olive oil over both sides. Drizzle with juice of ½ lime and sprinkle with garlic salt.

- Cook on oiled grill over medium heat for about 3 to 5 minutes per side until fillets flake easily with fork. Do not overcook. Serve with mango salsa. Serves 4.

Mango Salsa:

2 ripe mangoes, peeled, finely chopped
1 jalapeno, seeded, finely chopped
4 green onions with tops, finely chopped
1 yellow bell pepper, seeded, finely chopped
1 lime, halved

- Mix all ingredients in bowl and squeeze juice of one-half lime over salsa. Refrigerate while fillets cook.

Dilled Grilled Fillets

1 pint plain yogurt
1 tablespoon lemon juice
2 cloves garlic, minced
1 tablespoon chopped fresh dill
Dash hot sauce
½ cucumber, peeled, thinly sliced
6 (8 ounce) fish fillets

• Combine yogurt with lemon juice, garlic, dill, ⅛ teaspoon each of salt and pepper and hot sauce in medium bowl. Gently stir in cucumber.

• Place large, sprayed foil on preheated grill over medium heat. Cook fish for 4 to 8 minutes per side until fish flakes easily. Spread yogurt dill sauce over fish before serving. Serves 6.

Lemon Barbecue Fish Fillets

½ cup lemon juice
½ cup vegetable or salad oil
¼ cup packed brown sugar
¼ cup grated onion
2 teaspoons dry mustard
½ teaspoon hot sauce
1½ - 2 pounds fish fillets

• Mix all ingredients except fish so sugar dissolves. Baste fish well while cooking.

• Cook fish on oiled grill over medium fire for about 3 to 5 minutes per side until fish just begins to flake with fork. Pour any remaining sauce over fish before serving. Serves 4 to 6.

Fish on the grill is perfect when the meat is opaque in the center. Cook fish about three minutes per side and check inside. Most people overcook fish which dries it out and toughens it. The rewards of grilling fish are well worth being extra careful with the timing.

Easiest Fish Tacos

1 pound white fish fillet, boned
6 corn tortillas
Coleslaw

- Season fish with a little salt and pepper. Cook fish on oiled, preheated grill over medium fire for about 3 to 4 minutes per side until fish flakes and meat is opaque.

- Place tortillas on grill away from heat while fish cooks. Shred fish and place in tortillas. Add coleslaw and serve. Makes about 6 tacos.

Easy Fish Tacos

1 pound boned white fish fillets
2 tablespoons lime juice
Garlic powder
6 soft corn tortillas
Shredded lettuce
Finely chopped tomatoes
Salsa

- Season fish with lime juice and garlic powder. Cook fish on oiled, preheated grill over medium fire for about 3 to 4 minutes per side until fish flakes. Shred fish and set aside.

- Place tortillas on grill away from heat while fish cooks. When ready to serve, place shredded fish, lettuce and tomatoes in tortilla and fold over. Serve with salsa. Makes about 6 tacos.

TIP: Crispy taco shells are a nice option.

It's good to use foil or a fish grate to grill fish. Poke holes in foil to let the smoke come through the foil and spray or oil the surface.

Italian Fish Packs

1 (14.5 ounce) can Italian stewed tomatoes
1 (2 ounce) can sliced olives, drained
⅓ cup pesto
2 pounds fish fillets

- Combine tomatoes, olives and pesto. Place fish on large, sprayed heavy-duty foil. Sprinkle with ½ teaspoon each salt and pepper. Pour tomato mixture over fish. Fold foil so air will circulate and juices are sealed in.

- Cook on grill away from direct medium heat for about 5 minutes, turn package and cook additional 5 minutes. Check fish and continue to cook until it starts to flake. Remove from heat and serve. (Fish will continue to cook after removed from heat.) Serves 6.

Grilled Cod Fillets

Cape Cod got its name from the abundance of cod in the area. You can use any kind of white fish.

1 - 1½ pound fish fillets
3 tablespoons butter
1 teaspoon tarragon
2 teaspoons capers
2 tablespoons lemon juice

- Season fish fillets with a little salt and pepper. Cook on oiled, preheated grill over medium-low fire for about 3 minutes per side. Continue to cook until fish flakes with fork.

- Melt butter with tarragon, capers and lemon juice in saucepan and simmer while fish cooks. Pour over fillets as soon as they come off grill. Serves 3 to 4.

> *The biggest mistake in grilling is to cook food too long.*
> *When this happens, food is usually dry and tough.*

Orange Roughy with Peppers

1 onion, sliced
1 red bell pepper, seeded, julienned
Canola oil
2 (1 pound) orange roughy fillets
¼ cup (½ stick) butter, melted
1 teaspoon dried thyme leaves

- Rub onion slices and bell pepper with a little oil and place on sprayed, foil-lined grill over medium-hot fire for about 5 to 10 minutes until vegetables get slightly tender.

- Cut fish into 4 serving-size pieces and place on top of vegetables. Pour butter over fish and season with thyme and ¼ teaspoon pepper. Move away from direct heat, fold foil over loosely and partially seal.

- Cook until fish flakes easily, about 5 to 10 minutes. If you want fish to brown, place directly on foil to cook. Serve with onions and peppers on top of fish. Serves 4.

Pacific Mahi Mahi

This is an excellent sauce for mahi mahi or any fish with a mild flavor.

¼ cup soy sauce
1½ tablespoons rice vinegar
1 tablespoon olive oil
2 tablespoons brown sugar
1 clove garlic, pressed
2 - 4 drops hot pepper sauce
4 (4 - 6 ounce) mahi mahi fillets

- Mix all ingredients except mahi mahi and pour into sealable bag. Place fish in bag and coat well with sauce. Marinate for about 30 minutes in refrigerator and bring to room temperature.

- Cook on oiled grill or in fish basket over medium fire for about 5 minutes per side until fish flakes easily with fork. Serves 4.

Mahi Mahi with Pistachio Butter

4 - 6 (6 ounce) mahi mahi fillets
Vegetable oil
½ cup (1 stick) butter, softened
¼ - ⅓ cup crushed pistachios

- Sprinkle fillets with oil and salt and pepper. Blend butter and pistachios in bowl. Cook fillets on oiled grill or foil over medium heat for about 3 to 5 minutes per side until fish flakes easily with fork. Place dollop of pistachio butter on each fillet just before removing from heat. Serves 4 to 6.

Lemon-Dill Fish Fillets

½ cup mayonnaise
2 tablespoons lemon juice
½ teaspoon lemon zest
1 teaspoon dill weed
1 - 1½ pound cod or flounder fillets

- Combine mayonnaise, lemon juice, zest and dill weed. Place fish on oiled grill over medium heat. Brush with half sauce. Grill 3 to 5 minutes, turn and brush with remaining sauce. Continue grilling 1 to 2 minutes if fish does not flake easily with fork. Serves 4.

Grilled Teriyaki Fish

This works well with any firm fish or large shrimp.

¼ cup plus 1 tablespoon honey
⅓ cup light soy sauce
⅓ cup Samuel Adams® Cream Stout
3 tablespoons olive oil
2 cloves garlic, crushed
⅛ teaspoon hot red chili flakes, ground
2 pounds mahi mahi, other firm fish or large shelled shrimp
⅓ cup flour

- Combine all ingredients except fish and flour. Brush half of marinade on both sides of fish and refrigerate for 2 hours.

- Dust fish with flour and cook on sprayed heavy-duty foil or oiled grill over medium fire for about 5 minutes per side until fish flakes easily. Baste often with remaining marinade. Do not overcook. Serves 4 to 6.

Cilantro-Flavored Flounder

4 (½ pound) flounder fillets
½ cup (1 stick) butter
¼ cup fresh snipped cilantro leaves
2 tablespoons lime juice

- Cook fillets on preheated grill covered with sprayed foil over medium fire. Melt butter with cilantro and lime juice and drizzle about one-fourth over fillets.

- Turn after about 3 minutes and continue to cook and baste with ¼ butter. Remove when fish flakes. Drizzle remaining butter over fillets just before serving. Serves 4.

Fire for Chicken and Fish

Coals for the fire should be red with a medium-thick layer of white ash on top. You should be able to hold your hand over the fire for three to four seconds.

Flounder Au Gratin

½ cup fine breadcrumbs
¼ cup grated parmesan cheese
1- 2 pounds flounder
⅓ cup mayonnaise

- Combine breadcrumbs and parmesan cheese in shallow dish. Brush both sides of fish with mayonnaise and coat with crumb mixture. Arrange fillets in single layer on oiled, preheated grill or on sprayed heavy-duty foil over direct medium heat. Cook for about 3 to 5 minutes per side until fish flakes easily. Do not overcook. Serves 2 to 4.

Spicy Halibut Steaks

4 (1 inch) thick fresh halibut steaks
2 tablespoons spicy brown mustard
1 teaspoon cumin
½ teaspoon cayenne
2 tablespoons butter, melted
1 lemon

- Rinse halibut steaks and pat dry with paper towels. Spread spicy mustard over top of steaks and sprinkle with cumin, cayenne and a little salt and pepper.

- Cook on oiled, preheated grill away from direct medium heat for about 3 minutes per side until fish flakes easily. (Do not overcook.) Remove fish, pour hot butter over top with a squeeze of lemon and serve with slices of lemon. Serves 4.

Lemon-Dill Halibut or Cod

½ cup mayonnaise
2 tablespoons lemon juice
½ teaspoon grated lemon peel
1 teaspoon dill weed
2 pounds halibut fillets

- Combine mayonnaise, lemon juice, lemon peel and dill weed in bowl and mix until they blend well.

- Place fish on oiled grill over medium heat for several minutes on both sides, then brush both sides with sauce. Continue grilling until fish flakes easily with fork. Serves 4.

First Place Lemon-Garlic Halibut

This is great with any fish steak including, swordfish and tuna.

1 cup (2 sticks) butter, melted
¼ cup fresh lemon juice
2 tablespoons sweet paprika
2 tablespoons dried parsley flakes
6 cloves garlic, pressed
4 (4 - 6 ounce) halibut steaks

- Mix butter, lemon juice, paprika, parsley flakes and garlic. Divide butter sauce in 2 bowls and use half to baste fish while cooking.

- Cook halibut on oiled grill over medium fire for about 5 to 8 minutes per side until fish flakes easily with fork. Pour any remaining sauce over fish before serving. Serves 4.

Halibut and Spring Greens with Raspberry Vinaigrette

4 (6 ounce) halibut fillets
½ teaspoon paprika
½ teaspoon freshly ground pepper
1 (10 ounce) package salad greens
¼ cup raspberry-flavored vinaigrette

- Sprinkle fillets with paprika and pepper. Cook fillets on oiled grill or sprayed heavy-duty foil over medium heat. Grill about 4 minutes on each side until fish flakes easily with fork.

- Arrange 4 equal portions of salad greens (and any other salad vegetables) on plate and top with sliced halibut and vinaigrette. Serves 4.

Closing the lid of a grill or smoker increases the temperature inside. Opening the lid decreases the temperature.

Bayside Red Snapper

1 (8 ounce) can tomato sauce
1 (4 ounce) can diced green chilies
1 clove garlic, minced
2 (1 pound) red snapper fillets

- Mix tomato sauce, green chilies and garlic in small saucepan and simmer over medium-low heat.

- Cook fillets on oiled, preheated grill away from direct medium heat for about 4 minutes per side. Turn and remove when fish flakes with fork. Serve with warmed sauce over top. Serves 4.

This Bud's for Snapper

1 potato, thinly sliced
1 large sweet onion, sliced
4 (6 ounce) red snapper fillets
½ cup (1 stick) butter
2 cloves garlic, minced
3 green onions with tops, minced
1 (12 ounce) bottle beer

- Lay out 4 pieces of sprayed, heavy-duty foil large enough to wrap fish and vegetables. Place two slices of potato in each foil packet, 1 thick onion slice on top of potato and 1 red snapper fillet over onion.

- Place 2 tablespoons butter on top of fish and sprinkle with garlic, green onions, and a little salt and pepper. Before sealing, add 3 ounces beer. Fold edges of foil over stack to seal in liquid.

- Place on preheated grill over medium fire. Cook until beer steams, about 5 minutes. (Do not let beer boil.) Test fish to see if it flakes. To cook more, move to indirect heat for several more minutes until fish flakes and potatoes are tender. Serve in foil if desired. Serves 4.

Controlling Temperature of a Fire

Increase temperature of fire by fanning or knocking white ash off coals and pushing coals closer together. Lower temperature of fire by spreading coals out.

Hobo Snappers

4 (6 ounce) red snapper fillets
3 - 4 red potatoes, thinly sliced
2 red bell peppers, seeded, chopped
1 bunch green onions with tops, chopped
2 teaspoons garlic salt
½ cup (1 stick) butter
1 (12 ounce) bottle or can light beer

- Place 1 fillet on large piece of sprayed, heavy-duty foil. Layer one-fourth of potatoes, one-fourth bell peppers and one-fourth green onions over fillet.

- Sprinkle with garlic salt. Dot with butter and pour one-fourth beer over ingredients. Fold foil loosely so air will circulate and seal tightly to hold juices. Repeat steps and prepare 3 more packages.

- Place on grill over medium-high heat for about 5 minutes. Move away from direct heat, shake package to redistribute and "steam" for additional 5 to 10 minutes. Packets are done when fish flakes easily and potatoes are tender. Serves 4.

Easy Grilled Stripers

1½ - 2 pounds striped bass fillets
2 -4 tablespoons butter, melted
Garlic powder
1 lemon
1 tomato, sliced

- Place fillets on sprayed heavy-duty foil and top with butter and garlic powder. Cook on preheated grill over medium fire about 3 to 5 minutes per side. (Don't overcook.)

- Squeeze a little lemon juice over fillets. Place tomato slices on top after fillets are turned and salt and pepper lightly. Cook until fillets are opaque and flake easily. Serves 4 to 6.

Always allow meats to stand for about 5 to 10 minutes before slicing. It will slice better and taste better.

Red Snapper with Fresh Salsa

4 (6 - 8 ounce) red snapper fillets
Canola oil
1 teaspoon ground cumin
½ teaspoon cayenne pepper

- Dry snapper with paper towels and rub a little oil on both sides of snapper. Sprinkle with cumin, cayenne pepper and ½ teaspoon salt.

- Cook on oiled grill over medium heat for about 5 minutes on each side until fish flakes easily with fork.

Fresh Salsa:

½ cup chopped fresh cilantro
1 (15 ounce) can great northern beans, drained
1 (15 ounce) can Italian stewed tomatoes, drained
⅓ cup chopped green olives
1 teaspoon minced garlic

- Combine cilantro, beans, tomatoes, olives and garlic in bowl and mix well. Serve with red snapper and garnish with slice of fresh lime. Serves 4.

Grilled Lemon-Peppered Catfish

Try grilling catfish instead of frying. You'll be surprised.

4 - 6 medium catfish fillets
Olive oil
½ teaspoon garlic powder
½ teaspoon lemon pepper

- Rub catfish fillets with olive oil and sprinkle seasonings and a little salt on all sides. Cover grill rack with sprayed foil. Cook fish on foil directly over medium heat for about 3 to 5 minutes per side until fish flakes easily. Do not overcook. Serves 4.

$ave Money! *Join your grocery store's loyalty program. It may seem like a hassle, but the savings can really add up.*

Spicy Catfish Amandine

¼ cup (½ stick) butter, melted
3 tablespoons lemon juice
6 - 8 catfish fillets
1½ teaspoons Creole seasoning
½ cup sliced almonds

- Combine butter and lemon juice and dip each fillet in butter mixture. Arrange in one layer on sprayed foil on grill and sprinkle both sides with Creole seasoning.

- Cook over direct medium heat for about 5 minutes and turn. Sprinkle almonds on top for last few minutes of cooking. Cook until fish flakes easily. Serves 6 to 8.

Easy Grilled Catfish

Olive oil
4 - 6 catfish fillets
1 teaspoon garlic salt or 1 - 2 fresh cloves garlic, pressed
½ teaspoon seasoned pepper
4 - 6 tablespoons butter

- Rub olive oil over fillets and sprinkle with garlic salt and pepper. Cook on oiled grill or sprayed heavy-duty foil over medium heat for about 3 to 5 minutes.

- Turn and cook just until fish flakes easily with fork. (Do not overcook.) Just before removing from grill, top each fillet with 1 tablespoon butter. Serves 4.

Easy Grilled Catfish with Tomatoes

- Use recipe for *Easy Grilled Catfish (page 255)* and add slice of tomato on top of fish when grilling. Eliminate butter and add lemon juice just before serving. Serves 4.

Easy Butter-Crusted Catfish

Everyone loves fried fish, but you'll be surprised to see how many raves you get with this easy grilling recipe.

8 - 10 catfish fillets
Butter, melted
3 lemons, juiced
1 teaspoon garlic powder

- Cook fish on sprayed, heavy-duty foil on grill over medium-hot fire for about 3 to 5 minutes per side. (Less if fillets are thin.)

- Pour melted butter, lemon juice and garlic powder over both sides of fish. If you want a crust to form, allow fish to char on outside just a little. When fish flakes easily, it is done. Serves 8 to 10.

Fisherman's Trout Fillets

Trout fillets
Butter, melted
Lemon pepper
Tomato Butter (recipe page 293)

- Soak mesquite wood chips for at least 1 hour. Place around outside of preheated charcoal fire. Season fillets with butter and lemon pepper. Cook on oiled grill over medium heat for about 3 minutes per side until fish is opaque and flakes with fork. Allow ⅓ to ½ pound fillet per person. Serve with Tomato Butter.

$ave Money! *Eat fruits and vegetables that are in season. The cheapest prices are at the peak of harvest.*

Campfire Rainbow Trout

½ cup (1 stick) plus 3 tablespoons butter, divided
1 - 2 large cloves garlic, minced
3 small green onions with tops, minced
3 tablespoons white wine
2 (1 pound) rainbow trout fillets
1 egg, lightly beaten
1 - 3 tablespoons oil
1 lemon, sliced, optional

- Melt ½ cup butter in cast-iron skillet and saute garlic and green onions over medium campfire or grill until they are translucent. Add white wine and pour into small saucepan. Simmer garlic sauce to one side of fire while fish cooks.

- Wash and pat dry trout fillets and set aside. Beat egg slightly with 1 tablespoon water in bowl and dip each fillet into egg mixture.

- In cast-iron skillet, heat oil and 1 tablespoon butter and cook fillets over hot coals or campfire. Turn once, add 1 to 2 tablespoons butter, if needed, and remove when fish flakes in thickest part.

- Arrange fish on platter and pour warm garlic sauce over fish just before serving. Garnish with lemon slices. Serves 4.

Rainbow Fillets in Caper Butter

½ cup (1 stick) butter
1 teaspoon tarragon
2 teaspoons capers
2 tablespoons lemon juice
1 pound trout fillets

- Melt butter, tarragon, capers and lemon juice in small saucepan. Make pouch or tray for fillets out of heavy-duty foil. Spray inside of foil and place fillets side by side. Pour half of butter sauce over fish. Seal foil pouch so no liquids escape.

- Cook on preheated grill over medium fire for about 5 minutes. Open pouch and turn; cook until fish flakes, but is not dry. Pour remaining caper-butter sauce over fish and serve. Serves 2 to 4.

Brook Trout Wrapped in Foil

1 onion, sliced
1 rib celery, chopped
1 carrot, chopped
¼ teaspoon thyme
1 bay leaf
3 sprigs parsley, snipped
2 (12 ounce) brook trout, dressed
½ cup wine
2 teaspoons butter
⅓ cup half-and-half cream
2 teaspoons flour

- Make 2 pouches out of heavy-duty foil large enough for vegetables and fish. Place half onion, celery, carrot, thyme, bay leaf and parsley in each pouch. Place trout on top and pour wine over fish.

- Seal foil packet so no liquids escape, but allow for air expansion. Cook on preheated grill over medium fire for about 20 minutes, rotating once, until fish flakes, but is not dry.

- A few minutes before fish is ready, melt butter in saucepan over low heat. Add half-and-half cream and flour slowly and whisk to dissolve lumps.

- Remove foil packets from heat and add liquid from packets to butter-cream mixture in saucepan. Whisk to combine well and pour over fish and vegetables. Serve immediately. Serves 4.

Sometimes it is best to sear the outside of the meat, cook on the grill for a limited time, then remove the food from the grill. Wrap meat in foil, place in pan and complete cooking in oven at 300° to finish the process. This gives you the flavor of the grill, but the tenderness of slow cooking.

Grilled Whole Rainbow Trout

This is very simple, but delicious.

Red cedar plank
Olive oil
4 (1 pound) whole, dressed rainbow trout
3 - 4 limes
Sea salt
Coarse ground black pepper

- Soak plank in water for about 30 minutes per side. Season plank with a little olive oil. Rub olive oil on outside and inside of trout. Douse with lime juice and sprinkle salt and pepper inside and out.

- Arrange trout on plank and place over medium-hot fire, close lid and cook for about 5 minutes. Check plank and reposition if it is burning. Cook additional 5 minutes, turn trout, close lid and continue cooking until trout is white and flaky on the inside. Serves 4.

Grilled Rainbow Trout

The whole grilled trout is an impressive main dish.

1 whole, cleaned rainbow trout
Onion, minced
Celery, diced
Parsley, snipped
Fresh garlic cloves, minced
Butter
Bacon

- Use these basic ingredients with any size trout. Fill cavity of fish with onion, celery, parsley, garlic and butter and season with a little salt and pepper.

- Wrap entire fish with bacon slices. Wrap several times in heavy-duty foil to prevent any leakage. Cook over hot charcoal fire for about 10 minutes on each side until fish flakes. The larger the fish, the longer it will need to cook. Serves 2.

Marinated Brook Trout

4 (1 pound) whole brook or rainbow trout, cleaned
2 - 3 limes
¼ cup butter, melted
1 tablespoon extra virgin olive oil
1 teaspoon snipped parsley
2 tablespoons slivered almonds, toasted
1 tablespoon hot sauce

- Prick fish with fork and salt both sides. Mix about ¼ cup lime juice, butter, oil, parsley, almond slivers and hot sauce and pour onto both sides of fish. Marinate at room temperature for about 20 minutes.

- Cook on oiled grill or foil over indirect, medium-high heat for about 5 minutes per side until fish just begins to flake with fork. Slice remaining lime and serve with fish. Serves 4.

Beer-Roasted Salmon

1 (1½ pounds) salmon fillets
3 - 4 cloves garlic, minced
2 tablespoons brown sugar
2 - 4 tablespoons butter
1 small onion, minced
1 (12 ounce) bottle or can beer

- Place enough foil in 9 x 13-inch baking pan to cover bottom and fold over sides. Spray foil and place salmon on top. Sprinkle minced garlic and brown sugar over salmon. Drop dabs of butter over top. Sprinkle with minced onion.

- Pour beer into pan and cover with foil. Place baking pan on medium grill and close lid. Cook for 5 minutes, remove foil cover and return pan to grill. Cover grill and cook for several minutes until salmon cooks through and is flaky. (Don't let beer boil or it will become bitter. Remove from direct heat if necessary.) Serves 4.

Salmon on a Plank

If you haven't tried cooking on a western red cedar or alder plank, you're missing a treat.

½ cup (1 stick) butter, softened
⅓ cup snipped fresh basil
4 - 5 cloves garlic, minced or crushed
1 (2 pound) salmon fillet

- Soak cedar plank in water for about 1 hour on each side. Prepare charcoal and oil grill while cedar plank soaks. Mix butter, basil and garlic in small bowl and spread on both sides of salmon. (If salmon has skin on 1 side, omit butter on that side.)

- When coals are red hot, but not flaming, place salmon on plank and plank on grill. Close lid and cook about 5 minutes. Check plank to make sure it's not burning. Reposition if it appears to be burning.

- Add a little salt and pepper on both sides and turn salmon to cook other side. Check again after 5 minutes or so and cook until salmon flakes, but is still moist inside. Serves 4.

Yaki Salmon

Teriyaki is a Japanese method of cooking. "Yaki" means grilled.

4 (4 - 8 ounce) salmon steaks
¾ cup teriyaki marinade
1 - 2 tablespoons brown sugar

- Place salmon and teriyaki marinade in sealable bag and marinate for about 30 minutes. Cook on oiled grill over medium heat for about 3 to 5 minutes per side.

- During last few minutes of cooking, sprinkle a little brown sugar on steaks and rub in. Salmon is done when it flakes easily. Do not overcook. Serves 4.

Grilled Salmon Caesar Salad

1 (8 ounce) salmon fillet
½ teaspoon garlic salt
12 leaves romaine lettuce
¼ cup shredded parmesan cheese
Caesar dressing
Croutons

- Season salmon with garlic salt and cook on oiled grill over medium fire for about 3 to 4 minutes per side. Do not overcook. Cut salmon into strips.

- Wash and pat romaine leaves dry with paper towels, tear leaves into pieces and place in salad bowl. Sprinkle with shredded parmesan and toss with dressing. When ready to serve, sprinkle croutons on top and place strips of salmon on top. Serves 2.

Tuna Steaks with Tomato Sauce

1 tablespoon olive oil
3 - 4 cloves garlic, crushed
2 teaspoons sugar
1 tablespoon dried basil
1 (18 ounce) can stewed tomatoes
4 (4 - 6 ounce) tuna steaks

- Heat olive oil in saucepan and add garlic, sugar, a little pepper and basil. Cook on low heat for 2 minutes. Add stewed tomatoes, bring to boil, reduce heat and simmer 20 minutes.

- Season fish with a little salt and pepper. Cook on oiled grill over medium-low heat for about 3 to 5 minutes per side. When fish flakes easily with fork, it is ready. Remove tuna steaks to platter and pour tomato sauce over top. Serves 4.

Grilled Tuna with Mediterranean Salsa

5 - 6 (1-inch) thick fresh tuna steaks
½ teaspoon minced garlic
Mediterranean Salsa (recipe follows)

- Sprinkle tuna steaks with minced garlic and ½ teaspoon each of salt and pepper. Cook on oiled grill over medium to high heat about 3 to 5 minutes.

- Gently turn steaks and continue grilling 3 to 5 minutes. Do not overcook. Tuna should be slightly pink in the middle. When serving, top each steak with Mediterranean salsa. Serves 5 to 6.

Mediterranean Salsa:

1 (4 ounce) can chopped ripe olives, drained
1 tomato, chopped
¼ cup olive oil
⅓ cup crumbled feta cheese
1 teaspoon dried basil

- In small bowl, combine ripe olives, tomato, oil, feta cheese and basil. Spoon salsa mixture over tuna steaks and refrigerate any leftover mixture. Makes about 1 cup.

To find out how hot your grill is, count the number of seconds that you can comfortably hold your hand over the grill. Carefully hold your hand as close to grill as you can without touching it and take your hand away before you burn it.

Hot	*2 - 3 seconds*
Medium	*4 - 5 seconds*
Low	*6 - 7 seconds*

Grilled Tuna with Salsa

2 bell peppers, seeded, chopped
1 small sweet onion, minced
3 cloves garlic, minced
2 teaspoons extra-virgin olive oil
½ cup snipped cilantro
1 lemon or lime, juiced
4 (1 inch thick) tuna steaks

- Mix bell pepper, onion, garlic, olive oil, cilantro, lemon or lime juice and a little salt and pepper. Place half salsa in saucepan and simmer.

- Make heavy-duty foil pouch for each steak and spray inside. Spread remaining half of salsa among pouches and place tuna on top. Seal pouch so liquid does not leak.

- Cook steaks on preheated grill over medium-hot fire for about 5 minutes. Open pouch and turn steaks. Reseal and continue cooking until steaks flake. Do not overcook and dry out fish. Serve hot with salsa on top. Serves 4.

TIP: For a colorful addition use red and orange bell peppers.

Marinated Swordfish

½ cup extra virgin olive oil
2 -3 cloves fresh garlic, chopped
1 lime, juiced
2 teaspoons chopped fresh basil
¼ cup chopped onion
4 (¼ pound) swordfish fillets

- Combine a little salt and pepper plus all ingredients except swordfish in flat dish and mix well. Add swordfish, turn several times and marinate, covered, in refrigerator for 2 to 3 hours.

- Discard marinade. Cook steaks on oiled, preheated grill over medium-high heat for 5 to 7 minutes on each side until fish flakes. (Don't overcook swordfish; it will dry out.) Serves 4.

Grilled Swordfish Steaks
with Avocado Salsa

2 ripe avocados, peeled, chopped
4 fresh green onions with tops, finely diced
8 - 10 grape tomatoes, quartered
5 - 10 pickled jalapeno slices, chopped
2 limes, juiced
¼ cup snipped fresh cilantro
4 (4 - 8 ounce) swordfish steaks

- Mix avocado, onion, tomatoes, jalapenos, lime juice, cilantro, ¾ teaspoon salt and a little black pepper in medium bowl; cover and refrigerate.

- Cook swordfish steaks on oiled grill over medium heat for about 5 minutes on each side until grill marks show. Check center of steaks and remove from grill when fish flakes easily. Do not overcook and dry out fish. Serve steaks with avocado salsa on top. Serves 4.

Swordfish-Bacon Kebabs

2 (1 pound, ½ - 1 inch thick) swordfish steaks
2 tablespoons lemon juice
2 tablespoons olive oil
1 tablespoon minced garlic
8 slices bacon
12 cherry tomatoes

- Cut fish into 2-inch pieces and combine in shallow bowl with lemon juice, oil and garlic. Cover and place in refrigerator; marinate about 20 minutes.

- Cook bacon until soft, but not crisp. Drain and reserve pan drippings. Cut bacon into 3-inch pieces. Wrap bacon around swordfish bites and thread with tomatoes on skewers. Brush kebabs with reserved bacon drippings.

- Cook on oiled, preheated grill over medium heat for about 3 to 4 minutes. Turn kebabs and grill another 4 minutes until swordfish cooks through. Serve immediately. Serves 4.

Zesty Herb Swordfish

1 (.5 ounce) package Zesty Herb Marinade Seasoning mix
¾ cup olive oil
¼ cup red wine vinegar
4 (4 to 6 ounce) swordfish steaks

- Mix marinade seasoning mix, oil and vinegar and pour into large sealable bag. Place fish in bag and coat with seasonings. Marinate for about 15 to 20 minutes. Discard marinade.

- Cook on oiled grill over direct medium heat for about 3 to 5 minutes per side until fish flakes easily with fork. (If steaks are thick, add more to cooking time.) Serves 4 to 6.

Swordfish with Lemon Baste

½ cup (1 stick) butter, melted
¼ cup lemon juice
½ teaspoon Worcestershire sauce
½ teaspoon hot sauce
4 (1 inch) thick swordfish steaks

- Combine butter, lemon juice, Worcestershire sauce, hot sauce, ½ teaspoon salt and ½ teaspoon pepper in saucepan over low heat and stir well.

- Brush steaks with lemon baste and cook on oiled, preheated grill over medium fire for about 3 to 5 minutes per side until fish flakes. Do not overcook. Baste liberally while cooking. Serves 4.

Sauces are usually thicker and heartier than marinades. They are basted, brushed, dabbled, sopped and smeared onto meats after they cook several minutes. Adding sauce halfway or more through the cooking time keeps it from burning or causing the fire to flare up.

Grilled Swordfish with Honey-Mustard Sauce

Terrific!

½ cup dijon-style mustard
½ cup soy sauce
½ cup rice wine vinegar
2 tablespoons olive oil
4 (4 - 6 ounce) swordfish steaks

- Combine mustard, soy sauce, wine vinegar and oil. Pour half of sauce into sealable bag with swordfish steaks and coat steaks well. Marinate for about 1 to 2 hours.

- Cook steaks on oiled grill over medium fire for about 8 to 10 minutes per side until fish is white and flakes easily with fork. Microwave remaining sauce for about 15 seconds and pour over fish before serving. Serves 4.

Grilled Swordfish with Veggie Kebabs

8 small white onions, peeled, halved
2 green bell peppers, seeded, quartered
1 (8 ounce) carton button mushrooms
Extra-virgin olive oil
4 (½ pound) swordfish steaks

- Coat vegetables with olive oil. Place veggies on skewers or in grilling basket. Cook on preheated, oiled grill over medium-hot fire. When veggies begin to soften, about 7 minutes, move to cooler part of grill.

- Place swordfish in grilling basket or on sprayed heavy-duty foil over medium heat. Season fish with salt and pepper and drizzle olive oil on top. Cook until vegetables are tender and fish flakes, about 10 to 15 minutes. Do not overcook. Serves 4.

Grilled Swordfish with Avocado Butter

½ cup light beer
1 lemon
¼ cup olive oil
2 cloves garlic, minced
2 tablespoons plus 2 teaspoons cumin, divided
4 (4 - 8 ounce) swordfish steaks
2 ripe avocados
2 tablespoons butter, softened
2 teaspoons coriander

- Combine beer, 1 tablespoon lemon juice, 1 teaspoon lemon zest, olive oil, garlic and 2 tablespoons cumin. Mix well and pour into sealable plastic bag. Add swordfish steaks, seal and refrigerate for 1 hour. Turn occasionally.

- When ready to cook fish, peel avocado, slice and place in blender. Add butter, 2 teaspoons cumin and coriander and process until smooth. Remove fish from marinade and drain well.

- Cook on oiled, preheated grill over medium-hot grill for about 3 to 5 minutes per side. Fish is done when it flakes easily. When fish is turned for final time, place dollop of avocado butter on top of each steak so it soaks into fish. Serves 4.

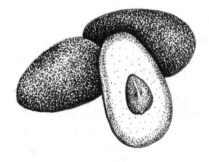

Grilled Swordfish with Mild Chile Sauce

Mild Chile Sauce:

2 red bell peppers, Colorado or poblano chilies
¼ cup mayonnaise
2 tablespoons dijon-style mustard

- Place peppers or chilies on oiled grill over medium-hot heat for about 5 minutes and turn several times. When peppers char on outside, remove from grill, place in plastic bag and seal for about 10 minutes.

- Remove from bag, peel skin away from chilies and drop in blender. Add mayonnaise and mustard and process until smooth. Serve over swordfish.

Fish:

4 (4 - 8 ounce) swordfish steaks
3 tablespoons olive oil
¾ teaspoon seasoned salt
½ teaspoon lemon pepper

- Rub swordfish with olive oil and sprinkle with seasoned salt and lemon pepper. Cook on oiled grill over medium-high heat for about 6 to 10 minutes total; turn once or twice. It is done when fish flakes easily. Serve with Mild Chile Sauce. Serves 4.

If your grilled fish is dry, tough or chewy, you have cooked it too long. It is the biggest mistake most people make when grilling fish.

Orange-Tipped Swordfish Steaks

½ cup soy sauce
½ cup orange juice
¼ cup ketchup
¼ cup fresh chopped parsley
2 tablespoons lemon juice
2 cloves garlic, minced
4 swordfish steaks

- Combine soy sauce, orange juice, ketchup, parsley, lemon juice, garlic and ½ teaspoon salt. Add fish, cover and marinate in refrigerator for 30 minutes. Remove fish and discard marinade.

- Cook fish on oiled grill away from medium hot coals for about 5 to 7 minutes per side depending on thickness. Steak is done when flakes easily with fork. Serves 4 to 6.

Quick Grilled Jambalaya Packs

1 pound uncooked shrimp
2 cups cooked rice
1 (14.5 ounce) can diced tomatoes with garlic and onions
½ cup chopped bell pepper
1 tablespoon Cajun seasoning

- Remove tails, shells and veins from shrimp. Combine all ingredients in large bowl. Place rice mixture evenly on 4 large heavy-duty foil sheets. Fold loosely for air to circulate and seal tightly. Grill about 12 minutes over medium heat until shrimp are pink; rotate packages once. Serves 4.

Extra Spicy Jambalaya Packs

- Use recipe for *Quick Grilled Jambalaya Packs (page 270)* and add 1 to 2 teaspoons red pepper sauce. Serves 4.

$ave Money! *Use coupons wisely. Don't use coupons for items you don't really need.*

Hot Spicy Grilled Shrimp

1 - 1½ pounds shrimp in shells
1½ cups (3 sticks) butter, melted
¼ teaspoon hot sauce
2 - 3 tablespoons barbecue sauce
1 cup white wine
2 - 3 cloves garlic, minced
1 lemon, sliced

• Prepare shrimp by washing well. In dish, combine all
  ingredients except shrimp and stir well. Add shrimp to mixture
  and marinate in refrigerator for 1 hour.

• Cook on oiled grill over medium heat for about 3 minutes
  per side until shrimp turn pink. Serve shrimp in soup bowls.
  Serves 3 to 4.

Stout-Marinated Shrimp

1 cup olive oil
1 (12 ounce) bottle Guinness® Extra Stout
1 - 2 jalapeno peppers, seeded*
2 cloves garlic, quartered
1 small onion, quartered
½ cup honey
1 bunch cilantro, stemmed
20 fresh medium - large shrimp, shelled, veined

• Place all ingredients except shrimp into blender and liquefy.
  Place shrimp in flat-bottomed dish and pour marinade over
  top of shrimp. Refrigerate for about 30 minutes and stir
  several times.

• Cook shrimp on oiled grill over medium heat until grill marks
  show and shrimp turn pink. Don't overcook. Serves 4.

*TIP: Wear rubber gloves when handling jalapenos.

> I always cook with wine. Sometimes I even add it to
> the food.
> –W.C. Fields

Grilled Butterflied Shrimp

16 - 18 uncooked medium - large shrimp, peeled, veined
Extra-virgin olive oil
Sea salt, cracked black pepper
2 limes
Butter, melted

- Butterfly shrimp by slicing halfway through shrimp lengthwise so they lay flat when open. Rub with olive oil and sprinkle with salt and pepper.

- Cook on oiled grill over medium hot fire about 2 minutes on each side until shrimp turn pink. Do not overcook or shrimp will be tough and not as flavorful.

- Slice limes in half and place cut side on grill while shrimp cooks. Remove shrimp and limes. Squeeze limes over shrimp. Serve with melted butter. Serves 4.

Grilled Garlic Shrimp

Great for an appetizer or main dish.

¼ cup (½ stick) butter
1 heaping teaspoon minced garlic
1 teaspoon dried parsley
¼ cup dry white wine
1 pound medium shrimp, peeled, veined

- Combine butter, garlic, parsley and wine in saucepan with ½ teaspoon black pepper. Cook mixture until butter melts, stir and set aside. Thread shrimp, once through top portion and once through bottom portion, onto metal skewers.

- Baste liberally with sauce and cook on oiled grill directly over medium-hot coals for about 3 to 5 minutes per side until pink. Brush shrimp frequently with sauce. Serves 4.

Gala Grilled Garlic Shrimp

Don't skimp on the garlic. It's wonderful.

½ cup extra virgin olive oil
10 - 12 cloves garlic, pressed
2 tablespoons dried parsley
2 pounds fresh shrimp, shelled, veined

- Combine olive oil, garlic, parsley and 1 teaspoon salt and pepper. Pour half into sealable bag, add shrimp and coat with seasonings. Marinate for about 30 minutes.

- Cook on oiled grill over medium-hot fire for about 3 minutes per side until shrimp turn pink and meat is white. Pour remaining garlic sauce over shrimp before serving or serve it on the side. Serves 4.

Easy Grilled Shrimp

1 - 2 pounds shrimp, peeled, veined
Old Bay® Seasoning

- Sprinkle shrimp with seasoning. Cook on oiled grill over medium heat for about 2 to 3 minutes until shrimp turn pink. Serves 4.

Grilled Lemon Shrimp

½ cup (1 stick) butter
2 tablespoons Worcestershire sauce
½ teaspoon minced garlic
2 tablespoons lemon juice
1½ - 2 pounds shelled shrimp, veined, drained

- Melt butter in saucepan and add Worcestershire sauce, garlic and lemon juice. Place shrimp in bowl and pour butter mixture on top. Marinate at room temperature for about 30 minutes.

- Cook shrimp on oiled grill over medium heat for about 3 to 5 minutes per side until shrimp turn pink. Serves 4.

Cajun Shrimp Boat

Couldn't be much simpler.

Tony Chachere's Original Creole Seasoning
2 pounds shrimp, shelled, veined
2 - 3 cloves garlic, pressed
½ cup (1 stick) butter, melted

- Sprinkle seasoning liberally over shrimp. Combine garlic and butter and pour into sealable bag. Add shrimp, coat with butter-garlic sauce and marinate for about 20 minutes.

- Cook on oiled grill over medium-hot fire for about 3 minutes per side until meat is white and shrimp turn pink. Serves 4.

Grilled Shrimp Scampi

½ cup (1 stick) butter
3 cloves garlic, pressed
¼ cup lemon juice
2 pounds shrimp, peeled, veined

- Melt butter in skillet, saute garlic and add lemon juice.

- Cook shrimp on oiled, preheated grill over medium heat until grill marks show and shrimp turn pink. Add shrimp to skillet, simmer for several minutes and turn several times. Serve with additional garlic butter. Serves 4.

Factors that determine the length of time foods should cook are below. Because of these variables, all cooking times in this cookbook are estimates.

- *Temperature of the grill.*
- *Grill covered or uncovered*
- *Direct or indirect heat*
- *Type of grill or smoker*
- *Amount of heat*
- *The heat source: charcoal, natural gas or hardwood*
- *Type of food*
- *Outside temperature*
- *Distance between food and heat source*
- *Personal preferences*

Barbecued Shrimp

2 (8 ounce) cans tomato sauce
1 cup corn oil
⅓ cup red wine vinegar
2 tablespoons ketchup
2 cloves garlic, minced
¼ cup minced cilantro
1 teaspoon freshly ground black pepper
18 - 22 medium to large shrimp

- Combine tomato sauce, corn oil, red wine vinegar and ketchup in bowl and mix well. Stir in garlic, cilantro, 1 teaspoon salt and black pepper and mix well. Add shrimp, cover with barbecue sauce and refrigerate for at least 30 minutes.

- Stir shrimp to coat with sauce several times while marinating. Cook shrimp on oiled, preheated grill over medium heat for 3 to 5 minutes per side until shrimp turn pink. Serve immediately. Serves 4.

Top-Shelf Tequila Shrimp

¼ cup (½ stick) butter
2 cloves garlic, minced
¼ cup tequila
1½ tablespoons lime juice
½ teaspoon chili powder
¼ cup coarsely chopped fresh cilantro
2 limes
1½ pounds medium shrimp, shelled, veined

- Heat butter in large skillet over medium heat. Add garlic, tequila, lime juice, ½ teaspoon salt, chili powder and cilantro and simmer for several minutes.

- Cook shrimp on oiled, preheated grill over medium fire until shrimp turn pink on both sides. Place shrimp in butter sauce, stir well to coat and serve immediately. Serves 4 to 6.

Tropical Shrimp Kebabs

½ cup soy sauce
¾ teaspoon paprika
Garlic salt
1 pound fresh, large peeled shrimp
2 large onions, quartered
1 large red pepper, cut into large pieces
16 - 20 whole mushrooms
20 pineapple chunks

- Mix soy sauce and paprika in small bowl. Marinate shrimp in soy sauce and sprinkle with garlic salt. Refrigerate for 30 minutes. Remove from refrigerator and let shrimp reach room temperature.

- Thread skewers with onion, pepper, mushrooms and pineapple pieces. Cook on oiled, preheated grill over medium fire for about 5 to 10 minutes per side until tender.

- Thread shrimp on skewers and cook over same fire for about 3 to 5 minutes per side until shrimp turn pink. Serves 4.

Glazed Shrimp Kebabs

Serve with margaritas!

2 - 3 limes
¼ cup (½ stick) butter, melted
½ cup honey
2 teaspoons curry powder
1½ pounds large shrimp, cleaned, peeled, veined

- Squeeze ¼ cup lime juice in small mixing bowl with melted butter. Add honey and curry powder and stir to mix.

- Thread shrimp on skewers. Cook on oiled grill over medium heat about 3 minutes per side until grill marks appear and shrimp are pink. Brush generously with glaze while grilling. Serves 4.

$ave Money! *Drink more water and less soft drinks. Simple and cost effective.*

Shrimp Kebabs with Beer Sop

Veggies:

1 (16 ounce) package grape or roma tomatoes
1 - 2 sweet onions, quartered
3 - 4 bell peppers, seeded, quartered

- Place tomatoes, onions and bell peppers on individual skewers to cook separately. Cook on oiled grill or foil over medium fire. Cook onions and bell pepper about 8 minutes per side and tomatoes about 3 to 5 minutes per side, until all are tender.

Shrimp Beer Sop:

1 (12 ounce) bottle or can beer
2 tablespoons oil
1 tablespoon Worcestershire sauce
¼ teaspoon hot sauce
2 cloves garlic, minced
2 pounds shrimp with tails, peeled, veined
Butter
Cocktail sauce

- Pour beer, oil, Worcestershire sauce, hot sauce and garlic in large sealable plastic bag and shake to mix. Add shrimp and refrigerate for 30 minutes; turn several times.

- Skewer shrimp through neck and tail and cook for about 3 minutes per side until they turn pink. Serve veggie and shrimp kebabs immediately with melted butter and cocktail sauce. Serves 6 to 8.

Shrimp with Basil Pesto

1 (6 ounce) jar basil pesto
2 pounds fresh shrimp with tails, peeled, veined

- Rub shrimp liberally with pesto and refrigerate for about 30 minutes. Cook shrimp on preheated, oiled grill over medium-hot fire until shrimp turn pink, about 3 to 5 minutes per side. Serves 4.

TIP: See recipe for Homemade Basil Pesto on page 308.

Soft Shrimp Tacos

1 pound small shrimp, shelled, veined
1 tablespoon taco seasoning
Flour tortillas
Shredded Mexican 4-cheese blend
Lettuce
Taco sauce or salsa

- Sprinkle shrimp with taco seasoning. Grill shrimp on oiled heavy-duty foil over medium heat for about 3 minutes per side until shrimp turn pink. Wrap in tortillas with cheese, lettuce and taco sauce. Serves 4.

Spicy Bacon Shrimp

1 clove garlic, minced
⅔ cup chili sauce
½ pound thin bacon strips
1 pound medium shrimp, cooked

- Add garlic to chili sauce and set aside for several hours. Broil bacon on 1 side only. Cut in half and drain. Dip shrimp in chili sauce and wrap with ½ bacon strip uncooked side out; fasten with toothpicks.

- Cook shrimp on oiled, preheated grill over medium fire about 3 to 5 minutes per side until bacon is crisp and shrimp turn pink. Serves 2.

Beef and pork aren't porous enough for marinades to penetrate very far into the meat, so sometimes they marinate overnight. Chicken and turkey are more porous and do not need to be soaked for a long time. Fish soaks up marinades quickly and thoroughly and marinades should be used sparingly.

Bacon-Wrapped Shrimp

12 - 16 medium - large shrimp, shelled, veined
1 bunch cilantro
1 large purple onion, thinly sliced
6 - 8 slices bacon, halved

- Take vein out of back of shrimp and make deeper cut down same area, but don't go all the way through. Open shrimp with hands, lay several pieces of cilantro and onion on 1 side of butterflied shrimp and close.

- Broil bacon in oven on 1 side. Wrap bacon around each shrimp, cooked side next to shrimp, and secure with toothpick. Cook on oiled grill over medium heat until bacon cooks and shrimp turn pink, about 3 to 5 minutes per side. Serves 2 to 4.

Quick Grilled Shrimp with Barbecue Sauce

1 (1 pound) package sliced bacon
3 - 4½ pounds fresh shrimp, peeled, veined
1 (14 ounce) jar barbecue sauce

- Cut bacon slices in half and wrap each half tightly around each shrimp. Place all shrimp on metal skewers and place on preheated, oiled grill over medium-low fire.

- Cook several minutes on each side, baste with barbecue sauce and cook several minutes more until shrimp turn pink and bacon cooks. Barbecue sauce may make fire flame, so watch carefully. Baste with remaining sauce before serving. Serves 6 to 8.

You need about ¾ pound fresh shrimp with peels and
½ pound without peels to feed one person.

Lemon-Garlic Shrimp

Great combination for shrimp.

2 pounds shrimp, shelled, veined
¼ cup (½ stick) butter, melted
¼ cup shredded parmesan cheese
2 tablespoons lemon juice
2 - 3 cloves garlic, pressed

- Cook shrimp on oiled grill over medium heat for about
  3 minutes per side until shrimp turn pink.

- Mix butter, parmesan, lemon juice and garlic in small bowl.
  Remove shrimp from grill and place in large bowl. Pour sauce
  over shrimp and stir to coat well. Serves 3 to 4.

Tropical Shrimp and Scallops Skewers

1 pound medium shrimp, veined, shelled
1 pound scallops
1 large lime
1 large lemon
1 large orange

- Put shrimp and scallops on skewers and place in glass dish.
  Mix juices of lime, lemon and orange and pour over seafood.
  Refrigerate for about 30 minutes; drain well.

- Cook on oiled grill or foil over medium heat for about 3 to
  4 minutes per side until shrimp turn pink and scallops are
  tender. Serves 4.

---

*Direct heat for grilling refers to food cooked directly
over the heat source. Indirect heat refers to food cooked
away from the heat source. With wood fires, move food
away from the fire for indirect heating. For gas grills,
light both sides of gas burners to preheat grill. Turn one
side off and place food on it for indirect heating.*

Scallop Kebabs

1 pound fresh or frozen (thawed) scallops
1 (15 ounce) can pineapple chunks, drained
1 (12 ounce) carton button mushrooms
1 green bell pepper
¼ cup canola oil
¼ cup lemon juice
¼ cup soy sauce
12 slices bacon, optional

- Place scallops and pineapple in bowl. Remove stems from mushrooms, cut bell pepper into 1-inch pieces and add to bowl with scallops.

- Mix oil, lemon juice, soy sauce and dash of pepper. Pour over scallops and marinate for about 30 minutes. Drain and discard marinade.

- Fry bacon to partially done and drain well. Cut each slice of bacon in half and wrap around a scallop.

- Run skewer through bacon and scallop and alternate with pineapple and vegetables. Cook on oiled grill over medium fire for about 5 to 8 minutes per side until grill marks show and scallops are opaque. (Do not overcook.) Serves 6.

Easy Grilled Clams

Fresh clams
Butter, melted
Lemon

- Scrub all sand and grit from clams. Place on oiled, preheated grill about 4 to 6 inches from hot coals. Turn clams after 4 minutes and continue to cook until shells open, about 5 minutes longer.

- When shells open, they are ready to eat. Discard clams that do not open. Serve with melted butter and lemon. Serve 6 to 8 clams per person.

Oysters on the Grill

- Wash outside of shells and discard any open shells. Leave oysters in shell and place on oiled grill when fire reaches white ash stage.

- Cover and cook for about 5 minutes until shells open. Discard any shells that do not open. Serve immediately with *Lemon Butter (recipe on page 290)*. Average 6 to 8 per person.

Frank's Special Grilled Oysters

- Use recipe for *Oysters on the Grill (page 282)*. Instead of lemon butter, place oysters on crackers and top with Frank's® RedHot Buffalo Wings Sauce. Average 6 to 8 per person.

Seafood species are interchangeable in the recipes in this cookbook. Use any species you have available in your area as substitutes for those called for in recipes.

$ave Money! *Buy generics. Store brands are usually of similar quality to name brands. Don't let more appealing packaging convince you to spend more when the items taste the same.*

Grilled Rock Lobster Tails

This is a special occasion treat when lobster is on sale. Just be patient and wait for the sale. It's worth it.

4 (6 - 10 ounce) rock lobster tails, thawed
1 cup (2 sticks) butter
Tabasco® Pepper Sauce

- Use kitchen shears to cut down center of soft lobster underbelly to 1 inch from tail. Do not cut through. Use fingers to separate meat from shell on sides and pull up meat a little. Push shell together underneath so meat sits on top.

- Make shallow cuts down center of lobster in 2 or 3 places so more meat shows and lays out. Run skewer through lobster to keep it from curling up. Melt butter in small saucepan and add several drops of Tabasco®. Use about *one-third* to baste while cooking.

- Baste lobster meat well and cook, shell side down, on oiled grill over medium heat with lid closed for about 10 to 15 minutes until meat is completely opaque and flakes with fork. Baste several times and serve with melted butter. Serves 4.

Lemon-Garlic Basted Lobster Tails

4 (6 - 10 ounce) rock lobster tails, thawed
1 cup (2 sticks) butter
2 - 3 cloves garlic, pressed
2 tablespoons minced parsley
1 teaspoon lemon juice

- Prepare lobster as in recipe for *Grilled Rock Lobster Tails (page 283)*. Melt butter and add garlic, parsley and lemon juice in small saucepan and infuse sauce into meat with liquid injector. Cook as in recipe for *Grilled Rock Lobster Tails (page 283)*. Serves 4.

Oriental Grilled Lobster Tails

4 (6 - 10 ounce) rock lobster tails, thawed
1 (6 ounce) can pineapple juice
1 - 2 teaspoons soy sauce
1 cup (2 sticks) butter, melted

- Prepare lobster as in recipe for *Grilled Rock Lobster Tails (page 283)*. Mix pineapple juice and soy sauce and baste lobster while cooking as in recipe for *Grilled Rock Lobster Tails (page 283)*. Serve with melted butter. Serves 4.

Celebration Lobster

Unless you live on the coast, lobster is rare on most tables. There is a time, however, when we throw caution to the wind (or frozen lobster tails are on sale) and celebrate with grilled lobster tail.

4 - 6 (8 - 10 ounce) frozen lobster tails, thawed
1 cup (2 sticks) butter
2 - 3 lemons, sliced

- Let thawed lobster stand at room temperature for about 20 minutes. Split thin shell on inside lengthwise down middle, but don't cut all the way through. Open shell and lay cut side down on oiled grill.

- Cook over medium fire for about 5 minutes and turn with shell side down to hold juices. Remove from grill when meat is opaque. Serve immediately with melted butter and lemon slices. Serves 4 to 6.

When making sauces, cook ingredients uncovered to thicken sauce and reduce to desired consistency.

Game

If you're tired of the same old game dishes,
you'll enjoy these great tasting recipes.

Grilled Jalapeno-Stuffed Doves

Marinade:

¾ cup vinegar
¼ cup Worcestershire sauce
½ cup sugar
2 teaspoons garlic powder
1 teaspoon seasoned salt
1 cup canola oil

- Combine all marinade ingredients in large glass bowl or baking dish and set aside.

Doves:

8 - 10 doves, cleaned
5 - 6 jalapenos, seeded, halved
1 (1 pound) package colby cheese, sliced
8 - 10 slices bacon

- Slice breasts off dove and drop in marinade. Cover bowl, refrigerate and marinate for 24 hours. Mix marinade and dove breasts several times to blend ingredients.

- Remove dove breasts from marinade and drain; discard marinade. Make a "sandwich" using one breast, one jalapeno half, one slice cheese and one breast together. Wrap with one slice bacon and secure with toothpick.

- Place on oiled grill over medium fire and cook until bacon is crispy, about 15 to 20 minutes, and internal temperature of dove is 165°. Turn several times while grilling. Serves 8 as appetizers and 4 as main dish.

Bacon-Wrapped Grilled Dove

10 - 12 doves, dressed
Worcestershire sauce
5 - 6 slices bacon, halved

- Sprinkle doves with Worcestershire, salt and pepper. Wrap each dove in ½ slice bacon and secure with toothpick.

- Cook on oiled, preheated grill over medium heat about 20 to 30 minutes until juices are clear and internal temperature reaches 165°. Turn occasionally. Serves 4 to 6.

Marinated Grilled Pheasant, Dove or Quail

1 cup canola oil
½ cup white wine
½ cup Worcestershire sauce
2 tablespoons vinegar
2 teaspoons sugar
4 cloves garlic, minced
½ cup minced onion
2 (2 pound) dressed pheasants, halved

- Combine all ingredients except pheasant with 2 teaspoons pepper in flat glass dish and mix well. Place pheasant halves in dish, turn in marinade several times and marinate for 3 hours. Drain and discard marinade.

- Sear outside of birds on oiled, preheated grill over medium-high heat. Reduce heat or move to indirect heat.

- Continue to cook slowly over low heat for about 5 to 8 minutes, turn once, until juices are clear and internal temperature is 165°. Serves 4.

$ave Money! *Look at the top and bottom of grocery shelves for the best deals. Store brands are usually at the top.*

Bacon-Grilled Duck Breasts

1 (10 ounce) can cream of onion soup
½ cup ketchup
¼ cup (½ stick) butter
4 drops hot sauce
2 cloves garlic, minced
2 ribs celery, sliced
8 wild duck breast halves, boned
8 slices bacon

- Combine soup, ketchup, butter, hot sauce, garlic, ¼ teaspoon each of salt and pepper, celery and ½ cup water. Bring mixture to a boil, reduce heat and simmer for 30 minutes. Cool.

- Wrap each breast half with slice of bacon and secure with toothpick. Cover breasts with sauce and marinate for 3 hours in refrigerator. Allow breasts to reach room temperature. Pour remaining sauce into saucepan and bring to a boil; set aside.

- Cook breasts on oiled, preheated grill over medium-low coals for about 5 to 8 minutes on each side until juices are clear and internal temperature is 165°. Pour boiled marinade over birds and serve immediately. Serves 8.

Dijon Quail

8 quail, dressed
½ cup Dijon-style mustard
⅔ cup dry white wine
⅓ cup olive oil
2 teaspoons dried thyme

- Sprinkle quail with a little salt and pepper. Mix mustard, wine, oil and thyme in bowl. Cook quail on oiled grill over medium fire for about 5 minutes.

- Baste liberally, turn and continue to cook about 3 to 5 minutes until internal temperature reaches 165° and juices are clear. Serves 4.

Wild Turkey Breast Bites

1½ - 2 pounds turkey breast
¼ cup deli-style hot mustard
1 tablespoon honey
2 tablespoons brown sugar
1 tablespoon balsamic vinegar

- Cut breast and surrounding meat from turkey and slice into 2 to 3-inch pieces.

- Mix mustard, honey, brown sugar and balsamic vinegar in bowl. Place turkey in sealable bag and pour mustard mixture into bag. Marinate overnight in refrigerator.

- Cook on oiled grill over medium heat for about 3 to 5 minutes per side until juices are clear and internal temperature is 165°. Serves 4.

Wild Turkey Bacon Bites

- Use recipe for *Wild Turkey Breast Bites (page 288)*. After removing turkey from marinade, wrap each piece of breast meat with half slice of bacon. Cook as recipe directs. Serves 4.

Grilled Venison Back Strap

1 (2 pound) venison back strap (loin)
Oil
2 large onions, sliced
4 slices bacon
Barbecue sauce

- Rub back strap with oil, salt and pepper. Add onion on top of back strap and wrap bacon around both. Secure with toothpicks.

- Cook slowly on oiled grill over medium low fire for about 10 to 15 minutes per side until most pink is gone and internal temperature is at least 160°. Cut in ¼-inch slices and serve with barbecue sauce and sliced onions. Serves 4 to 6.

Smoked Venison Ham or Roast

1 (4 - 6 pound) venison ham or roast
4 - 5 cloves garlic, pressed
¼ cup canned jalapeno slices

- Cut small slits all over ham and insert pieces of garlic and jalapenos in each. Rub thoroughly with salt and pepper.

- Cook on oiled grill over oak wood fire and water pan away from direct heat for 3 hours at about 250°. Baste well with sauce below. Remove from grill, wrap in foil and cook in oven baking dish at about 300° for another 2 hours until tender. Serves about 10.

Basting Sauce:

1 cup red wine
⅔ cup red wine vinegar
Juice of 2 - 3 limes
½ cup (1 stick) butter, melted
2 - 3 cloves garlic, pressed
1 tablespoon hot sauce

- Mix all ingredients and 1 teaspoon salt. Divide into 2 bowls. Baste venison ham well with half sauce while on grill. Pour all remaining sauce over venison in its foil wrapping before cooking in oven.

Venison Jerky

Any of the beef jerky recipes on page 173 work well with venison. One of the best spice mixes is Hi-Country Jerky Spice Kit, Original Flavor.

Grilled Rack of Lamb

2 (6 - 8 rib) racks of lamb, trimmed
Rosemary
Thyme

- Rub lamb with salt and pepper and stuff rosemary and thyme in cuts of meat.

- Cook on oiled grill over medium fire for about 10 to 15 minutes per side until internal temperature is at least 145°. Serves 4.

Sauces, Marinades, Rubs and More

Barbecue has more sauces and
marinades than most food categories.
Find your special "secret" sauce right here.

Fast, Easy Basting Butters

Use these butters to baste fish, pork, chicken and vegetables
while cooking. If you have a burner attached to your grill, it's
very easy to melt butter while you're grilling. Choose any of the
combinations below for a real flavor boost.

• Combine all ingredients with wooden spoon, blender or mixer.
  Place mixture on parchment or wax paper and roll into log
  shape. Wrap paper around log and twist ends together to
  seal. Refrigerate for up to 1 month or freeze for up to 3 months.
  Makes 1 cup.

Lemon Butter

½ cup (1 stick) unsalted butter,
    softened
2 tablespoons lemon juice
1 teaspoon lemon zest
Salt and pepper

Cilantro Butter

½ cup (1 stick) unsalted butter,
    softened
3 - 4 cloves garlic, crushed
¼ - ⅓ cup snipped cilantro
Juice of 1 lemon
½ teaspoon kosher salt
Fresh ground black pepper

Continued next page...

Continued from previous page...

Dijon Butter

½ cup (1 stick) unsalted butter,
    softened
3 tablespoons dijon-style
    mustard
1 - 2 tablespoons minced green
    onions
2 teaspoons lemon juice

Pistachio Butter

½ cup (1 stick) butter, softened
¼ - ⅓ cup crushed pistachios

Butter-Gorgonzola Baste

½ cup (1 stick) unsalted butter,
    softened
2 tablespoons shredded
    gorgonzola cheese
½ teaspoon sea salt

Bacon-Butter Baste

½ cup (1 stick) unsalted butter,
    softened
¼ cup chopped pecans
¼ cup crushed, crispy bacon or
    real bacon bits

Fresh Herb Butter Baste

½ cup (1 stick) unsalted butter,
    softened
2 tablespoons minced fresh
    green onions with tops
1 tablespoon snipped parsley
½ teaspoon sea salt

Fresh Onion Butter

½ cup (1 stick) unsalted butter,
    softened
½ cup red wine
3 green onions with tops,
    minced
1 teaspoon dried parsley
Salt and pepper

Honey Butter

½ cup (1 stick) unsalted butter,
    softened
¼ cup honey

Chile-Lime Butter

½ cup (1 stick) unsalted butter,
    softened
2 tablespoons diced green
    chilies
1 tablespoon lime juice
½ teaspoon sea salt

Sun-Dried Tomato Butter

½ cup (1 stick) unsalted butter,
    softened
¼ cup diced sun-dried tomato
1 teaspoon crushed basil
½ teaspoon kosher salt,
    optional

Continued next page...

Continued from previous page...

Garlic-Basil Butter

½ cup (1 stick) unsalted butter,
    softened
1 tablespoon minced or
    crushed garlic
1 teaspoon minced basil

Poblano Butter

½ cup (1 stick) unsalted butter,
    softened
¼ cup diced poblano chilies
½ teaspoon sea salt

Chipotle Butter

½ cup (1 stick) unsalted butter,
    softened
2 chipotles in adobo sauce,
    minced
1 teaspoon minced cilantro
1 teaspoon lime juice
½ teaspoon sea salt

Lemon-Garlic Butter

½ cup (1 stick) unsalted butter,
    softened
1 clove garlic, crushed
2 tablespoon lemon juice
½ teaspoon lemon zest
¼ teaspoon fresh cracked
    pepper

Butter-Pecan Spread

½ cup (1 stick) unsalted butter,
    softened, softened
¼ cup finely chopped pecans
½ teaspoon kosher salt,
    optional

Peach Butter

2 pounds peaches, pitted

- Peel or parboil peaches and remove skin. Place in large saucepan with one-third amount of water to peaches. Simmer to soften peaches; stir frequently. Puree in food processor or blender.

- Pour into baking pan and bake, uncovered, at 325° for 30 minutes. Remove from oven, stir well and continue to bake, stirring every 10 to 15 minutes, until mixture is thick and reddish amber color. Makes about 4 pints.

Tomato Butter

½ cup (1 stick) butter, softened
2 tablespoons tomato paste
¼ teaspoon sugar

- Process butter, tomato paste, sugar and ½ teaspoon salt in blender until light and fluffy. Refrigerate. Makes about ½ cup.

Basic Barbecue Rub

This basic rub is great with chicken, pork, beef and vibrant fish steaks.

¼ cup packed brown sugar
¼ cup kosher or sea salt
¼ cup Hungarian paprika
¼ cup black pepper
1 tablespoon garlic salt
1 tablespoon onion flakes
1 - 2 teaspoons cayenne pepper

- Mix all ingredients and rub liberally over outside of meat before cooking. Let meat rest at room temperature with rub for at least 20 minutes before cooking. Makes about 1 cup.

Easy Ready-Rub

Great for beef or pork roasts.

½ cup salt
½ cup garlic salt
¼ cup garlic powder
¼ cup pepper

- Combine all ingredients in airtight container. Apply at least 30 minutes before cooking. Makes 1½ cups.

One of the easiest ways to enhance flavors of grilled meats and vegetables is to add compound butters at the end of cooking.

Barbecue Dry Rub

¼ cup paprika
2 - 3 tablespoons light brown sugar
2 tablespoons chili powder
2 tablespoons cracked black pepper
1 tablespoon cayenne pepper
1 tablespoon ground cumin
1 - 2 tablespoons garlic powder
1 tablespoon celery salt
1 - 2 teaspoons dry mustard

- Combine all ingredients with 1 tablespoon salt in bowl and mix thoroughly. Rub mixture into meat of your choice and wrap in plastic wrap. Refrigerate for several hours or overnight. Makes 1 cup.

Brisket Dry Rub

Great for brisket and heavier beef cuts.

½ cup dried, ground red chile peppers or chili powder
¼ teaspoon paprika
¼ cup freshly ground black pepper
3 tablespoons garlic salt
¼ cup sugar
1 tablespoon dry mustard
1 teaspoon oregano

- Mix all ingredients in large bowl. Rub into beef at least 1 hour before cooking. Cover all sides of brisket with seasonings. Makes about 1 cup.

You can grill almost anything: beef, chicken, turkey, pork, seafood, game, lamb, vegetables, fruits, breads and even cheese. (Look for cheese especially for grilling.)

Louisiana Cajun Rub

½ cup kosher or sea salt
¼ cup black pepper
¼ cup paprika
1 - 2 tablespoons cayenne
1 tablespoon celery salt
1 tablespoon onion flakes
1 teaspoon crumbled bay leaf
1 teaspoon dried thyme

- Mix all ingredients and rub liberally over outside of meat
  before cooking. Wrap in plastic wrap and refrigerate overnight
  or let meat rest at room temperature with rub for at least
  20 minutes before cooking. Makes about 1 cup.

Blue Blazes Brisket Rub

Chipotle peppers are dried jalapenos and are wonderful.

4 chipotle peppers, stemmed, seeded, ground
2 ancho chile peppers, stemmed, seeded, ground
½ cup sea salt or coarse salt
3 tablespoons cracked black pepper
3 tablespoons garlic powder
2 tablespoons paprika
1 tablespoon ground cumin
1 tablespoon dried oregano

- Combine all ingredients in bowl and whisk well. Store in
  air-tight jar. Sprinkle on briskets and heavy beef cuts several
  hours before cooking. Sprinkle on steaks just before grilling.
  Use sparingly for chicken. Makes about 1 cup.

*Dry rubs are mixes of various seasonings applied to
meat before it cooks. Rubs are applied very liberally
and usually coat the outside of the meat.*

No-Nonsense Texas Rub

Authentic Texas-style rubs don't use sugar.

½ cup kosher or sea salt
½ cup cracked black pepper
¼ cup chili powder
2 tablespoons cayenne pepper
2 tablespoons garlic salt
1 tablespoon cumin
1 tablespoon paprika

- Mix all ingredients and use liberally over meats. Let meat stand at room temperature for about 20 to 30 minutes before cooking. Rub will keep in airtight container for 4 to 6 weeks. Makes about 1½ cups.

Rosemary-Thyme Rub

Great with beef roasts and steaks.

¼ cup kosher or sea salt
¼ cup dried rosemary
2 tablespoons dried oregano
1 tablespoon onion flakes
1 tablespoon dried sage
1 teaspoon garlic salt

- Mix all ingredients and add 1 tablespoon pepper. Rub liberally over outside of meat before cooking. Let meat rest at room temperature with rub for at least 20 minutes before cooking. Makes about 1 cup.

Parsley-Pepper Rub with Dijon

Great for pork or chicken.

½ cup chopped fresh parsley
¼ cup dijon-style mustard
2 tablespoons cracked peppercorns
3 - 4 cloves garlic, minced

- Combine all ingredients and add salt to taste. Rub mixture into meat and refrigerate about 1 hour. Let meat reach room temperature before grilling. Makes about ½ cup.

Southwest Seasoning Mix

This mix is great on vegetables, tossed salads, roast beef, grilled chicken, seafood or pork. Use sparingly.

3 tablespoons ground red chilies
2 tablespoons paprika
1 tablespoon ground coriander
1 tablespoon dried parsley, crushed
1 tablespoon ground cumin
1 teaspoon dried oregano leaves, crushed
¼ teaspoon cayenne pepper
¾ teaspoon garlic powder

- Mix all ingredients plus 1 teaspoon salt in bowl well. Store in air-tight container.

Dry Rub for Pork

This is exceptionally good on pork tenderloin.

1 teaspoon chili powder
1 teaspoon ground cumin
1 teaspoon Italian seasoning
1 teaspoon garlic powder
1 tablespoon oil

- Combine all seasonings plus 1 teaspoon salt and mix in oil. Rub all over tenderloin. Makes ¼ cup.

Pork Rub

1 cup seasoned salt
1 cup lemon-pepper
½ cup garlic salt

- Combine these ingredients for the best rub around. Store in airtight container. Makes 2½ cups.

Quick Ham Glaze

½ cup packed brown sugar
¼ cup vinegar
2 tablespoons dry mustard

- Combine all ingredients and spread over ham in last few minutes of grilling. Makes about ½ cup.

Golden Citrus Glaze

This will give chicken a golden brown glaze that's wonderful.

1 (6 ounce) can frozen pineapple-grapefruit juice
    concentrate, thawed
¼ teaspoon ginger
3 tablespoons lemon juice
6 tablespoons butter

- Combine all ingredients and baste while grilling. Discard unused glaze. Makes about 1 cup.

Simple Meat Marinade

1 (12 ounce) bottle or can beer
¼ cup snipped parsley
⅓ cup soy sauce
1 tablespoon minced garlic

- Mix all ingredients and pour over meat. Cover and marinate beef in refrigerator overnight; chicken about 30 minutes. Turn meat several times. Allow meat to reach room temperature before grilling. Discard marinade before cooking. Makes 1¾ cups.

> *Marinades are mixtures of a liquid and seasonings to enhance the flavor of foods before it cooks on the grill. The simplest marinade is oil, salt, pepper and other seasonings. Foods need to soak in marinades for minutes to overnight (depending on the type of food) so flavors infuse into the food.*

Four-Herb Marinade

Great with beef or chicken.

4 - 5 lemons
1 teaspoon sea salt
1 teaspoon cracked black pepper
1 tablespoon ground, dried red chile flakes
4 cloves garlic, minced
½ cup cilantro, minced
¼ cup fresh oregano
¼ cup fresh basil
¼ cup fresh chives
½ cup extra virgin olive oil

- Juice lemons to equal ⅓ cup and pour in bowl. Add sea salt and whisk until salt dissolves. Add all remaining ingredients and whisk thoroughly.

- Use immediately. Marinate for several hours for beef and 30 minutes for chicken. Discard marinade before cooking. Makes 1½ cups.

Best Marinade Ever

Put this on just about everything.

½ cup extra virgin olive oil
¼ cup lemon juice
¼ cup chopped cilantro
¼ cup chopped parsley
4 cloves garlic, pressed
1 teaspoon cayenne pepper
1 teaspoon lemon zest
½ teaspoon sea salt

- Mix all ingredients in bowl and stir well. Pour over meats and marinate in refrigerator for about 1 hour. (To baste with same marinade, set aside enough for basting later.) Discard marinade before cooking. Makes about 1 cup.

Lemon-Beer Marinade

This goes well with chicken, beef and fish.

¼ cup (½ stick) butter
2 tablespoons minced garlic
1 bunch green onions with tops, chopped
1 (12 ounce) bottle beer
1 cup packed brown sugar
1 orange
1 lemon
1 lime
¼ cup teriyaki sauce
1 tablespoon fresh chopped parsley

- Heat butter in skillet and saute garlic and green onions until translucent. Add beer, brown sugar, juice from 1 orange, juice from 1 lemon, juice from 1 lime and teriyaki sauce. Simmer for 2 minutes, remove from heat and set aside to cool before using. (Do not boil.)

- For chicken, marinate meat for about 45 minutes. For beef, use as a basting sop or marinate for about 1 hour 30 minutes. For fish, marinate for about 10 minutes. Discard marinade before cooking. Makes 2½ cups.

Amber-Citrus Marinade

2 (12 ounce) bottles amber ale
1 tablespoon red wine vinegar
2 tablespoons orange juice
1 teaspoon orange zest
½ cup canola oil
1 tablespoon horseradish sauce
½ cup minced onion
3 - 4 cloves garlic, minced
1 - 2 teaspoons cayenne pepper

- Puree all ingredients in blender. Set aside 1 cup for basting meat while cooking. Marinate beef or lamb in refrigerator for several hours before cooking. Discard marinade before cooking or grilling. Makes about 1 quart.

Steak Marinade

3 cloves garlic
3 tablespoons olive oil
3 teaspoons soy sauce
Dash Worcestershire sauce

- Chop garlic and let stand in olive oil for 30 minutes. Remove garlic; add soy sauce and Worcestershire sauce. Pour over steak and permit meat to marinate in sauce for 2 hours. Discard marinade before cooking. Makes about ¼ cup.

Ginger-Lime Marinade

Great with pork.

⅓ cup soy sauce
⅓ cup olive oil
1 tablespoon crystallized ginger, finely chopped
1 tablespoon lime juice
Few drops garlic juice from pressed garlic clove

- Mix all ingredients and pour over pork loin. Marinate several hours in refrigerator. Discard marinade before cooking. Makes about 1 cup.

Homer's Best Beef Marinade

Use this marinade on any beef you plan to grill or smoke.

1 cup red wine
2 teaspoons Worcestershire sauce
2 teaspoons garlic powder
1 cup canola oil
¼ cup ketchup
2 teaspoons sugar
2 tablespoons vinegar
1 teaspoon marjoram
1 teaspoon rosemary

- Mix all ingredients with 1 teaspoon salt in bowl and stir well. Marinate beef for several hours before cooking. Discard marinade before cooking. Makes about 2 cups.

Light Vinegar and Oil Marinade

This is great for a light marinade on beef.

2 cloves garlic, minced
⅔ cup soy sauce
¼ cup canola or virgin olive oil
¼ cup packed light brown sugar
2 tablespoons red wine vinegar

- Mix all ingredients and marinate beef for 1 to 2 hours. Discard marinade before cooking. Makes about 1 cup.

Chiquita's Fajita Marinade

1 (8 ounce) bottle Italian salad dressing
1 (12 ounce) bottle beer
Juice of 3 limes
1 medium onion, minced
3 cloves garlic, minced
3 tablespoons chili powder
2 tablespoons lemon pepper
1 tablespoon Worcestershire sauce
2 teaspoons ground cumin
1 teaspoon cayenne pepper

- Pour salad dressing and beer in 1-quart jar. Add remaining ingredients and shake vigorously. Pour over fajita meat and refrigerate for at least 8 hours. Turn several times while marinating. Discard marinade when ready to grill. Makes about 3 cups.

Lamb Chop Marinade

You may wish to double this recipe

¼ cup oil
1 tablespoon lemon juice
1 small bay leaf
1 teaspoon chopped parsley
1 clove garlic
1 small onion, sliced

- Combine oil, lemon juice, 1 teaspoon salt, ½ teaspoon pepper, bay leaf and parsley. Mash garlic or put through press. Add garlic and onion to marinade.

- Pour marinade over 2 lamb chops and refrigerate at least 3 hours. Turn once or twice. Discard marinade before cooking. Makes about ½ cup.

Marinade Sauce

1½ cups canola oil
¾ cup soy sauce
¼ cup Worcestershire sauce
2 tablespoons dry mustard
½ cup wine vinegar
1½ teaspoons parsley flakes
2 cloves garlic, crushed
⅓ cup fresh lemon juice

- Combine oil, soy sauce, Worcestershire sauce, dry mustard, vinegar, parsley flakes, garlic, lemon juice and ¼ teaspoon salt and mix well. Cover meat with marinade and refrigerate several hours.

- Before cooking, drain off all liquids and allow meat to come to room temperature before grilling. Discard marinade before cooking. Makes 3½ cups.

$ave Money! *Don't waste leftovers!*

Basting Sauce

⅓ cup wine vinegar
⅓ cup fresh lemon juice
⅓ cup corn or olive oil
½ teaspoon soy sauce
Coarsely ground black pepper

• Combine vinegar, lemon juice and oil in bowl. Add soy sauce
  and black pepper to taste. Use brush or wooden spoon with
  small towel wrapped around it to sop on basting sauce while
  cooking. Makes about 1 cup.

Marinade for Steaks or Burgers

This is good for filets, minute steaks and hamburgers.

1 cup olive oil
2 teaspoons minced parsley
¼ teaspoon marjoram
1 onion, chopped
Juice of 1 lemon
1 clove garlic, crushed

• Combine olive oil, ½ teaspoon black pepper, parsley, marjoram,
  onion, lemon juice, thyme garlic and 1 teaspoon salt in bowl.
  Allow steak to marinate in mixture for several hours. Discard
  marinade before cooking. Makes about 1¼ cups.

$ave Money! Pay attention while checking out at the
grocery store. Make sure sales items and coupons scan
correctly. Also, make sure things aren't mistakenly
scanned multiple times. Checkers are humans too and
accidents happen.

Homemade Salsa

This is great over grilled chicken, pork, beef and even vegetables.

3 large tomatoes, peeled, seeded, chopped
3 - 4 fresh green chilies, roasted, seeded, minced
2 cloves garlic, minced
1 jalapeno chile, seeded, minced
1 bunch green onions with tops, minced
1 bunch fresh cilantro, snipped
½ teaspoon cumin

- Mix all ingredients and a little salt and pepper in large bowl
  and refrigerate for several hours for flavors to blend. Serve
  in small bowls with chips or over meat or vegetables. Makes
  about 1½ cups.

Pineapple Salsa

Great with grilled pork chops.

1 (20 ounce) can pineapple tidbits, drained
¼ cup balsamic vinegar
⅓ cup maple syrup
2 tablespoons Asian sesame oil

- Combine pineapple, vinegar, maple syrup and oil in bowl.
  Bring mixture to a boil, lower heat and simmer for 5 minutes.
  Makes 3 cups.

Texas Hot Chunky Salsa

2 quarts (about 12) peeled, cored, chopped, ripe tomatoes
1 large white onion, chopped
4 - 5 large jalapenos, seeded, chopped
½ cup sugar
1¾ cups vinegar

- Combine all ingredients in large saucepan, add 1½ tablespoons
  salt and cook on low for about 25 minutes; stir frequently.
  Makes about 6 pints.

Chunky Salsa

3 pounds tomatoes, blanched, peeled, diced
1 green bell pepper, cored, diced
1 red bell pepper, cored, diced
1 large white onion, diced
½ large bunch cilantro, minced
1 - 2 tablespoons minced garlic
2 teaspoons ground cumin
1½ cups apple cider (5% acidity) vinegar
⅓ cup lemon juice

- Combine all ingredients in large saucepan and bring to a
  boil. Reduce heat and simmer for about 10 minutes. Makes
  about 4 pints.

Pico de Gallo

1 whole jalapeno, seeded, diced*
½ cup minced fresh cilantro
1 bunch green onions with tops, chopped
2 large tomatoes, chopped, drained
Juice of 2 limes
½ teaspoon garlic salt
½ teaspoon seasoned salt

- Stir together all ingredients and ¼ teaspoon pepper or to taste.
  Cover and refrigerate to blend flavors.

- Serve with tortilla chips, over guacamole salad or with grilled
  meats or fish. Makes about 1 cup.

*TIP: Wear rubber gloves when removing seeds from jalapenos.

For the best results, make sure that meat is at room
temperature before grilling.

Classic Guacamole

Traditional guacamole is mashed with a fork to get the right chunky texture. It is simple, fresh and unbelievably good.

4 - 5 ripe avocados
1 lemon
1 tomato, peeled, seeded, diced, drained
2 green onions with tops, minced
½ - 1 teaspoon minced garlic

- Peel, remove seeds and mash avocados in bowl with fork. Squeeze juice of lemon over avocados and mix well.

- Add tomato, green onions and garlic and mix thoroughly. Add salt to taste. Serve on bed of lettuce as individual salads or with chips as an appetizer. Serves 4.

Onion Relish

This is a gorgeous amber color and is delicious.

2 pounds large white onions, diced
1 cup vinegar
1 cup sugar

- Prepare enough diced onions to equal 4 cups. Pour just enough boiling water over onions to cover and let stand 5 minutes; drain.

- Pour vinegar, sugar and ½ teaspoon salt in large saucepan, add onions and simmer for 15 minutes. Makes about 3 pints.

Dad's Favorite Jalapeno Relish

The "hot" factor is totally dependent on mild to hot jalapenos.

2½ pounds jalapenos, cored, seeded, minced
1 pound onions, peeled, minced
3 pods garlic, separated, peeled, minced
¼ cup sugar
1 (16 ounce) bottle vinegar
2 tablespoons mustard seed

- Mix all ingredients in large saucepan and cook over medium heat for 30 minutes. Makes about 6 pints.

Spicy Basil Pesto with Lemon

Great with pork or chicken.

2 cups fresh basil leaves
1 cup shredded parmesan cheese
3 cloves garlic, peeled
½ cup pine nuts, slightly crushed
1 - 2 tablespoons lemon zest
1 - 2 teaspoons red pepper flakes, crushed
½ cup extra-virgin olive oil

- Remove any long stems on basil, wash leaves and dry with paper towels. Coarsely process parmesan, garlic and pine nuts in blender or food processor.

- Add remaining ingredients to mixture and process, while pouring oil into mixture, until entire mixture is coarsely ground.

- Add a little salt and pepper to taste and add more lemon zest or crushed red pepper flakes if needed. Store in refrigerator for up to 2 to 3 days. Makes about 1 cup.

Homemade Basil Pesto

2 cups fresh basil leaves
1 cup shredded parmesan cheese
3 cloves garlic, peeled
½ cup pine nuts, slightly crushed
½ cup extra-virgin olive oil

- Remove any long stems on basil, wash leaves and dry with paper towels. Coarsely process parmesan, garlic and pine nuts in blender or food processor.

- Add basil to mixture and process, while pouring oil into mixture, until it is coarsely ground. Add a little salt and pepper to taste. Store in refrigerator for up to 2 to 3 days. Makes about 1 cup.

Mornay Sauce

Great over seafood or vegetables.

1 tablespoon butter
1 tablespoon flour
1 cup milk
1 egg yolk, beaten
2 tablespoons whipping cream
2 tablespoons shredded Swiss cheese
3 tablespoons grated parmesan cheese

- Melt butter in saucepan, add flour and cook for about 1 minute, stirring constantly. Gradually add milk, ½ teaspoon salt, cook and stir constantly until mixture thickens.

- Combine egg yolk and whipping cream in bowl and very gradually add a little at a time to hot mixture, stirring constantly, until thick. Remove from heat, add cheeses and stir until cheese melts. Makes about 1¼ cups.

Blender Hollandaise Sauce

Great for sauce on vegetables.

½ cup (1 stick) butter
4 egg yolks
2 - 3 tablespoons fresh lemon juice

- Melt butter in small saucepan just enough to melt, but not enough to separate. Place egg yolks, lemon juice and pinch of salt with a dash of pepper in blender and pulse several times.

- Pour butter in slow, thin stream into blender while processing on high speed. Serve immediately. Makes 1 cup.

Basting sauces are used to keep meats moist, add flavor and tenderize to some degree while meats are cooking. They also help to add a brown, crispy glaze to meats. Any sauces with sugar may cause charring and burning and should be applied to the meat toward the end of cooking time.

Cocktail Sauce for Seafood

This is a quick cocktail sauce for any seafood.

3 tablespoons ketchup
1 tablespoon horseradish
1 tablespoon Worcestershire sauce
1 tablespoon lemon juice
¼ tablespoon hot pepper sauce

- Combine all ingredients and refrigerate before serving. Serves 4.

Easy Homemade Tartar Sauce

Great with grilled or fried fish.

3 cups mayonnaise
1 cup minced chopped onion
¾ cup sweet pickle relish
⅓ cup lemon juice

- Combine all ingredients, cover and refrigerate until ready to serve. Makes about 2 cups.

Steaming Garlic Butter

Hot butter sauces make a nice presentation, not to mention the delicate flavors added.

4 - 6 cloves garlic, pressed
½ cup (1 stick) butter

- Saute garlic in butter until it's translucent. Add a little salt and pepper. Makes about ½ cup.

Trim most of the fat off meat. Excess fat drips into fire and can cause flare-ups. If a flare-up occurs, move the food away from the fire until the flare-up dies out. If necessary, take the food off the grill and leave lid open until the flare-up burns out. Never use water on a grease fire; it can cause an explosion.

Hot Tomato-Salsa Butter

2 large tomatoes, peeled, seeded, diced
4 - 6 green onions with tops, chopped
1 fresh jalapeno, stemmed, cored, seeded, diced
⅓ cup chopped cilantro
¾ cup (1½ sticks) butter

- Combine all ingredients in saucepan and cook on low until butter melts. Add a little salt and pepper. Makes about 1 cup.

Caper-Butter Sauce

Wonderful over grilled, sauteed or baked chicken.

2 tablespoons butter
2 tablespoons capers, drained
Juice of ½ lemon
1 cup olive oil, divided
1 teaspoon cornstarch

- Melt butter with capers in saucepan over moderate heat for 1 to 2 minutes. Stir in juice of ½ lemon and olive oil. Continue cooking over moderate heat until just before it boils and reduce heat.

- Add cornstarch to small amount of cold water and stir to dissolve. Add cornstarch to sauce and cook until it is right consistency to pour over grilled, sautéed or baked chicken. Makes 1 cup.

Lemon-Butter Sauce with Capers

Great with grilled chicken or seafood.

½ cup (1 stick) butter
1 (3.5 ounce) jar capers
2 tablespoons lemon juice

- Melt butter in small saucepan, add capers and lemon juice and mix well. Makes about ½ cup.

Asian Sauce

½ cup sesame oil
½ cup corn oil
½ cup plus 2 tablespoons duck sauce
⅓ cup chili-flavored oil
¼ cup soy sauce

• Blend all ingredients well. Makes about 2 cups.

TIP: Duck sauce is easy to find in the Asian foods section at the
     grocery store.

Creamy Cucumber Sauce

This is a nice light sauce for fish, chicken or vegetables.

1 seedless cucumber, peeled, coarsely grated, drained
½ cup plain yogurt
¼ cup finely grated onion, drained
2 teaspoons dill weed

• Combine cucumber, yogurt, grated onion, 2 teaspoons salt and
  dill weed and refrigerate until ready to use. Makes 1 cup.

Currant-Raisin Sauce

Great with ham and pork.

1 cup sugar
1 cup raisins
2 tablespoons butter
3 tablespoons vinegar
½ cup currant jelly
1½ teaspoons Worcestershire sauce
¼ teaspoon ground cloves

• Put sugar and ½ cup water in saucepan and boil. Add
  remaining ingredients and cook 5 minutes until jelly dissolves.
  You can substitute ½ cup red wine for currant jelly. Makes
  about 1 cup.

All-Purpose Barbecue Sauce

Works well on anything grilled.

2 tablespoons butter
1 medium onion, minced
1 small green bell pepper, minced
2 tablespoons brown sugar
2 tablespoons mustard
1 tablespoon Worcestershire sauce
¾ cup ketchup

- Combine butter, onion, bell pepper, brown sugar, mustard, Worcestershire sauce, 1 teaspoon salt and ketchup in pan and simmer 15 minutes. Makes about 1 cup.

Basic Barbecue Sauce

1 (15 ounce) can tomato sauce
1 cup canola oil
½ cup vinegar
½ cup Worcestershire sauce
1 clove garlic, minced
1 small onion, minced

- Combine all ingredients in large bowl and mix well with whisk. Refrigerate until ready to use. Makes 4 cups.

Backyard Barbecue Sauce

This is a great sauce for strong-flavored meats.

1 cup tomato ketchup
¾ cup packed brown sugar
½ cup corn oil (not other vegetable oil)
¼ cup vinegar
3 tablespoons Worcestershire sauce
¼ cup chili powder
1 tablespoon prepared mustard

- Combine all ingredients and stir well. Add a little salt and pepper to taste. Apply to meats during final minutes of cooking. Makes about 1 pint.

Easy Two-Alarm Barbecue Sauce

1 cup Chinese plum sauce
2 teaspoons dry mustard
½ - 1 teaspoon cayenne pepper
8 ounces beer

- Combine all ingredients in saucepan and heat almost to boiling. (Do not boil or beer will become bitter.) Cook on low until sauce thickens a little. Strain to remove lumps. Makes 1½ to 2 cups.

Grandma's Secret Barbecue Sauce

½ cup white vinegar
¼ cup sugar
1½ (32 ounce) cans tomato sauce
1½ (28 ounce) cans whole tomatoes, pureed
1 large onion, minced
½ pound jalapenos, seeded, chopped
3 - 5 cloves garlic, minced

- Combine all ingredients in saucepan with ½ cup water and bring to a boil. Cook on medium for 15 to 30 minutes; stir continuously to prevent scorching or sticking. Store in refrigerator for up to 1 month. Makes about 5 pints.

Old-Style Barbecue Sauce

1 (28 ounce) bottle ketchup
1 (12 ounce) can beer
1 small onion, diced
1½ cups packed dark brown sugar
½ cup prepared mustard
3 tablespoons barbecue seasoning
2 tablespoons distilled white vinegar
1 teaspoon garlic powder

- Combine ketchup, beer, onion, brown sugar, mustard, barbecue seasoning, vinegar and garlic powder. Simmer for several hours and brush onto chicken or beef. Makes about 3 pints.

Range Barbecue Sauce

Works well with pork.

½ cup dill pickle juice
½ cup chili sauce
1 tablespoon Worcestershire
1 teaspoon hot sauce

- Mix all ingredients and baste over pork. Makes about 1 cup.

Raspberry Barbecue Sauce

1 (12 ounce) jar seedless raspberry preserves
½ cup barbecue sauce
2 tablespoons raspberry or cider vinegar
2 tablespoons dijon-style mustard

- Combine all ingredients in bowl. Baste chicken with sauce during last minutes of cooking or spread sauce on chicken before serving. Makes 2 cups.

Rodeo Cowboy Barbecue Sauce

2 onions, finely minced
1 clove garlic, finely minced
¼ cup (½ stick) butter
1 (14 ounce) bottle ketchup
⅓ cup Worcestershire sauce
2 tablespoons canola oil
1 - 3 teaspoons chili powder
½ cup packed brown sugar

- Cook onions and garlic in butter in saucepan until they are translucent. Add ketchup, 1 cup water, Worcestershire sauce and oil and bring almost to a boil, stirring constantly. Reduce heat, add 2 tablespoons salt and chili powder and mix well.

- Slowly add brown sugar while stirring and simmer for about 20 to 30 minutes. Makes 4 cups.

$ave Money! *Always send in your rebates!*

Steak Barbecue Sauce

3 tablespoons dry mustard
3 tablespoons garlic powder
1 teaspoon cayenne pepper
½ teaspoon paprika
½ cup (1 stick) butter
2 tablespoons vinegar
1 tablespoon lemon juice
1 tablespoon Worcestershire sauce

- Mix dry mustard, garlic powder, cayenne pepper, paprika,
  1 tablespoon salt and 2 teaspoons pepper in bowl. Melt
  butter with vinegar, lemon juice and Worcestershire sauce in
  saucepan. Add dry ingredients and let cook 1 minute. Makes
  about 1 cup.

Stout Barbecue Sauce

½ cup molasses
¼ cup mustard
½ cup chili sauce
1 teaspoon Worcestershire sauce
¼ cup onion flakes
½ cup oatmeal stout*

- Combine all ingredients in saucepan and heat, but do not boil.
  Spread over meat and cook as desired. Makes about 1½ cups.

*TIP: Guinness® is the most famous brewer of stout. It is a dark,
    heavy beer that originated in the British Isles. Oatmeal
    stout is sweeter and has a silky-smooth texture.

Put oil or heavy-duty foil on the grill to keep foods from
sticking. You can use a paper towel, a sopping rag or
towel or vegetable such as onion or potato with oil on it
to rub across the grate.

Western Barbecue Sauce

Good with beef, pork and chicken.

1 (5 ounce) bottle Worcestershire sauce
1 cup cider vinegar
¾ cup lemon juice
¼ cup oil
¼ cup packed brown sugar
1 teaspoon garlic salt

- Combine all ingredients plus 2 cups water, 2 teaspoons salt and ½ teaspoon pepper in saucepan over medium-high heat and bring to boil.

- Reduce heat and simmer, uncovered, for about 10 minutes. Use immediately or store in airtight container in refrigerator for 1 to 2 weeks. Makes 2½ cups.

Basic Ranchero Sauce

2 tablespoons butter
1 onion, chopped
½ cup chopped celery
2 cloves garlic, minced
2 jalapeno peppers, seeded, chopped
1 tablespoon Worcestershire sauce
1 (28 ounce) can chopped stewed tomatoes

- Combine all ingredients plus ½ teaspoon salt in saucepan. Heat to boil, reduce heat and simmer for 1 hour until sauce thickens. Serve as is or cool and puree. Makes about 4½ cups.

TIP: Wear rubber gloves when removing seeds from jalapenos.

The best way to tell if meat is done is to insert a meat thermometer in the thickest part of the meat away from a bone. When the meat reaches the right temperature, take it off the grill. It's best not to cut into the meat and let those wonderful juices drip into the fire. (See Cooking Times on pages 8-9.)

Louisiana Red Sauce

¼ cup (½ stick) butter
3 cloves garlic, pressed
½ cup chopped celery
½ cup chopped green onions with tops
1 tablespoon chili powder
1 - 2 tablespoons Louisiana hot sauce
1 (28 ounce) can crushed Italian tomatoes

- In large saucepan, melt butter and sauté garlic, celery and onions until garlic and onions are translucent.

- Add chili powder, hot sauce and crushed tomatoes and bring to a boil. Cook for several minutes and reduce to low. Cook 30 to 45 minutes until sauce thickens. Pour over flank before serving. Makes about 4½ cups.

Peppercorn Sauce

Great with pork.

1 cup olive oil
6 whole peppercorns, crushed
6 cloves garlic, crushed
1 cup lemon juice
Hot sauce

- Blend oil, peppercorns, garlic, lemon juice, 1 tablespoon salt and a dash of hot sauce until smooth. Use for basting pork on grill or in oven. Makes about 2 cups.

Mint Sauce

This has a delightfully fresh taste and is very nice with lamb.

1 tablespoon dried mint
4 tablespoons cider vinegar
1 teaspoon sugar
1 small green onion, chopped

- Muddle dried mint with vinegar until vinegar turns greenish. Add sugar and onion. Let stand for several hours. Use as marinade or baste. Makes about ¼ cup.

Chicken Dipping Sauce

Great for dipping grilled chicken strips.

1 cup prepared barbecue sauce
½ teaspoon mustard
¾ cup apricot preserves

- Place barbecue sauce, mustard and preserves in microwave-safe bowl and microwave on HIGH for 30 seconds until hot; stir occasionally. Makes about 2 cups.

Chili Sauce for Chicken

¾ cup chili sauce
¾ cup packed brown sugar
1 (1 ounce) packet onion soup mix
⅛ teaspoon cayenne pepper

- Combine chili sauce, brown sugar, onion soup mix, cayenne pepper and ¼ cup water in bowl and spoon over chicken. Use as basting sauce for grilling or cover chicken with sauce for roasting. Makes about 1½ cups.

Dipping Sauce for Ham

¾ cup peanut butter
2 tablespoons soy sauce
½ cup honey
3 tablespoons lime juice

- In bowl, combine all dip ingredients and mix well. Cut ham in bite-size chunks and use toothpicks for ham and dip-dip-dip! Makes about 1 cup.

Sops are similar to sauces, but the sop is applied multiple times during the cooking time. Sauces may be brushed on halfway through the cooking process or just before the meat is ready to eat.

Garlic-Parmesan Dressing

This is a great dressing for grilled beef, chicken or pork over spring greens as a main dish.

½ cup olive oil
¼ cup red wine vinegar
½ cup shredded parmesan cheese
2 tablespoons lemon juice
3 cloves garlic, pressed
1 teaspoon red pepper flakes

- Combine all ingredients and stir well before serving. Makes about 1¼ cups.

Horseradish Sauce

This is great with beef.

½ cup mayonnaise
¼ cup prepared horseradish, drained
2 tablespoons light corn syrup
2 tablespoons dry sherry or tarragon vinegar
2 teaspoons prepared mustard

- Combine all ingredients and a little salt and refrigerate before serving. Makes 2 cups.

Grilling with Horseradish

Prepared horseradish may be used to coat all sides of the meat you are planning to grill. With a paper towel, pat dry the meat and then pat on the prepared horseradish. The liquid and the horseradish will keep the meat moist.

It is your option whether you want to eat the horseradish or to scrape it off the grilled meat. Either way, it adds a lot of flavor.

Fresh Horseradish Sauce

Horseradish roots, peeled, cut into chunks
Vinegar
Canned evaporated milk
Sugar

• Grate horseradish in food processor or blender. Add just enough vinegar and canned milk to make paste. For each pint, add 3 teaspoons sugar and 2 teaspoons salt.

Dr Pepper Tastes-Good Sauce

Great for chicken and pork.

2 cloves garlic
2 tablespoons oil
½ cup Dr Pepper®
¼ cup dry mustard
2 tablespoons ketchup
1 tablespoon vinegar
2 tablespoons soy sauce

• Saute garlic in oil; add Dr Pepper®, dry mustard, ketchup, vinegar, soy sauce, 1¼ teaspoons salt and ¼ teaspoon black pepper and stir well. Pour marinade over meat and refrigerate 6 to 24 hours. Turn several times. Makes about 1 cup.

Dr Pepper is the world's oldest major soft drink in the world. It originated at Morrison's Corner Drug Store in Waco, Texas in 1885 when a young pharmacist combined enough syrups and flavors to get a beverage that tasted and smelled right. It was introduced at the 1904 World's Fair in St. Louis. There are 23 fruit flavors in Dr Pepper.

Old-Fashioned Chili Sauce

3 pounds tomatoes, diced
½ large white onion, minced
¾ cup sugar
½ teaspoon nutmeg
½ teaspoon hot pepper sauce
¼ teaspoon curry powder
1 cup vinegar
1 teaspoon ginger
½ teaspoon cinnamon
½ teaspoon dry mustard

- Prepare enough pureed tomatoes to equal 2 quarts. Add all ingredients with 2 teaspoons salt to large saucepan and gently boil for 1 hour; stir frequently to prevent scorching. Makes about 6 pints.

Philly Veggie Sauce

½ cup milk
1 (8 ounce) package light cream cheese, cubed
¼ cup shredded parmesan cheese
½ teaspoon onion powder

- Heat milk and cream cheese over low heat and stir until smooth. Blend in parmesan cheese and onion powder. Serve over hot cooked vegetables. Makes about 1½ cups.

While trying to manufacture Neufchatel cheese in 1872, William Lawrence of Chester, New York accidentally invented cream cheese. He wrapped it in a foil package and gave it the name Philadelphia Brand Cream Cheese in 1880. By 1928 the cheese was well known and James Kraft, who invented pasteurized cheese, bought the brand and the company and pasteurized cream cheese. Today it is the most popular cream cheese used in cheesecakes.

Pineapple Sauce

Great for chicken, pork and ham.

½ cup (1 stick) butter
1 teaspoon grated lemon peel
¼ cup lemon juice
2 tablespoons chopped onion
1 teaspoon soy sauce
1 (15 ounce) can pineapple slices with juice
1 teaspoon cornstarch

- Mix all ingredients except pineapple slices and cornstarch in small saucepan. Pour ⅓ cup pineapple juice in saucepan. Cook on medium for about 3 minutes.

- Mix cornstarch with 2 tablespoons water and stir well. Add to sauce and cook for about 5 to 10 minutes until sauce thickens. Grill canned pineapple slices and serve on top of meat with sauce. Makes about 1 cup.

Raisin Sauce

Great with pork.

1 cup raisins
¼ cup vinegar
¼ cup packed brown sugar
1 teaspoon mustard
1 teaspoon Worcestershire sauce
1 tablespoon flour
1 tablespoon butter

- Cook raisins in 1 cup water for 10 minutes over medium heat. Remove from heat and set aside. Combine ½ teaspoon salt and remaining ingredients in bowl and add to raisins. Cook mixture until thick and add butter, if desired. Makes 2½ cups.

$ave Money! Make a list and stick to it. Shopping lists help you avoid impulse buys and save money.

Seafood Sweet and Sour Marinade

⅓ cup honey
¼ cup soy sauce
¼ cup orange juice
1 teaspoon cayenne powder

- Combine honey, soy sauce, orange juice and cayenne powder and mix well. Use as marinade. Makes about ¾ cup.

Secret Tomato Sauce

3 (8 ounce) cans tomato sauce
½ (12 ounce) can beer
2½ tablespoons brown sugar
¼ cup honey
2 teaspoons seasoned pepper
1 teaspoon garlic salt
1 teaspoon chili powder

- Combine all ingredients in saucepan with 2 teaspoons salt. Bring to a boil and simmer for about 5 to 10 minutes until sauce thickens. (If sauce gets too thick, add a little water.) Makes about 4 cups.

Smoky Onion Sauce

This is a great way to add a little something extra to vegetables.

1 medium onion, sliced
1 tablespoon flour
1 cup milk
1 tablespoon butter

- Cook onion on oiled grill or on foil over medium-hot heat until tender and coarsely chop onions. Blend flour and milk, pour slowly, in skillet over low heat and stir to remove lumps.

- Add butter and cook, stirring constantly, until mixture thickens. Add onion and salt and pepper to taste. Serve over vegetables. Makes 1 cup.

Worcestershire Butter Sauce

Serve this over fish or vegetables.

½ cup (1 stick) butter
2 tablespoons lemon juice
1 tablespoon chopped parsley
1½ teaspoons Worcestershire sauce

- Melt butter in small saucepan and add remaining ingredients. Makes about ½ cup.

Jack Daniel's Special Sauce

This is a general, all-purpose sauce for meats.

1 cup pineapple juice
½ cup Jack Daniel's® Tennessee Whiskey
¼ cup soy sauce
1 tablespoon ginger
1 teaspoon garlic powder

- Mix all ingredients and baste meats while cooking. Makes about 1¾ cups.

Kitchen-Sink Beef Basting Sauce

½ cup barbecue sauce
½ cup steak sauce
½ cup balsamic vinegar
¼ cup hot sauce
1 (12 ounce) bottle or can beer
4 cloves garlic, minced

- Mix barbecue sauce, steak sauce, balsamic vinegar, hot sauce and beer well. Rub fresh garlic over beef and pat down. Pour sauce over beef, cover and marinate in refrigerator for several hours. Discard marinade. Makes 3¼ cups.

Secret Sauce

1 (10 ounce) bottle A1® Steak Sauce
1 cup ketchup
½ cup packed brown sugar
3 tablespoons vinegar
6 - 12 drops hot sauce
2 tablespoons Worcestershire
2 tablespoons dry mustard
1 shot bourbon

- Mix all ingredients and add salt and pepper to taste. Brush on during last minutes of cooking or grilling. Makes about 2 cups.

Barbecue Sauce with Mustard

Good for beef and pork.

1 cup vinegar
⅔ cup lemon juice
2 teaspoons minced garlic
1 onion, finely grated
1 cup packed brown sugar
4 cups ketchup
1 teaspoon cayenne pepper
¼ cup mustard
2 teaspoons liquid smoke

- Combine vinegar, lemon juice, garlic, onion and brown sugar in saucepan and bring to a boil. Add remaining ingredients, 1 tablespoon salt and 1 tablespoon pepper and boil for 5 minutes. Makes 1½ quarts.

All-Purpose Mopping Sop

2 (14 ounce) cans beef broth
1 (10 ounce) bottle Worcestershire sauce
¾ cup oil
½ - ¾ cup vinegar
1 tablespoon dry mustard
1 tablespoon paprika
2 teaspoons garlic powder
2 teaspoons chili powder
2 teaspoons hot sauce
1 teaspoon crushed bay leaves

- Mix all ingredients in saucepan and cook on medium for about 5 minutes. Cool and refrigerate overnight.

- Use basting brush or wrap cloth around wooden spoon to baste meat thoroughly while cooking. Makes about 4 cups.

Beer Brisket Sop

Just sop this on a brisket when you are grilling or smoking to keep it moist during the cooking process. Brisket should be cooked slow and long so it will be fork tender.

1 onion, minced
3 cloves garlic, minced
1 (12 ounce) can beer
¼ cup canola oil
¼ cup vinegar
2 tablespoons Worcestershire sauce
Chili powder

- Place vegetables in large saucepan with ½ cup water, a little salt and pepper and bring to a boil. Reduce heat to low, pour all remaining ingredients in saucepan and mix well.

- Put sop on brisket with pastry brush or rag wrapped around wooden spoon. Sop brisket 3 to 4 times while cooking. Makes enough for 1 (4 - 5 pound) brisket.

Cayenne Grilling Sop

Works well with beef.

2 tablespoons lime juice
2 tablespoons vegetable oil
1 tablespoon tequila
1½ teaspoons cayenne pepper
1½ teaspoons brown sugar
1 teaspoon chili powder
1 teaspoon coarse black pepper

- Combine all ingredients and marinate with beef for at least 1 hour. Makes ½ cup.

Pop's Big Time Slatherin' Sop

Great for beef and ribs.

1 (15 ounce) can tomato sauce
1 (18 ounce) bottle steak sauce or barbecue sauce
1 (14 ounce) bottle ketchup
½ cup canola oil
1 cup (2 sticks) butter
1 - 2 tablespoons hot sauce
1 tablespoon mustard
3 onions, minced
2 cloves garlic, minced
2 - 3 cups packed brown sugar

- Combine tomato sauce, barbecue sauce, ketchup, oil, butter, hot sauce and mustard in saucepan over medium heat and bring almost to a boil and mix well. Lower heat, add onions and garlic and stir well.

- Slowly pour in brown sugar, stirring constantly, a little at a time. When sugar dissolves, turn heat to simmer. Cover and cook for about 1 to 2 hours. Makes about 8 cups.

Pop's Easy Slatherin' Sop

Great for beef, ribs and chicken.

1 (14 ounce) bottle spicy ketchup
½ cup canola oil
1 cup (2 sticks) butter
1 tablespoon mustard
2 cloves garlic, minced
1 cup packed brown sugar

- Combine all ingredients, except brown sugar, in saucepan over medium heat, bring almost to a boil and mix well. Lower heat and stir well.

- Slowly pour in brown sugar, stirring constantly, a little at a time. When sugar dissolves, turn heat to simmer. Cover and cook for about 1 hour. Makes about 3 cups.

Smoke-Gets-In-Your-Eyes Brisket Sop

1 cup (2 sticks) butter
3 cloves garlic, minced
1 - 2 jalapenos, stemmed, seeded, minced or 2 teaspoons hot sauce
2 - 3 teaspoons liquid smoke

- Melt butter in small saucepan over low heat, add garlic and cook until clear and stir constantly. Add all remaining ingredients and cook for 2 to 3 minutes. Remove from heat and baste meat with brush. Makes about 1 cup.

TIP: Wear rubber gloves when removing seeds from jalapenos.

Do not baste meats with tomato-based sauces until meat is at least half done. Sugars and sweeteners in ketchups and barbecue sauces will burn and become too crusty for the best flavor.

Texas-Style Sop

This is used for short ribs, brisket and just about anything you put on a grill. Don't be scared by the number of ingredients. It's easy.

½ cup (1 stick) butter
1 Texas SuperSweet or Vidalia® onion, minced
4 - 6 cloves garlic, pressed
1 tablespoon sweet paprika
1 tablespoon chili powder
1 cup beef broth
⅓ cup Shiner Bock or Lone Star® beer
¼ cup lightly packed brown sugar
2 tablespoons ketchup
¼ cup apple cider vinegar
¼ cup steak sauce
¼ cup Worcestershire
1 teaspoon hot sauce

- Melt butter in medium saucepan, add onion and garlic and cook until onion is transparent. Mix paprika, chili powder and 1 teaspoon pepper. Add butter and stir to mix well.

- Add beef broth and beer and stir in brown sugar until it dissolves. Add ketchup, vinegar, steak sauce, Worcestershire and hot sauce and stir to mix well. Simmer for 15 to 20 minutes. Baste liberally. Makes about 2½ cups.

Fair Wind Seafood Sop

1 cube chicken bouillon
1 (12 ounce) bottle lager
¾ cup fresh lime juice (about 6 medium limes)
6 garlic cloves, minced
1 tablespoon hot sauce
1 teaspoon Worcestershire sauce
1 teaspoon soy sauce
1 teaspoon ground black pepper

- Dissolve chicken bouillon cube according to package directions. Mix with remaining ingredients and refrigerate for several hours before using. Baste seafood while grilling. Makes 2 cups.

"Wet" Barbecued Pork Rib Sop

In many places in the South, particularly in Tennessee, the question "Wet or dry?" will be asked whenever one orders ribs. "Wet" means a sauce applied just before serving and "dry" means a dry seasoning mixture applied liberally before cooking.

1 bunch green onions with green stems, chopped
2 cloves garlic, minced
2 tablespoons bacon drippings or canola oil
1 (14 ounce) spicy ketchup
⅓ cup Worcestershire sauce
⅓ cup dry white wine
2 tablespoons vinegar
2 tablespoons brown sugar
1 teaspoon hot sauce
1 teaspoon dry mustard
1 teaspoon ground cumin
¼ teaspoon crushed red pepper flakes
Chili powder to taste, optional

- Saute onions and garlic in bacon drippings in large skillet until translucent. Add remaining sauce ingredients and cook over low heat until mixture reduces. Makes about 3 cups.

White Barbecue Sauce for Brisket

This is a neat change-of pace from the normally tomato based barbecue sauce and can be used with chicken, turkey or pork.

1½ cups mayonnaise
¼ cup white wine vinegar
1 tablespoon Creole mustard
1 tablespoon horseradish
1 tablespoon cracked black pepper
1 tablespoon minced garlic
1 teaspoon sugar

- In bowl, combine all barbecue ingredients and use as a marinade for the brisket or use it for basting the brisket. Bake or grill as you normally would when cooking a brisket. Makes about 2 cups.

Desserts

You can even grill desserts at a
backyard barbecue. These recipes keep
you out of the kitchen and in the party.

Grilled Chocolate Sandwich

Butter, softened
4 large slices French bread
4 (1 ounce) squares bittersweet or semi-sweet chocolate, grated
Powdered sugar

- Lightly butter bread slices on 1 side. Top unbuttered side
  evenly with grated chocolate. Place other slice, buttered-side
  out, on top.

- Cook sandwiches on oiled grill or sprayed foil over medium
  heat until golden brown, about 5 to 10 minutes; turn and grill
  until chocolate melts.

- Sprinkle with powdered sugar. Cut sandwiches in halves or
  fourths and serve immediately. Serves 2.

Chocolate-Banana Dana Sandwich

- Use recipe for *Grilled Chocolate Sandwich (page 332)* and add
  sliced banana on top of chocolate. Serves 2.

Chocolate-Raspberry Sandwich

- Use recipe for *Grilled Chocolate Sandwich (page 332)* and add
  raspberry preserves. Serves 2.

Jammin' Strawberry-Chocolate Sandwich

- Use recipe for *Grilled Chocolate Sandwich (page 332)* and add strawberry jam. Serves 2.

Nutty Chocolate Sandwich

- Use recipe for *Grilled Chocolate Sandwich (page 332)* and add ¼ cup chopped nuts. Serves 2.

Nutella Fella

- Use recipe for *Grilled Chocolate Sandwich (page 332)* but skip the chocolate and add hazelnut spread (Nutella®). Serves 2.

Bread Twist for Grilled Chocolate Sandwich

- Use recipe for *Grilled Chocolate Sandwich (page 332)* but use raisin bread or any firm bread. Serves 2.

Peanut Butter Cup S'Mores

1 peanut butter cup
2 thin chocolate chip cookies

- Place 1 peanut butter cup between cookies. Cook on oiled grill or sprayed foil over medium-hot fire for about 3 to 5 minutes with lid closed until chocolate begins to melt. Flip and cook additional 2 to 3 minutes. Makes 1 s'more.

Dieting is wishful shrinking.
–Author Unknown

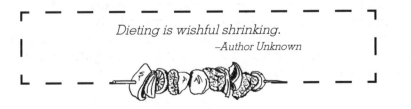

Grilled Banana S'Mores

2 firm bananas
Canola oil
½ cup Nutella® hazelnut spread
8 cinnamon graham crackers

- Cut bananas (with peels on) in half lengthwise. Coat with a little oil. Cook banana side down on clean oiled grill or sprayed foil over medium-high heat for about 6 to 8 minutes with lid closed. (Peel will turn dark.) Remove banana halves from peels and slice.

- Spread Nutella® on ½ cinnamon graham cracker, place grilled banana slices on Nutella® and press remaining half of cinnamon graham cracker on top. Makes 8.

Ginger-Nutella S'Mores

Marshmallows
Gingersnap cookies
Nutella® hazelnut spread

- Place marshmallow on end of long skewer and cook over medium-hot fire until brown on outside. Place marshmallow on gingersnap cookie. Spread Nutella® on another cookie and press together with marshmallow.

Hot Peanut Butter Grahams

Fix several helpings for the kids, but you better have extras for the grown-ups.

8 square graham crackers
½ cup peanut butter
⅓ cup miniature marshmallows

- Spread graham crackers with peanut butter and scatter marshmallows on top. Place on preheated, oiled grill or sprayed foil away from direct heat, close lid and cook about 4 minutes until marshmallows melt and turn a little brown on top. Serve at once. Makes 4.

Grilled Chocolate Chip Cookies

1 (16.5 ounce) package refrigerated chocolate chip cookie dough

- Preheat grill to medium heat (about 350 degrees).

- Shape dough into balls and place on large piece of heavy-duty foil. Grill about 15 minutes until golden brown. Serves 6 to 8.

Favorite Grilled Cookies

- Use recipe for *Grilled Chocolate Chip Cookies (page 335)* and replace chocolate chip cookie dough with your favorite prepared cookie dough. Serves 6 to 8.

Grilled Fruits

Grilling fruits reduces their juices, caramelizes natural sugars and intensifies the flavors.

Grilled fruits make great appetizers as well as side dishes and desserts. They are wonderful with the luscious dipping sauces on pages 343-346.

All fruits may cook directly on clean, oiled grills, but using foil makes cleanup much easier.

Basics of Grilling Fruits

- Always use ripe fruits.

- Before grilling, marinate in 1 cup water for about 30 minutes so fruit won't dry out.

- Always brush with canola oil or butter before grilling.

- Always use a very clean grill or foil so flavors and charring from meats will not transfer.

- Firm fruits (apples, pears, pineapple) take longer to cook.

- Soft fruits (peaches, plums, strawberries) can get mushy if cooked too long.

- Brown sugar caramelizes best for fruits.

Easy Basic Grilled Fruit

Grilled fruit works as an appetizer, side dish or dessert.

Apples
Pears
Pineapple
Strawberries
Peaches
Plums
Bananas

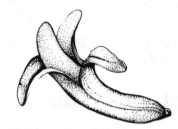

- Leave peel on fruits and eat fruit out of peel if you normally don't eat peel. Cut in half, remove seeds, core and stem. Soak in enough water to cover for about 30 minutes.

- A drop or two of lemon juice will keep fruit from turning dark. Cook on oiled grill over medium heat or away from direct heat until grill marks show.

- Be careful not to burn or overcook soft fruits like peaches or they will get mushy. Cooking times will vary between 5 to 10 minutes per side; the harder the fruit, the longer it will take to cook.

Grilled Fruit Kebabs

12 strawberries with stems
3 kiwifruit, peeled
2 peaches with peel
1 (15 ounce) can pineapple chunks, drained
Balsamic vinegar or balsamic glaze

- Soak bamboo skewers in water for about 30 minutes before grilling. Divide fruit equally among 4 portions. Use 2 skewers for each portion (so fruit doesn't slip or fall off) and arrange fruit on skewers.

- Cook on oiled grill over medium fire for about 5 minutes per side until grill marks show. Drizzle balsamic vinegar or balsamic glaze over grilled fruits before serving. Serves 4.

Turtle Brownies with Grilled Tropical Fruit

¼ cup (½ stick) butter, melted
3 tablespoons orange juice
2 tablespoons brown sugar
6 cups tropical fruit, cut in 1-inch chunks (pineapple,
      mangoes, bananas)
8 brownies, warmed
1 cup caramel topping

- Combine butter, orange juice and brown sugar. Place fruit on skewers and coat with butter mixture.

- Cook on oiled grill over medium heat for about 5 to 10 minutes per side until soft, but not mushy. Baste frequently with butter mixture. Place brownies on plate and top with fruit and caramel topping. Serves 8.

Grilled Tropical Fruit Sundaes

- Use recipe for *Turtle Brownies with Grilled Tropical Fruit (page 337)* and substitute ice cream or sorbet for brownies. Serves 8.

Apple Wedges

3 delicious, gala, or Fuji apples
Lemon juice
Butter, melted

- Core apples and slice into bite-size wedges. Soak fruit in 1 cup water and 1 tablespoon lemon juice for about 30 minutes before grilling.

- Butter both sides of apples and cook on clean, oiled grill or foil on grill over medium fire for about 2 to 4 minutes per side until apples are tender. Remove from grill and cool slightly before dipping in chocolate or other sauces on pages 343-346. Serves 4 to 6.

Brown Sugar Apples

- Use recipe for *Apple Wedges (page 337)* and sprinkle brown sugar and cinnamon on apple wedges before grilling. Serves 4 to 6.

Gingered Apples

- Use recipe for *Apple Wedges (page 337)* and sprinkle crystallized ginger on apple wedges before grilling. Serves 4 to 6.

Fancy Grilled Apricots

4 ripe apricots
Lemon juice
Canola oil

- Cut apricots in half and remove pits. Soak fruit in 1 cup water and 1 tablespoon lemon juice for about 30 minutes before grilling.

- Rub with canola oil and cook on clean, oiled grill or foil, cut side down, over medium-high heat for about 3 to 4 minutes per side until tender. Cut each in half again for dipping. Use wonderful fruit dipping sauces on pages 343-346. Serves 4 to 6.

Honeyed Apricots

- Use recipe for *Fancy Grilled Apricots (page 338)* and add a little honey over grilled apricots before serving. Serves 4 to 6.

Banana Bites

2 firm bananas
Canola oil

- Cut one slit through peel lengthwise. Spread open just a little. Cook on clean oiled grill or foil, open side down, over medium-high heat for about 6 to 8 minutes. (Peel will turn dark.)

- Remove peel and cut into bite-size pieces for dipping. Use wonderful fruit dipping sauces on pages 343-346. Serves 4.

Kwik Kool Kiwi

3 ripe kiwifruit
Canola oil

- Cut kiwis in half. Soak fruit in 1 cup water for about 30 minutes before grilling. Rub with canola oil.

- Cook on clean, oiled grill or foil, cut side down, over medium-high heat for about 2 to 4 minutes per side until warm. Slice to dip in chocolate sauce. Or use the wonderful fruit dipping sauces on pages 343-346. Serves 4 to 6.

Mango Supreme

2 ripe, soft mangoes
Canola oil

- Cut mangoes in half and remove seeds. Soak fruit in 1 cup water for about 30 minutes before grilling.

- Rub with canola oil and cook on clean, oiled grill or foil, cut side down, over medium-high heat for about 2 to 3 minutes per side until tender. Cut into bite-size pieces before dipping. Use wonderful fruit dipping sauces on pages 343-346. Serves 4 to 6.

Nectarine Slices

3 ripe nectarines
Canola oil

- Cut nectarines in half and remove pits. Soak fruit in 1 cup water for about 30 minutes before grilling.

- Rub with canola oil and cook on clean, oiled grill or foil, cut side down, over medium-high heat for about 4 to 5 minutes per side until tender. Cut into bite-size pieces before dipping. Use wonderful fruit dipping sauces on pages 343-346. Serves 4 to 6.

Brown Sugar Nectarines

- Use recipe for *Nectarine Slices (page 339)* and sprinkle brown sugar and cinnamon on nectarine halves before grilling.

Papaya Surprise

2 ripe papayas
Canola oil

- Cut papaya in half and remove pit. Soak fruit in 1 cup water for about 30 minutes before grilling.

- Rub with canola oil and cook on clean, oiled grill or foil, cut side down, over medium-high heat for about 3 to 4 minutes per side until tender. Cut into bite-size pieces before dipping. Use wonderful fruit dipping sauces on pages 343-346. Serves 4 to 6.

Papaya with Balsamic Vinegar

- Use recipe for *Papaya Surprise (page 340)* and pour balsamic vinegar over grilled papaya.

Peach Surprise

2 - 3 ripe peaches
Canola oil

- Cut peaches in half and remove pit. Soak fruit in 1 cup water for about 30 minutes before grilling.

- Rub with canola oil and cook on clean, oiled grill or foil, cut side down, over medium-high heat for about 3 to 5 minutes per side until tender. Cut into bite-size pieces before dipping. Use wonderful fruit dipping sauces on pages 343-346. Serves 4 to 6.

Brown Sugar Peaches

- Use recipe for *Peach Surprise (page 340)* and sprinkle brown sugar and cinnamon on peach halves before grilling. Serves 4 to 6.

Grilled Peaches with Cinnamon Cream

- Use recipe for *Peach Surprise (page 340)* and add a dollop of Cinnamon Cream (recipe below) in center of peaches.

Cinnamon Cream:

1 (4 ounce) package cream cheese, softened
1 (6 ounce) container vanilla yogurt
¼ cup sugar
1 teaspoon cinnamon

- Mix all ingredients and serve with grilled fruit.

Pear Party Pieces

2 - 3 ripe pears
Canola oil

- Cut pears in half and remove pit. Soak fruit in 1 cup water for about 30 minutes before grilling.

- Rub with canola oil and cook on clean, oiled grill or foil, cut side down, over medium-high heat for about 5 to 6 minutes per side until tender. Cut into bite-size pieces before dipping. Try dipping sauces on pages 343-346. Serves 4 to 6.

Brown Sugar Pears

- Use recipe for *Pear Party Pieces (page 341)* and sprinkle brown sugar and cinnamon on pear halves before grilling. Serves 4 to 6.

Ginger Pears

- Use recipe for *Pear Party Pieces (page 341)* and sprinkle crystallized ginger on pear halves before grilling. Serves 4 to 6.

Pineapple Delight

1 whole fresh pineapple
Canola oil

- Cut ½ to 1 inch from top and bottom of pineapple. Set pineapple on its base and cut down just behind dark eyes on sides. Soak fruit in enough water to cover for about 30 minutes before grilling.

- Cut pineapple in 1 to 2-inch slices. Rub with canola oil and cook on clean, oiled grill or foil over medium-high heat for about 4 to 5 minutes per side until grill marks show and fruit is soft.

- Cut white center core away from pineapple. Cut remaining pineapple into bite-size pieces before dipping. Use wonderful fruit dipping sauces on pages 343-346. Serves 4 to 6.

Brown Sugar Pineapple

- Use recipe for *Pineapple Delight (page 342)* and sprinkle brown sugar and cinnamon on pineapple slices before grilling. Serves 4 to 6.

Ginger Pineapple

- Use recipe for *Pineapple Delight (page 342)* and sprinkle crystallized ginger on pineapple slices before grilling. Serves 4 to 6.

Dipped Strawberries

12 large firm strawberries, hulled
Canola oil

- Soak fruit in 1 cup water for about 30 minutes before grilling. Cook on clean, oiled grill or foil over medium-high heat for about 1 to 2 minutes per side until warm.

- Eat whole or slice strawberries into bite-size pieces before dipping. Use wonderful fruit dipping sauces on pages 343-346. Serves 6 to 8.

Sugar-Coated Strawberries

- Use recipe for *Dipped Strawberries (page 342)* and pour balsamic vinegar and granulated sugar over strawberries before serving. Serves 6 to 8.

Grilled Strawberry-Cake Sundae

Grilled strawberries (use recipe for Dipped Strawberries, page 342)
Pound cake
Ice cream
Whipped cream

- Grill slices of prepared pound cake on oiled grill over medium heat just until each side gets a little toasty. Place in individual dish and top with ice cream, grilled strawberries and whipped cream.

Terrific Watermelon Wedges

1 small ripe watermelon
Canola oil

- Cut 1 to 2-inch slices across width of watermelon. Cut in half and again in half and rub with canola oil. Cook on clean, oiled grill or foil over medium-high heat for about 1 to 2 minutes per side until warm. Cut rind off and slice wedges into bite-size pieces before dipping. Use wonderful fruit dipping sauces on pages 343-346. Serves 6 to 8.

Dipping Sauces for Grilled Fruits

Try any of these delicious dipping sauces for fabulous, fun desserts with grilled fruit recipes in this section.

Favorite Creamy Fruit Dip

1 (8 ounce) package cream cheese, softened
¾ cup packed brown sugar
1 teaspoon vanilla

- Beat cream cheese until fluffy and slowly pour in brown sugar and vanilla. Continue beating until dip mixes well. Use with grilled fruit recipes on pages 335-343. Makes about 1 cup.

Favorite Marshmallow Crème Dip

1 (8 ounce) package cream cheese, softened
1 (7 ounce) jar marshmallow crème
1 teaspoon vanilla

- Beat cream cheese until fluffy and fold in marshmallow crème and vanilla. Use with grilled fruit recipes on pages 335-343. Makes about 1½ cups.

Lemon Marshmallow Dip

1 (8 ounce) package cream cheese, softened
1 (7 ounce) jar marshmallow crème
1 tablespoon sugar
1 tablespoon lemon juice
1 teaspoon grated lemon peel

- Beat cream cheese until fluffy and fold in marshmallow crème, sugar, lemon juice and lemon zest. Use with grilled fruit recipes on pages 335-343. Makes about 1½ cups.

Orange Marshmallow Dip

- Use recipe for *Lemon Marshmallow Dip (page 344)*, but add orange juice and zest instead of lemon.

Creamy Pina Colada Fruit Dip

1 (8 ounce) package cream cheese, softened
1 (7 ounce) jar marshmallow crème
⅓ cup frozen pina colada drink mix concentrate
2 tablespoons light rum

- Beat cream cheese until fluffy and fold in marshmallow crème, drink mix and rum. Use with grilled fruit recipes on pages 335-343. Makes about 2 cups.

Seize the moment. Remember all those women on the Titanic who waved off the dessert cart.

–Erma Bombeck

Amaretto Fruit Dip

1 (8 ounce) package cream cheese, softened
1 (7 ounce) jar marshmallow crème
2 tablespoons amaretto liqueur

- Beat cream cheese until fluffy and fold in marshmallow crème and amaretto. Use with grilled fruit recipes on pages 335-343. Makes about 2 cups.

Ice Cream Truck Fruit Dip

1 (8 ounce) container frozen whipped topping, softened
1 (3.5 ounce) package instant vanilla pudding mix
1 (6 ounce) package frozen orange juice concentrate

- Mix all ingredients and serve with grilled fruit. Use with grilled fruit recipes on pages 335-343. Makes about 2 cups.

Easy Chocolate Sauce

This is great for dipping grilled fruit, as well as dressing up a casual and pleasant dessert like ice cream or pound cake.

1 cup semi-sweet chocolate chips
¾ cup whipped (heavy) cream
1 teaspoon vanilla

- Melt chocolate with cream over low heat in saucepan until smooth. Remove from heat and add vanilla. Serve hot. Makes 1¾ cups.

Ginger Fruit Dip

1 (3 ounce) package cream cheese, softened
1 (7 ounce) jar marshmallow creme
½ cup mayonnaise
1 teaspoon ground ginger
1 teaspoon grated orange peel

- Beat cream cheese in bowl on medium speed until smooth, add marshmallow creme, mayonnaise, ginger and orange peel. Stir until smooth. Use with grilled fruit recipes on pages 335-343 or with fresh fruit. Makes about 2 cups.

Juicy Fruit Dip

Delicious!

1 (8 ounce) package cream cheese, softened
2 (7 ounce) cartons marshmallow creme
1 teaspoon ground cinnamon
½ teaspoon ground ginger
Nectarines and apples, grilled

- Beat cream cheese in bowl until smooth. Add marshmallow creme, cinnamon and ginger and mix well. Refrigerate. Serve with slices of nectarines or apple slices. Serves 8.

Kahlua Fruit Dip

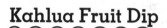

1 (8 ounce) package cream cheese, softened
1 (8 ounce) carton whipped topping
⅔ cup packed brown sugar
⅓ cup Kahlua® liqueur
1 (8 ounce) carton sour cream
Fresh fruit, grilled

- Beat cream cheese in bowl until creamy and fold in whipped topping. Add brown sugar, Kahlua® and sour cream and mix well. Refrigerate for 24 hours before serving. Use with grilled fruit recipes on pages 335-343. Serves 8.

Creamy Pineapple Crush

1 (8 ounce) package cream cheese, softened
1 (7 ounce) jar marshmallow crème
1 (8 ounce) can crushed pineapple with juice

- Beat cream cheese until fluffy and fold in marshmallow crème. Drain juice from crushed pineapple and add to mixture. Drain 1 tablespoon crushed pineapple to mixture and stir gently. Use with grilled fruit recipes on pages 335-343. Makes about 2 cups.

$ave Money! Be aware of portion sizes. This will not only help your waistline, but also stretch your budget!

Banana-Strawberry Grilled Pizza

1 firm banana
Canola oil
Lemon juice
8 - 10 fresh strawberries, halved
¼ cup hazelnut spread
1 (14 ounce) refrigerated pizza dough

- Cut one slit through banana peel lengthwise. Spread open just a little and rub a little oil over banana. Cook on clean, oiled grill or heavy-duty foil, open side down, over medium-high heat for about 3 to 5 minutes per side. (Peel will turn dark.) Remove from grill, peel and slice. Sprinkle a little lemon juice on top.

- Oil one side of pizza dough. Lay out dough, oiled side down, on sprayed heavy-duty foil over cookie sheet or on clean oiled grill. Cook dough on preheated grill over medium-high fire for about 5 to 8 minutes until dough is light brown. Oil top side of dough, flip and cook another 5 to 8 minutes.

- Cover crust with hazelnut spread and top with strawberries and bananas. Grill about 3 to 5 minutes to warm hazelnut spread. Slice and serve immediately. Serves 4 to 8.

Tropical Supreme Pizza

1 (14 ounce) refrigerated pizza dough
Canola oil
½ - ¾ cup peach preserves
1 ripe mango, peeled, pitted, sliced
1 ripe papaya, peeled, seeded, sliced

- Oil one side of pizza dough. Lay out dough, oiled side down, on sprayed heavy-duty foil over cookie sheet or on clean oiled grill. Cook dough over medium-high fire for about 5 to 8 minutes per side until dough is light brown. Oil top side of dough, flip and cook another 5 to 8 minutes.

- Spread peach preserves over crust and position mango and papaya over top. Grill for about 5 minutes with lid closed until preserves are warm. Slice and serve immediately. Serves 4 to 8

Roasted Cooked Apples

6 Fuji, Jonathan or golden delicious apples
⅓ cup (⅔ stick) butter
⅔ cup packed brown sugar, divided
2 tablespoons lemon juice

- Cut apples in half and trim core from apple into bowl shape, but don't cut through apple. Soak in 1 cup water for about 30 minutes before grilling. Mix butter, ⅓ cup brown sugar, lemon juice and ¼ cup water in large saucepan.

- Cook on low, stirring constantly, until butter melts and sugar dissolves. (Do not burn.) Pour butter mixture into center of each apple and sprinkle generously with brown sugar on top.

- Wrap loosely in sprayed, heavy-duty foil and seal tightly so it will not leak. Cook on preheated grill over medium fire until apple is tender, about 10 to 15 minutes; rotate over heat. Unwrap carefully and cool slightly before serving. Serves 6.

TIP: To prevent butter from leaking from bottom of apple, stuff a marshmallow in cavity before pouring in butter.

Grilled Apple Slices

4 Fuji, gala, or Granny Smith apples, cored
2 tablespoons lemon juice
2 tablespoons brown sugar
2 teaspoons cinnamon
Ice cream or whipped topping

- Cut apples into 1-inch slices. Soak in 1 cup water for about 30 minutes before grilling. Mix remaining ingredients and baste apples liberally while cooking.

- Cook on sprayed foil over medium-hot fire for about 5 to 10 minutes per side until apples are tender. Sprinkle with a little extra cinnamon before serving. Serves 4 to 8.

Marinated Apples

1 cup orange juice
3 tablespoons honey
1 tablespoon vanilla
2 teaspoons cinnamon
3 apples, sliced ½-thick

- Combine orange juice, honey, vanilla and cinnamon in large sealable plastic bag. Add apples slices and mix well. Refrigerate 2 hours, turn occasionally.

- Place apple slices on oiled grill or sprayed foil. Grill about 4 minutes per side; baste frequently with marinade. Serves 3 to 6.

Marinated Peaches

- Use recipe for *Marinated Apples (page 350)* and replace apples with firm peaches. Reduce marinade time to 1 hour. Serves 3 to 6.

Roasted Apple Dessert

4 apples
4 tablespoons brown sugar
4 tablespoons butter
Cinnamon
Whipped cream

- Wash apples and remove cores, but do not pierce bottom. Fill center of each apple with 1 tablespoon brown sugar, 1 tablespoon butter and sprinkle cinnamon on top. Wrap in heavy-duty foil so juices do not leak.

- Cook on preheated grill over indirect medium heat about 20 to 30 minutes until apples are tender. Turn several times. Serve with whipped cream. Serves 4 to 8.

Spicy Apple Dessert

- Use recipe for *Roasted Apple Dessert (page 350)* and drop Red Hots candies in apples with other ingredients. Sprinkle a little lemon juice on top of apples. Serves 4 to 8.

Roasted Apples with Banana Slices

- Use recipe for *Roasted Apple Dessert (page 349)* and add banana slices with brown sugar and butter. Serves 4 to 8.

Jelly-Belly Apple Desert

- Use recipe for *Roasted Apple Dessert (page 349)*, but stuff miniature marshmallows in apple cavity first, then add a little of your favorite jam, jelly or marmalade before adding brown sugar and butter. Serves 4 to 8.

Tropical Roasted Apple Crunch

- Use recipe for *Roasted Apple Dessert (page 349)*, but stuff miniature marshmallows in cavity first, then add drained, crushed pineapple with brown sugar and butter. Serves 4 to 8.

Camp Fire Girl Apples

6 - 8 large delicious apples
12 - 16 marshmallows
6 - 8 tablespoons brown sugar
6 - 8 teaspoons Red Hots candies
Cinnamon

- Core apples, but don't cut through bottom. Stuff 1 marshmallow into core at bottom. Add 1 tablespoon brown sugar, 1 teaspoon Red Hots and stuff 1 marshmallow in top.

- Sprinkle with cinnamon, wrap in heavy-duty foil and cook in campfire coals or on medium grill over campfire for about 20 minutes until tender. Turn several times. Serves 6 to 8.

$ave Money! *Cook from scratch and avoid processed foods. Frozen and prepared entrees cost a premium.*

Apricot Tart

1 (9 inch) refrigerated pie crust
1 (21 ounce) can apricot pie filling
2 tablespoons chopped pecans

- Roll out pie crust to about 13 inches. Place on large sprayed piece of heavy-duty foil. Pour pie filling in middle of pie crust and top with pecans. Fold edges of crust up and over so only a small circle of filling is visible.

- Place foil on grill away from medium heat. Cover and cook about 45 minutes until crust is golden brown. Serves 4 to 6.

Berry Cobbler

1 cup crushed graham crackers
⅓ cup flour
¼ cup packed brown sugar
⅓ cup butter
6 cups fresh berries (blueberries, raspberries, blackberries or
    strawberries)
½ cup sugar
2 tablespoons quick-cooking tapioca
1 teaspoon cinnamon

- Combine graham crackers, flour and brown sugar. Cut in butter and set aside. Combine berries, sugar, tapioca, cinnamon and ¼ teaspoon salt. Set aside for 15 minutes, stir occasionally.

- Place berry mixture in sprayed disposable foil pan and cover with foil. Grill 5 inches away from medium heat for about 30 minutes; rotate once. Remove foil and sprinkle with graham cracker mixture. Cover and grill additional 15 minutes. Serves 6.

Chocolate Chip Banana Boats

4 firm bananas
Mini-chocolate chips
Canola oil
Ice cream
Chocolate ice cream syrup

- Cut one slit through banana peel lengthwise. Spread open a little and stuff with mini-chocolate chips. Cook on clean, oiled grill or foil, open side up, over medium-high heat for about 2 to 3 minutes with lid closed. (Peel will turn dark.)

- Remove from grill when chocolate chips melt a little. Remove banana from peel and serve on individual plates with ice cream and chocolate syrup on top. Serves 4.

Grilled Rum-Banana Split

4 firm bananas
Canola oil
¼ cup dark rum
¼ cup honey
Vanilla ice cream

- Cut bananas in half lengthwise. Cook on clean oiled grill or foil, cut side down, over medium-high heat for about 6 to 8 minutes. (Peel will turn dark.)

- Remove banana from peel and place each half on 2 sides of banana split dish. Combine rum and honey in small saucepan and warm over low-medium heat. Place 2 to 3 scoops of ice cream in center of bananas and pour rum-honey mixture over top. Serves 4.

Chocolate-Nut Banana Split

- Use recipe for *Grilled Rum-Banana Split (page 352)* and replace rum and honey with chocolate sauce and chopped walnuts. Serves 4.

Caramel Banana Delight

- Use recipe for *Grilled Rum-Banana Split (page 352)* and replace rum and honey with caramel ice cream sauce and chopped peanuts. Serves 4.

Coconut-Banana Split

- Use recipe for *Grilled Rum-Banana Split (page 352)* and top with flaked sweetened coconut. Serves 4.

Pina Colada Banana Split

- Use recipe for *Grilled Rum-Banana Split (page 352)* and replace rum with coconut-flavored rum. Serves 4.

Kid-Friendly Banana Split

- Use recipe for *Grilled Rum-Banana Split (page 352)* and remove rum. Top each banana split with maraschino cherries. Serves 4.

Bananas were first exported to America around 1900. Dr. David Strickler worked at Tassel Pharmacy in Latrobe, Pennsylvania filling prescriptions, jerking sodas and scooping ice cream. He made several ice cream concoctions, but none were as popular as the one he served with a banana split lengthwise and placed parallel on a dish. He added scoops of vanilla, strawberry and chocolate ice cream between the bananas. To top it, he added crushed pineapple, chocolate syrup and strawberry sauce. To finish it off, he put a dollop of whipped cream on top of each scoop of ice cream and a stemmed maraschino cherry on top. August 25 is National Banana Split Day.

Grilled Banana Sundaes with Chocolate Sauce

4 ripe bananas
8 teaspoons unsalted butter, cut into small pieces
4 tablespoons light brown sugar
4 tablespoons brandy
½ cup chocolate sauce
4 scoops vanilla ice cream
¼ cup toasted pecans, optional

- Cut lengthwise down each banana with 1-inch uncut at both ends. Keep peel intact. Open cut and place 2 tablespoons butter pieces, 1 tablespoon brown sugar and 1 tablespoon brandy within each banana peel.

- Cook on preheated, oiled grill or foil over medium heat for about 8 to 10 minutes until butter melts and bananas heat through. Warm chocolate sauce in saucepan.

- Pour about half of chocolate sauce on 4 individual serving plates. Remove banana from peel and place on each plate. Divide ice cream evenly among servings and place next to banana. Pour remaining chocolate sauce over top and add nuts. Serve immediately. Serves 4 to 8.

Honey-Glazed Cinnamon Peaches

3 large, ripe peaches
Canola oil
½ - 1 cup honey
1 - 2 tablespoons cinnamon

- Cut peaches in half and remove pit. Soak fruit in 1 cup water for about 30 minutes before grilling.

- Cut into large slices, rub with canola oil and cook on sprayed, heavy-duty foil on grill over medium-high heat for about 3 to 5 minutes per side until soft. Combine honey and cinnamon and baste while cooking. Serves 4.

Honey-Glazed Cinnamon Apples

- Use recipe for *Honey-Glazed Cinnamon Peaches (page 354)*, but substitute apples. Grill apples about 4 to 6 minutes per side until soft. Serves 4.

Honey-Glazed Cinnamon Mangoes

- Use recipe for *Honey-Glazed Cinnamon Peaches (page 354)*, but substitute mangoes. Grill mangoes about 3 to 5 minutes per side. Serves 4.

Honey-Glazed Cinnamon Pears

- Use recipe for *Honey-Glazed Cinnamon Peaches (page 354)*, but substitute pears. Grill pears about 4 to 6 minutes per side until soft. Serves 4.

Grilled Grapefruit Cups

4 pink or ruby red grapefruit
3 oranges
1 lime
½ cup sherry
¼ cup plus 1 tablespoon packed light brown sugar
4 tablespoons butter

- Cut grapefruit in half, scoop out flesh over bowl to catch juice and set grapefruit shells aside. Remove any pithy white parts from flesh and separate into sections. Peel oranges and lime, remove pith and separate into sections. Add to grapefruit.

- Leave fruit and juice in bowl and pour sherry over top. Cover and refrigerate for about 1 hour, stir occasionally.

- Stir mixed fruit and scoop into grapefruit shells. Sprinkle brown sugar and bits of butter on top. Grill away from direct medium heat with lid closed just long enough for butter to melt and sugar to crystallize, about 15 minutes. Serves 4.

Creamy Peach-Fired Crepes

3 large, ripe peaches
Canola oil

- Cut peaches in half and remove pits. Soak in 1 cup water for about 30 minutes before grilling.

- Cut into large slices, rub with canola oil and cook on sprayed foil on grill over medium-high heat for about 3 to 5 minutes per side until soft.

Cream Filling:

1 (8 ounce) box cream cheese, softened
¼ cup powdered sugar

- Beat cream cheese until fluffy and mix in powdered sugar. Cut peaches into small pieces and mix with cream filling.

Crepes:

1 cup flour
4 large eggs, beaten lightly
1⅓ cups milk
2 tablespoon canola oil

- Combine flour and ¼ teaspoon salt, whisk in eggs, milk and oil and mix well. Pour about ¼ cup batter into sprayed crepe pan or small skillet and cook on grill over medium-high heat for about 1 to 2 minutes, flip and cook until light brown. (Crepe should be flexible, not crisp.)

- Remove from pan, stack and cover. Continue cooking all crepes. Divide peach cream filling equally among crepes, roll and serve. Serves 8 to 10.

Spiced Pears

1 (15 ounce) can pear halves
⅓ cup packed brown sugar
¾ teaspoon ground nutmeg
¾ teaspoon ground cinnamon

- Drain pear syrup into saucepan and set aside. Wrap pears in sprayed foil and place on grill away from medium heat. Turn package and heat all sides for about 5 minutes until hot.

- Place brown sugar, nutmeg and cinnamon in saucepan with syrup and bring to a boil. Reduce heat and simmer uncovered for 5 to 8 minutes; stir frequently. Place pears in bowl, pour syrup over top and serve immediately. Serves 4.

Roasted Spiced Pears

4 ripe pears
¼ cup brown sugar
¼ cup chopped nuts
¼ cup butter, softened
Ground nutmeg
Ground cinnamon

- Remove stem and core pear carefully without cutting through bottom. Mix brown sugar, nuts and butter and stuff equal amounts of mixture into each cavity.

- Sprinkle nutmeg and cinnamon on top. Wrap pears in sprayed foil and place on grill away from medium heat. Turn package and heat all sides for about 5 minutes per side until soft. Serves 4.

Pear-Ricotta Tart

1 (16 ounce) container ricotta cheese
⅓ cup plus 2 tablespoons sugar, divided
1 package refrigerated pizza dough
2 tablespoons butter, melted, divided
2 (15 ounce) cans sliced pears, drained
2 teaspoons cinnamon

- Combine ricotta cheese and ⅓ cup sugar; refrigerate. Roll out pizza dough and brush top with 1 tablespoon butter. Grill butter-side down for about 5 minutes. Brush remaining butter on top of dough; flip and grill about 5 minutes.

- Place pears on dough and sprinkle with cinnamon and remaining sugar. Grill for about 10 minutes until dough browns and pears heat through. Top with ricotta mixture. Serves 6 to 8.

TIP: Remove tart from grill by sliding onto baking sheet.

Nutty Pear Tart

- Use recipe for *Pear-Ricotta Tart (page 358)* and top pears with ½ cup chopped pistachios or walnuts before grilling. Serves 6 to 8.

Peach-Ricotta Tart

- Use recipe for *Pear-Ricotta Tart (page 358)* and replace pears with sliced peaches. Serves 6 to 8.

Research tells us that 14 out of 10 people like chocolate.
–Sandra Boynton

Roasted Coconut Pineapple

1 fresh whole pineapple
¼ - ½ cup canned coconut milk
¼ cup packed brown sugar
Cinnamon

- Cut ½ to 1 inch from top and bottom of pineapple. Set pineapple on its base and cut down just behind dark eyes on sides. Cut pineapple in 2-inch thick slices. Cut core from slices.

- Dip in coconut milk, dip in brown sugar (press into fruit) and sprinkle cinnamon on both sides. Cook on clean, oiled grill or foil over medium-high heat for about 4 to 5 minutes per side until soft. Serves about 6 to 8.

Pineapple-Coconut Paradise

1 (1½ - 2 pound) whole pineapple
Canola oil
1 pint vanilla yogurt
½ cup shredded coconut, lightly toasted
½ cup slivered almonds, lightly toasted

- Cut ½ to 1 inch from top and bottom of pineapple. Set pineapple on its base and cut down just behind dark eyes on sides. Cut pineapple in 2-inch slices. Cut center white core from pineapple.

- Soak pineapple in 1 cup water for about 30 minutes before grilling. Rub with canola oil.

- Cook on clean, oiled grill or foil over medium-high heat for about 4 to 5 minutes per side until tender. Place dollop of yogurt in center and sprinkle with toasted coconut and almonds. Serves 6 to 8.

Easy Grilled Pineapple

1 fresh whole pineapple
Cinnamon
Rum-Butter Sauce (recipe follows)

- Cut ½ to 1 inch from top and bottom of pineapple. Set pineapple on its base and cut down sides just behind dark eyes. Remove all dark eyes and remaining outer skin. Soak in water for about 30 minutes.

- Dust with cinnamon. Cook whole pineapple on clean, oiled grill or foil over medium-high heat for about 4 to 5 minutes per side until tender. Baste often with rum-butter sauce while cooking. Serves 6 to 8.

Rum-Butter Sauce:

½ cup (1 stick) butter
2 tablespoons light rum

- Melt butter in small saucepan, remove from heat and add rum. Pour over pineapple or use basting brush.

Fiery Pineapple Logs

1 fresh whole pineapple
Brown sugar

- Cut ½ to 1 inch from top and bottom of pineapple. Set pineapple on its base and cut pineapple in half vertically. Hold each half and cut in half again to get 4 pieces; remove core from each piece.

- Press brown sugar into pineapple and cook on clean, oiled grill or foil over medium-high heat for about 4 to 5 minutes per side until tender. Serves 4.

Grilled Pineapple with Rum Sauce

1 fresh whole pineapple
½ cup light rum
1 cup packed brown sugar
2 teaspoons vanilla
Cinnamon

- Cut ½ to 1 inch from top and bottom of pineapple. Set pineapple on its base and cut down sides just behind dark eyes. Cut pineapple horizontally into 1 to 1½-inch thick slices and remove core. Mix rum, brown sugar and vanilla.

- Cook pineapple slices on oiled grill over medium heat for about 5 to 7 minutes per side until heated through. Baste liberally with rum sauce while cooking. Sprinkle cinnamon on top of each slice before serving. Serves 6 to 8.

Coconut-Rum Pineapple Grill

1 fresh whole pineapple
⅓ cup coconut rum
¼ cup packed brown sugar
2 tablespoons cinnamon
Shredded coconut

- Cut ½ to 1 inch from top and bottom of pineapple. Set pineapple on its base and cut down sides just behind dark eyes. Cut pineapple in 2-inch thick slices, remove core and place in sealable bag.

- Combine rum, brown sugar and cinnamon, pour over pineapple and marinate in refrigerator overnight. Cook on clean, oiled grill or foil over medium-high heat for about 4 to 5 minutes per side until soft. Sprinkle shredded coconut on top before serving. Serves 6 to 8.

If no one sees you eat it, do you still have to count the calories?

Grilled Strawberry Short Tart

1 (9 inch) unbaked piecrust
1 (21 ounce) can strawberry pie filling
1 (10 ounce) carton whipped topping

- Place unbaked piecrust into 6 to 7-inch disposable foil pan and lap crust beyond edge of dish. Pour strawberry pie filling into unbaked crust and bring excess piecrust over pie filling for several inches.

- Cook on preheated, oiled grill over medium fire with lid closed for about 15 to 20 minutes until crust is crispy. (Crust may not look real brown, but should still be crispy when done.)

- Pull piecrust from grill onto cookie sheet to remove from grill. (Foil pie pan may not hold weight.) Cool for about 10 minutes before slicing and top with whipped topping. Serves 6 to 8.

Grilled Angel Fruit

8 (1 - 2 inch) pieces watermelon
8 large strawberries, hulled
½ cup fresh blueberries
1 (14 ounce) prepared angel food cake
Whipped topping

- Soak fruit in 1 cup water for about 30 minutes before grilling. Place fruit on sprayed heavy-duty foil away from direct heat and place 4 large pieces angel food cake on clean, oiled grill or foil over medium-hot fire. Grill fruit and cake for about 3 to 5 minutes per side until cake is toasty.

- Remove from grill, place on individual plates. Divide fruit equally and top with whipped topping. Serves 4.

James Cook introduced pineapple to Hawaii in 1770, but commercial harvesting of pineapple did not begin until the development of the steam engine. By 1903 James Dole began canning pineapples in Hawaii and business was booming by the 1920's. The last commercial pineapple crop in Hawaii was harvested in 2008 to make room for Hawaii's ever expanding tourist industry.

Strawberry Napoleon

2 (6 ounce) cartons vanilla yogurt
¼ cup honey
1 (16 ounce) carton sliced strawberries, drained
3 tablespoons sugar
4 frozen phyllo sheets, thawed

- Combine yogurt and honey; refrigerate. Combine strawberries and sugar; refrigerate. Coat 1 phyllo sheet with cooking spray. Top with another phyllo sheet and coat with cooking spray. Cut into 4 squares. Repeat with remaining 2 phyllo sheets.

- Grill phyllo "stacks" on oiled grill or sprayed heavy-duty foil over medium heat for about 2 minutes on each side until golden brown. Layer one phyllo "stack" with one-fourth strawberry slices and one-fourth yogurt mixture and top with another phyllo "stack". Repeat with remaining phyllo "stacks", strawberries and yogurt mixture. Makes 8.

Double Strawberry Delight

- Use recipe for *Strawberry Napoleon (page 363)* and replace vanilla yogurt with strawberry yogurt. Makes 8.

Favorite Berry Napoleon

- Use recipe for *Strawberry Napoleon (page 363)* and replace strawberries with blueberries or raspberries. Makes 8.

Glazed Watermelon Wedges

1 small ripe watermelon
Canola oil
Balsamic glaze

- Cut 1 to 2-inch slices across width of watermelon. Cut in half and again in half and rub with canola oil.

- Cook on clean, oiled grill or foil over medium-high heat for about 1 to 2 minutes per side until warm. Pour balsamic glaze over watermelon before removing from grill. Serves 6 to 8.

Fruit Medley Delight

2 apples, cored, halved
2 peaches, seeded, halved
2 pears, seeded, halved
2 mangoes, seeded, halved
Brown sugar
Butter, softened, or canola oil

- Rub each half with a little butter or oil. Cook on sprayed foil over medium fire for about 3 to 5 minutes per side until soft. Sprinkle brown sugar over fruit before serving. Serves 4.

Cake and Fruit Kebabs

½ cup peach preserves
1 tablespoon butter
¼ teaspoon cinnamon
1 loaf frozen pound cake, thawed
4 peaches, quartered
4 plums, quartered

- Heat preserves, butter and cinnamon over medium heat until they blend well. Cut pound cake into 2-inch cubes. Alternately thread fruit and cake on skewers. Coat with preserves mixture.

- Cook on sprayed, heavy-duty foil over grill with medium heat for about 2 minutes per side until fruit and cake are hot. Baste frequently with preserves. Serves 6 to 8.

Life is uncertain. Eat dessert first.
–Ernestine Ulmer

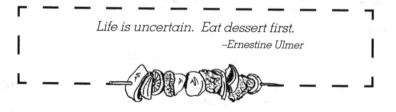

Bibliography

Barbecue Bible. Steven Raichlen. Workman Publishing. 1998.

Great Ribs Book. Hugh Carpenter, Teri Sandison. Tem Speed Press. 1999.

Grilling Encyclopedia. Cort Sinnes. Atlantic Monthly Press. 1992.

More Chicken Breasts. Diane Rozas. Harmony Books. 1991.

The Best Little Grilling Book. Karen Adler. Celestial Arts. 2000.

The Encyclopedia of Sauces for Your Foods. Charles Bellissino. Marcus Kimberly Publishing, 1997.

The Grilling Book, The Techniques, Tools, and Tastes of the New American Grill. Cort Sinnes. Aris Books. 1985.

The Little Chicken Cookbook. Iona Nixon. Ventura Books. 1982.

Thrill of the Grill. Chris Schlesinger, John Willoughby. William Morrow,. 1990.

Weber: The Art of the Grill. Chronicle Books,. 1999.

www.recipepizza.com

www.jokeshaha.com

www.usda.gov (United States Department of Agriculture)

www.whatscookingamerica.com

The story goes that at a baseball game in New York in 1901, an ice cream vendor who wasn't selling much started selling sausages. He would yell out, "They're red hot. Get your red hot dogs!" Another man was selling sausages and bread and called them "meat sandwiches". A voice in the crowd yelled out "Give me a hot dog," and that seems to have solidified the name for eternity.

Index

C

D

Desserts

G

H

N

P

S

T

Cookbooks Published by Cookbook Resources, LLC
Bringing Family and Friends to the Table

The Best 1001 Short, Easy Recipes
1001 Slow Cooker Recipes
1001 Short, Easy, Inexpensive Recipes
1001 Fast Easy Recipes
1001 America's Favorite Recipes
1001 Easy Inexpensive
Grilling Recipes
Easy Slow Cooker Cookbook
Busy Woman's Slow Cooker Recipes
Busy Woman's Quick & Easy Recipes
365 Easy Soups and Stews
365 Easy Chicken Recipes
365 Easy One-Dish Recipes
365 Easy Soup Recipes
365 Easy Vegetarian Recipes
365 Easy Casserole Recipes
365 Easy Pasta Recipes
365 Easy Slow Cooker Recipes
Super Simple Cupcake Recipes
Leaving Home Cookbook
and Survival Guide
Essential 3-4-5 Ingredient Recipes
Ultimate 4 Ingredient Cookbook
Easy Cooking with 5 Ingredients
The Best of Cooking with 3 Ingredients
Easy Diabetic Recipes
Ultimate 4 Ingredient
Diabetic Cookbook
4-Ingredient Recipes
for 30-Minute Meals
Cooking with Beer
The Washington Cookbook
The Pennsylvania Cookbook
The California Cookbook
Best-Loved New England Recipes
Best-Loved Canadian Recipes
Best-Loved Recipes
from the Pacific Northwest
Easy Homemade Preserves
(Handbook with Photos)
Garden Fresh Recipes
(Handbook with Photos)

Easy Slow Cooker Recipes
(Handbook with Photos)
Cool Smoothies
(Handbook with Photos)
Easy Cupcake Recipes
(Handbook with Photos)
Easy Soup Recipes
(Handbook with Photos)
Classic Tex-Mex and Texas Cooking
Best-Loved Southern Recipes
Classic Southwest Cooking
Miss Sadie's Southern Cooking
Classic Pennsylvania Dutch Cooking
The Quilters' Cookbook
Healthy Cooking with 4 Ingredients
Trophy Hunter's Wild Game Cookbook
Recipe Keeper
Simple Old-Fashioned Baking
Quick Fixes with Cake Mixes
Kitchen Keepsakes
& More Kitchen Keepsakes
Cookbook 25 Years
Texas Longhorn Cookbook
The Authorized Texas
Ranger Cookbook
Gifts for the Cookie Jar
All New Gifts for the Cookie Jar
The Big Bake Sale Cookbook
Easy One-Dish Meals
Easy Potluck Recipes
Easy Casseroles Cookbook
Easy Desserts
Sunday Night Suppers
Easy Church Suppers
365 Easy Meals
Gourmet Cooking with 5 Ingredients
Muffins In A Jar
A Little Taste of Texas
A Little Taste of Texas II
Ultimate Gifts for the Cookie Jar

cookbook
≋resources LLC
www.cookbookresources.com
Toll-Free 866-229-2665
Your Ultimate Source for Easy Cookbooks

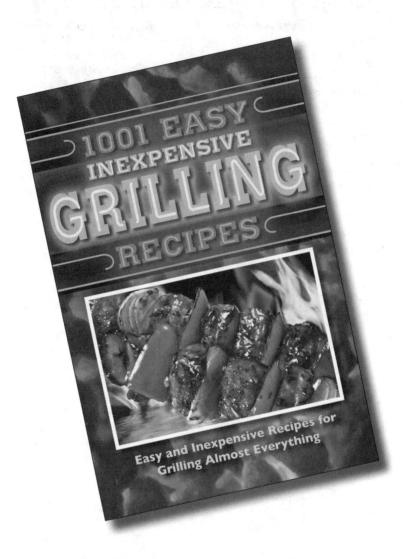

Easy and Inexpensive Recipes for Grilling Almost Everything

cookbook
resources LLC
www.cookbookresources.com
Toll-Free 866-229-2665
Your Ultimate Source for Easy Cookbooks